HIDDEN
WARBIRDS

The Epic Stories of Finding, Recovering, and Rebuilding WWII's Lost Aircraft

Nicholas A. Veronico

ZENITH PRESS

For Caroline and Ray and
Armand and Karen

Quarto is the authority on a wide range of topics.

Quarto educates, entertains and enriches the lives of our readers—enthusiasts and lovers of hands-on living.

www.quartoknows.com

© 2013 Quarto Publishing Group USA Inc.
Text © 2013 Nicholas A. Veronico

Unless noted otherwise all archival photos are from the author's collection and all contemporary photos were taken by the author.

First published in 2013 by Zenith Press, an imprint of Quarto Publishing Group USA Inc., 400 First Avenue North, Suite 400, Minneapolis, MN 55401 USA. Telephone: (612) 344-8100 Fax: (612) 344-8692

quartoknows.com
Visit our blogs at quartoknows.com

Zenith Press titles are also available at discounts in bulk quantity for industrial or sales-promotional use. For details contact the Special Sales Manager at Quarto Publishing Group USA Inc., 400 First Avenue North, Suite 400, Minneapolis, MN 55401 USA.

10 9 8 7 6 5 4

Library of Congress Cataloging-in-Publication Data

Veronico, Nick, 1961-
  Hidden warbirds : the epic stories of finding, recovering, and rebuilding WWII's lost aircraft / Nick Veronico.
     pages cm
  Includes bibliographical references and index.
  ISBN 978-0-7603-4409-5 (hbk.)
  1. Airplanes, Military--Conservation and restoration--United States. 2. Airplanes, Military--Accidents--United States--History--20th century. 3. World War, 1939-1945--Aerial operations. I. Title.
  UG1243.V469 2013
  623.74'60288--dc23
                            2012050971

Editor: Scott Pearson
Design: Chris Fayers
Cover design: Jason Gabbert

On the front cover: Shot down in February 1942, this B-17E became known as the *Swamp Ghost* and was the object of many failed recovery attempts. *Charles Darby*

On the back cover: *Glacier Girl* in the ice (*Lou Sapienza*) and back in the air (*A. Kevin Grantham*).

On page 2: Battle of Midway veteran SBD-2 Dauntless BuNo 2106 is returned to dry land after more than fifty-one years resting on the bottom of Lake Michigan. *A&T Recovery via National Museum of Naval Aviation*

Printed in China

Contents

Acknowledgments

When assembling a book like *Hidden Warbirds*, many old friends and many new friends are called upon for information, opinions, photos, and other resources. Their generosity is shown on these pages and woven into each of the stories. A special thanks to: Ian Abbott; Denis Arbeau; Frank Arrufat; Jim Azelton; Brian Baker; Gerald Balzer; Darlene and Roger Cain; Bob Cardin; Mike, Francis, Steve, and Robert Coutches; Charles Darby; Ed Davies; Mike DeCastro; Robert F. Dorr; Jim Dunn; Linda and Bruce Fenstermaker; Bill Fischer—EAA Warbirds; Rasa and Craig Fuller—Aviation Archaeological Investigation and Research; Denny Ghiringhelli; Erik Gilg; Ric Gillespie—TIGHAR; Wayne Gomes; Jackie and Kevin Grantham; Dan Hagedorn; Fred Hagen; Lori Hahn; Eric Hammel—Pacifica Military History; John Harjo; Alice Hendricks; Ted Holgerson; Vallarie Kilkenney-Jukes and Norm Jukes; Mike Kellner; Martin Kyburz; John Lane—Airpower Unlimited; Peter Langsdale; Gary Larkins; Tillie and William T. Larkins; Dave Leininger; Gerry Liang; Ed Lindsay; Michael H. Marlow; Rob Mears; Yvonne and Dale Messimer; Ken Miller; Gina Morello; John C. Morgan; National Museum of Naval Aviation—Bill Dunbar and Shelley Ragsdale; Robert Nishimura; Bob O'Hara; Michael O'Leary; Allan Olson and Taras Lyssenko—A. and T. Recovery; Scott Pearson; Milo Peltzer; Bruce Pruitt; Jim Pyle; George Radovich; Taigh Ramey—Vintage Aircraft; Chris Rathbun; Mike Rawson; Lou Sapienza; Carl Scholl and Tony Ritzman—Aero Trader; Lee Scales; Butch Schroeder; Doug Scroggins; Dik Shepherd; Doug Siegfried; Bill Stanczak; Russ Strine; Ron Strong; John Tallichet; Justin Taylan—PacificWrecks.com and PacificGhosts.com; Anthony Taylor; Cal Taylor; Scott Thompson; Dave Trojan; Rick Turner; Mike VadeBonCoeur—Midwest Aero; Richard VanderMeulen; Armand and Karen Veronico; Betty Veronico; Tony Veronico; Gary Verver; Chuck Wahl—Vultures' Row Aviation; and Tom Wilson.

With great appreciation.

Nicholas A. Veronico
San Carlos, California

Introduction
How the Hunt for Hidden Warbirds Has Evolved

By the end of June 1946, Storage Depot 41 at Kingman, Arizona, was home to 5,553 aircraft. Of the more than eighteen thousand B-24 Liberators built during the war, today only two are regularly flown with fifteen surviving aircraft plus some nose sections. All of the warbirds at Kingman were gone by the fall of 1948.

They're out there . . . you just need to know where to look. Missing fighters with names like Lightning and Warhawk; bombers large and small—Havoc, Marauder, Flying Fortress, and Liberator; and navy carrier planes—Hellcats, Wildcats, and Dauntlesses; all are scattered across the former battlegrounds of World War II.

Friend and foe alike, the hands of fate have also hidden Hurricanes and Spitfires, Stukas and Zeros, and dozens of other types. They sit in humid swamps and jungles, on sweltering desert hard scapes, submerged under water, or buried under tons of ice. Even the location names sound remote and foreboding; places like Dobodura, Saidor, Narsarsuaq, and the Calanshio Sand Sea.

RF-6C-10-NT 44-10911 was sold at Kingman to aircraft dealer Lee Cameron and dismantled. *William T. Larkins*

The aircraft was transported to Los Angeles where it was rebuilt and sold, becoming N5528N *Thunderbird*. The plane competed with pilot Joe DeBona at the controls with sponsorship from the actor Jimmy Stewart. *Burke-Smith Studios*

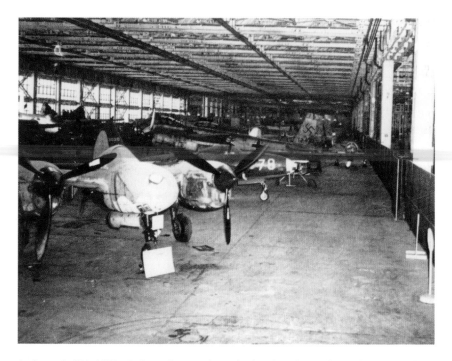

At the end of World War II, the air force and navy had gathered aircraft significant to each service's history, including enemy aircraft. Dozens of the collection's aircraft were stored in the former C-54 plant at Park Ridge, Illinois, and when the space was needed to build C-119 Flying Boxcars for the Korean War, the collection was evicted. Most of the aircraft were dismantled, including this P-38, and shipped to Silver Hill, Maryland, for storage. *National Archives via A. Kevin Grantham*

In the field, what might be impossible-to-overcome obstacles to many would-be explorers are mere hurdles to others. Insects, reptiles, snakes, sharks, hostile natives, and poor or primitive living conditions are only some of the problems facing aircraft recovery teams. Imagine trying to dismantle a 65,000-pound B-17 sitting in a swamp with the nearest hard ground a four- or five-mile trek through razor-sharp Kunai grass that grows taller than most men. Once out of the swamp and on terra firma, the aircraft then has to be transported half a world away before restoration work can begin.

The cost of recovering a World War II warbird is beyond the reach of the average aviation enthusiast. But that's not to say that there are not warbirds closer to home that are awaiting discovery. Closer to home they are in lakes, hidden in the trees, in hangars, garages, and sitting on abandoned airfields. They are out there . . .

When Warbirds Were a Dime a Dozen

The United States had built more than three hundred thousand planes between 1941 and 1945. At the close of World War II, the military had more than twenty-five thousand aircraft that were surplus to its postwar needs. The planes were parked on fields across the United States, Europe, and islands in the Pacific. Learning from its mistakes after World War I, the U.S. government was careful not to flood the market with surplus aircraft and sold a relatively few tactical aircraft types to civilian operators. It did, however, release huge amounts

A number of warbirds sat unnoticed into the late 1950s and early 1960s at trade schools such as the Northrop Technical Institute near Los Angeles' Mines Field (today's Los Angeles International Airport). There is a B-24M, B-25H, and P-61 in the foreground with a training glider, C-78, and BT-13 facing the hangar. In between the hangars can be seen a P-61 fuselage and center section and an AT-6. *Gerald Balzer Collection*

Ed Maloney from The Air Museum-Planes of Fame rescued B-17F 42-3374 from the MGM film studio when it was divesting itself of everything on Backlot Number Five.

of single- and multi-engine trainers. The remaining tactical aircraft were scrapped, including more than twenty-one thousand sold in a bulk sale in June 1946. These aircraft were parked at Kingman, Arizona; Walnut Ridge, Arkansas; Ontario, California; Albuquerque, New Mexico; and Clinton, Oklahoma. Once the sale had concluded, the scrapping contractors were given from eighteen to twenty-four months to clear the fields. America's aerial armada, the likes of which the world has not seen since 1945, was reduced to aluminum ingots to feed the demands of the postwar economy.

Of the World War II fighters that escaped the scrappers' torch, most were sold to pilots interested in competing in the National Air Races at Cleveland, Ohio. The races had been held Labor Day weekend in the years leading up to World War II. The last prewar race was held in 1939, as conflict in Europe canceled the 1940 air races and those for the duration of the war.

While the United States demobilized from World War II, the announcement was made that the National Air Races would resume in 1946. Pilots with the financial wherewithal could purchase a surplus P-38, P-39 or P-40 for $1,250, and a P-51 for $3,500. Once title was acquired, the fighters were flown home and stripped of all military equipment.

Former World War II fighters were involved in two different types of competition at the 1946 National Air Races—cross-country and closed-course. The cross-country race, sponsored by the Bendix

Company and known as the Bendix Trophy Race, started at Van Nuys, California (a Los Angeles suburb), and ended at the race site in Cleveland. Twenty-two aircraft showed up to race in the cross-country dash, including fourteen Lockheed P-38s, four North American P-51s, a pair of Bell P-63s, one Goodyear FG-1D Corsair, and a Douglas A-26. Paul Mantz won the race in a P-51C Mustang with an average speed of 435.50 mph—an unheard of speed when compared to those of the prewar racers.

The closed-course race consisted of ten laps of a thirty-mile course laid out over the suburbs of Cleveland. The field for the 1946 race consisted of one P-38 and one P-39, four P-51s, four P-63s, and a lone FG-1D Corsair. Alvin "Tex" Johnston took the checkered flag with an average speed of 373.908 mph.

Air racing only made the former fighters of World War II more attractive to potential race pilots and aviation enthusiasts. The events were hugely popular and enjoyed tremendous success. The races and racers were extensively covered in local and national media, making

Maloney traded the aircraft to Gary Larkins in exchange for a new steel building for his museum in 1981. Larkins subsequently traded the B-17F to the Air Force Heritage Program, which had Larkins deliver the aircraft, display ready, to the Beale Air Force Base museum. The aircraft subsequently transferred to Offutt AFB and was rededicated as *Homesick Angel* in 1989. *Scott Thompson*

celebrities out of many of the pilots. Demand for former World War II fighters grew as the publicity from the air races attracted more pilots confident they could claim a share of the prize money.

Interest in, and the value of, former World War II fighters was lost in an instant. During the second lap of the 1949 Thompson Trophy Race, Bill Odum's highly modified P-51C *Beguine* dove into a house in Brea, Ohio, killing young mother Jeanne Laird and her infant son Gregg. The accident, combined with the North Korean invasion of South Korea on June 25, 1950, ended air racing and effectively extinguished interest in warbirds of World War II. Jet fighters and bombers and the Cold War now dominated the aviation world.

At the end of World War II, the Army Air Forces and the navy had gathered their own collections of important Allied and enemy aircraft at various locations across the country. To accommodate these collections under the management of one organization, Public Law 722, signed by President Harry S. Truman on August 12, 1946, established the National Air Museum as part of the Smithsonian Institute. Subsequently, both services transferred their collections to the newly formed National Air Museum. The Smithsonian consolidated these aircraft from West and Gulf Coast collection points at the former Douglas C-54 plant at Park Ridge, Illinois.

A few years later, America's entry into the Korean War forced the eviction of the collection from Park Ridge when the U.S. Air Force wanted the facility to build C-119 cargo planes for the war effort. Paul E. Garber, curator of the collection, was forced to move the aircraft as quickly as possible. Garber selected a site at Silver Hill, Maryland, that was to temporarily house the National Air Museum's collection, including aircraft rounded up from Park Ridge. Unfortunately, the train Garber was given to transport the Park Ridge planes would not accommodate all of the aircraft and he had to make choices, such as what to do with the Mitsubishi G4M "Betty" bomber. There wasn't enough room to move the entire aircraft, so Garber took the nose section and the tail gunner's compartment and had to scrap the rest. Garber got everything he could out of Park Ridge by his deadline, and the nucleus of the Smithsonian's World War II collection was saved.

The death of the postwar air races and the consolidation of the National Air Museum's collection saw a complete lack of national interest in World War II aircraft, and P-38s, P-51s, and others of their kind languished on airfields across the United States.

"Mustang Mike" Coutches bought surplus P-51s, licensed them, and sold them for $3,995 in the late 1950s. His aircraft sales business was at the Hayward airport, also a California Air National Guard base, home to the 194th Fighter Squadron, which flew lightweight P-51Hs. Coutches wanted one and spent years gathering H-model Mustang parts. His son Steve is seen at the controls of the Coutches family P-51H following the 2012 Mustang Days gathering in Vacaville, California.

Through this lack of interest in America's military aviation history, a number of significant aircraft types became extinct. Of the nearly 18,500 Consolidated B-24 Liberators built, there was a time when only one was on display and none were flying in the United States. The B-17, of which more than 12,700 were constructed, saw less than a dozen flying as fire bombers. The Curtiss P-36, one of the first aircraft to take the fight to the Japanese during the attack on Pearl Harbor, was gone. Combat veteran B-32s that brought the fight to the Japanese in the closing days of the war were extinct as well. By the middle of the 1950s, many other aircraft were on the brink of disappearing—the P-38 was nearly gone, as were the P-40, B-26, P-61, and so many others.

The Beginnings of the Warbird Movement
Bob Bean, Jack Hardwick, Paul Mantz, and Bob Sturges were but four of the men in the warbird business at the end of World War II. These gentlemen were flying aircraft in the postwar races and supplying war surplus planes to others. Mantz bought the surplus aircraft at

Stillwater, Oklahoma, 475 in all, and from this haul of aircraft he selected a pair of P-51Cs that he would successfully campaign in the postwar air races.

Jack Hardwick was at Cleveland with a P-38 one year, and a P-51C the next. Hardwick picked up whatever ex–World War II aircraft he could. The P-59 Airacomet that had been sent to the Hancock College of Aeronautics in Santa Maria, California, was acquired by Hardwick when it became surplus to the school's needs. He also scoured the country looking for unused, old stock aircraft parts. His stash of B-25 parts was acquired by Carl Scholl and Tony Ritzman of Aero Trader in Chino, California. Hardwick's parts enabled Aero Trader to build a B-25 repair and restoration business that dominates the market today.

Later, Bob Bean was wheeling and dealing warbirds, sending Corsairs south of the border and bringing back P-38s and P-63s that

P-51D 44-73264 was delivered to the Army Air Forces in March 1945. After World War II, 44-73264 flew with a number of Air National Guard units until sold as surplus at McClellan AFB in 1957. In 1977 the P-51 was donated to the Commemorative Air Force. Regis F. A. "Reg" Urschler (Brig. Gen. USAF ret.) was the aircraft's sole sponsor for thirty years and he is seen lifting off the Oshkosh runway in 2006. The aircraft is painted in the markings of the 343rd Fighter Squadron, 55th Fighter Group, 66th Fighter Wing, 8th Air Force.

The Commemorative Air Force (CAF) flies more than sixty different World War II aircraft types. The aircraft that started it all was P-51D 44-73843. Lloyd P. Nolen and friends bought the aircraft on October 17, 1957. The plane is affectionately known as "Old Red Nose" and the sixty-five-plus-year-old warbird is flown to airshows on a regular basis.

would eventually feed the warbird market. Bean was also buying obsolete planes from technical schools. In the mid-1950s, he acquired the B-24M and P-61 Black Widow from the Northrop Institute at Hawthorne, California. After Bean's passing, Carl Scholl and Tony Ritzman rescued the remains of the Black Widow, and those parts eventually went to the P-61 restoration at the Mid-Atlantic Air Museum in Reading, Pennsylvania.

By the mid-1950s, a number of visionaries in the aircraft preservation movement began to emerge. Their vision was to preserve, preferably in flying condition, the aircraft of World War II for future generations to see. Sure, people wondered what they were going to do with so much junk, but they persevered, dragging discarded aircraft home and saving them from a certain fate. Airport managers and community leaders were more than happy to rid themselves of the obsolete eyesores that littered the weed-covered corners of airfields across the country.

Living near Cal Aero Field, today's Chino Airport, during the 1930s and 1940s, Ed Maloney read about aviation's heroes from Charles Lindbergh to Howard Hughes. After the war he saw more than 1,300 aircraft scrapped at Chino Airport. His dream was to save these aircraft for future generations. To do that, Maloney started dragging home aircraft that others considered utterly worthless. He also attended surplus sales and bought aircraft with whatever money he had. In 1957, Maloney opened The Air Museum with just ten aircraft on display. As he managed his collection of planes, he was carting home German and Japanese aircraft that nobody wanted and cultivating relationships with people who would eventually decide whether the planes were scrapped, sold, or donated to Maloney's fledgling museum. Through his efforts he built one of the world's largest collections of Japanese World War II aircraft and rescued dozens of other extremely rare planes. Maloney also horse-traded to fill holes in his collection, and many a surviving aircraft owes its existence to his efforts.

Walter Soplata in Newbury, Ohio, was a carpenter by trade and an aviation enthusiast of the highest order. Soplata collected numerous extremely rare aircraft from the area, ranging from Dick Becker's Goodyear F2G Corsair to a Vought F7U Cutlass, a pair of P-82 Twin Mustangs, and the front half of a YB-36 brought home in the back of a Chevy El Camino over the course of six months. He rarely entertained visitors and maintained the aircraft as best he could while raising a family and earning a living. He was extremely passionate and very vocal about how various government agencies let historic aircraft be scrapped and railed against many of the volunteer organizations that flew their planes. It killed him to learn of a warbird crash. Soplata passed away in 2010, and a number of exceedingly rare aircraft from his collection are now under restoration, some to fly once again.

And there is "Mustang Mike" Coutches of American Aircraft in Hayward, California. Beginning in 1957, "Mustang Mike" was buying surplus P-51s from government sales at McClellan AFB for $750 to $1,000. He'd inspect and repair them as necessary, then turn around and sell the Mustangs for $3,995, licensed and ready to fly. A glance at the histories of surviving P-51s will show how deeply Coutches was involved in the civilian warbird business. Many Mustangs flying today owe their existence to Coutches.

In Texas, a group of former World War II military pilots headed by Lloyd Nolen got together and purchased a P-51 Mustang. They then bought a pair of surplus Grumman F8F Bearcats, and in 1960 set out to acquire one flyable example of every World War II aircraft type. As they searched, the group quickly learned just how rare the planes had become, with many types down to only one flying example. In

The Continental Can Company had used an LB-30 (B-24A) version of the Consolidated Liberator as a corporate aircraft. When flown by Continental Can, the aircraft was registered N1503.

Petróleos Mexicanos (PEMEX, the Mexican state-owned oil producer) acquired N1503 in April 1959 and registered it XC-CAY. The CAF bought the B-24 from PEMEX in 1967, and restored it as *Diamond Lil*. It underwent a major rework from LB-30 to B-24A configuration in 2006, headed by the late Gary Austin. *Roger Cain*

The 20th Century Fox film *Tora, Tora, Tora* was one of three big budget aviation movies in the late 1960s and early 1970s that brought a lot of attention to World War II aircraft. More than thirty BT-13s and AT-6s were modified to look like Japanese Kate torpedo bombers and Zero fighters for the movie. In addition, a number of PBYs and Curtiss P-40s were rounded up for the Ford Island scenes. *Challenge Publications/Bob O'Hara*

September 1961, Nolen and his friends incorporated their efforts as the Confederate Air Force. Today the group has more than nine thousand members and flies or is restoring more than sixty different World War II aircraft types. The Confederate Air Force changed its name to the Commemorative Air Force (CAF) in 2002.

Over the years, the CAF has flown its aircraft for millions of people at airshows across North America. Its collection is most impressive with nearly all types of World War II planes represented. The CAF can boast a pair of B-17s, a B-24, a B-29, and at one time or another nearly every major type of World War II fighter from the P-47 and P-63, to the Spitfire, Hurricane, and versions of the Messerschmitt 109. The group operates an impressive museum in Midland, Texas.

Former 100th Bomb Group B-17 pilot David C. Tallichet built an empire on theme restaurants and then began to collect World War II aircraft on a grand scale. Tallichet acquired a B-29 from the dozens sitting on the target ranges at China Lake, California; scoured the countryside for derelict planes; and financed expeditions from

After filming of Paramount Pictures' *Catch-22* wrapped, the B-25s were flown to the Tallmantz facility at Orange County Airport. Seen in April 1971, the fleet of Mitchell bombers was put up for sale for prices between $5,000 and $10,000. This movie saved fifteen B-25s, and many more, from being scrapped. *Scott Thompson*

Greenland to New Guinea, Canada, and India to locate and recover rare aircraft. At one time, Tallichet and his Military Aircraft Restoration Corp. (MARC) owned more than 120 World War II aircraft. And not just one of an aircraft type: MARC's compound at the Chino Airport had so many P-39s at one time they looked like they were stacked like firewood. There were a trio of B-24 Liberators—one flying and two complete fuselages—a B-17, B-29, an A-20 Havoc or two, and some Martin Marauders, plus additional types stashed in hangars around the country.

There were many other individuals across the United States who made an impact upon the beginning of the warbird movement, and a debt of gratitude is owed each and every one.

As the warbird movement gathered momentum, a trio of Hollywood films brought an increased awareness of the contributions of World War II aircraft, airmen, and their ground crews. The producers of the $17 million *Battle of Britain* (United Artists, 1969) needed to gather enough Spitfires, Hurricanes, Messerschmitt 109s, and Heinkel He-111 bombers to make the film believable. Group Captain

Grumman FM-2 BuNo 16161, flown by Ens. Robert L. Woodruff, was approaching the training carrier USS *Wolverine* on April 12, 1945. Woodruff was given the wave-off signal, but the tail hook caught an arresting wire and the plane went over the side into Lake Michigan. Woodruff survived the crash without serious injury. After recovery, the National Museum of Naval Aviation traded this aircraft to David Tallichet for a Brewster SB2A Buccaneer. The FM-2 is on display at Tucson, Arizona's Pima Air and Space Museum.

The Brewster SB2A Buccaneer was not a combat success and remained stateside in the training role. This aircraft was used to train Royal Navy pilots at Tullahoma, Tennessee. It was pushed off into the weeds and located and recovered by David Tallichet in the mid-1970s. Restoration progress was slow, and in 2004 the National Museum of Naval Aviation acquired the project. The aircraft was restored by museum volunteers, seen here, and placed on display in 2007.

Hamish Mahaddie scoured the globe and found the Spanish Air Force retained a sizeable inventory of Heinkels and Messerschmitts. Between 1940 and 1956, the Spanish had license-built 236 Rolls-Royce Merlin engine-powered Heinkel 111s as the Construcciones Aeronáuticas SA (CASA) 2.111. The CASA 2.111s were cast alongside Spanish license-built Messerschmitt Bf-109s, known as the Hispano Aviación HA-1112. At the conclusion of filming, the majority of the Battle of Britain air force was put up for sale.

On the heels of *Battle of Britain*, 20th Century Fox released *Tora! Tora! Tora!*, an epic film depicting the attack on Pearl Harbor from both the American and the Japanese perspective. More than $25 million was spent to produce the film, which included crews on the mainland United States, in Hawaii, and in Japan. With no authentic flying Japanese aircraft from the Pearl Harbor attack era, the producers had more than thirty North American AT-6/SNJs modified to resemble the Mitsubishi A6M Zero, and dozens of Vultee BT-13s became Nakajima Kate bombers. The film opened to mixed reviews and was a box office bomb in the United States, but a financial success in Japan. Once the studio had completed filming and the picture was in theaters, the replica aircraft were put up for sale. The Commemorative Air Force acquired a number of ex-*Tora! Tora! Tora!* planes and using its B-17s developed an entertaining airshow act re-creating the events of December 7, 1941.

The film based upon Joseph Heller's novel *Catch-22* was also released in 1970 by Paramount Pictures. Frank Tallman, partner in Tallmantz Aviation with the late Paul Mantz, gathered sixteen flyable B-25 Mitchell bombers and flight crews and headed down to Mexico to film *Catch-22*. Although the film was not a critical or box office success, it certainly is the best B-25 footage ever captured. A replica air base was built on the coast near Guaymas, Mexico, about an hour flight south of the border. From here, Tallman staged a number of mass formation takeoffs of all sixteen bombers. Coupled with the over-water formation flights, *Catch-22* is an aviation lover's dream film. After the production, the B-25s were gathered at the Tallmantz facility at Orange County Airport and sold for prices ranging from $5,000 to $10,000.

The release of three aviation movies so close together spawned other productions that were responsible for saving other aircraft from the smelter. Most notable is *Baa Baa Black Sheep*, the story of Marine Corps Ace Gregory "Pappy" Boyington. Seven Corsairs were used in the filming of a TV movie and later series (also known as *Black Sheep Squadron*), which undoubtedly rescued many other derelict Corsairs.

Film use saved these aircraft from the scrappers' torch and presented an inventory of rare aircraft. In the early 1970s these ex-film stars were not fast movers on the secondary aircraft market, but they were survivors, and ones that would quickly appreciate once the warbird movement got into full swing in the following decades.

Chasing Wrecks and Restorations

The July 1, 1976, opening of the Smithsonian Institute's National Air and Space Museum on the National Mall in Washington, D.C., gave the world a high visibility destination to see aviation history under one roof. Many of the collection's major milestone aircraft were presented to the public on opening day, from the Wright Flyer to the *Spirit of St. Louis*, to the Bell X-1, serial number 46-062, *Glamorous Glennis,* in which then-Capt. Charles "Chuck" Yeager broke the sound barrier, to Amelia Earhart's Lockheed Vega 5B in which she crossed the Atlantic solo.

More than five million streamed through the museum's doors in the first six months. And two of the highlights of the museum are and have been the World War II Aviation and the Sea-Air Operations galleries. The Sea-Air gallery replicates an aircraft carrier island and deck and displays a Boeing F4B-4 biplane, Grumman F4F Wildcat, Douglas SBD-6 Dauntless, and Douglas A-4 Skyhawk.

Across the catwalk from the navy-themed Sea-Air gallery is the World War II Aviation gallery. Dominating the backdrop of this space is artist Keith Ferris's near life-sized, 25-foot by 75-foot mural of the airwar over Germany titled *Fortress under Fire*. The mural features the 303rd Bomb Group B-17 *Thunderbird* under attack by Luftwaffe fighters after bombing Wiesbaden, Germany.

The opening of the National Air and Space Museum and its phenomenal attendance, on the heels of so many aircraft on the silver screen, energized the warbird movement. Soon the U.S. Air Force began its Heritage Program, where nearly every major air base started its own museum and set about collecting aircraft for display.

Simultaneous to the uptick in interest in warbirds and the air force's efforts to flesh out its base museums, many working in the aviation community who were experienced in aircraft recoveries formed themselves into teams, much like contracting companies. For a fee they would research, locate, and recover a warbird. Once recovered,

F3F-2 BuNo 0976 was assigned to Marine Fighter Squadron 2 *VMF-2* at NAS North Island, San Diego. On approach to USS *Saratoga*, pilot First Lt. Robert E. Galer (later Brig. Gen. and Medal of Honor recipient) switched fuel tanks, causing the engine to cough. Without enough altitude to restart the engine, Lt. Galer was forced to ditch in the Pacific Ocean. The fighter sank more than 1,800 feet to the bottom. The plane was raised on April 5, 1990, and sent to the nearby San Diego Air and Space Museum for restoration. *U.S. Navy*

After the plane was restored, it was displayed at the San Diego Air and Space Museum in Balboa Park for three years before moving to the National Museum of Naval Aviation in Pensacola, Florida.

This Sikorsky S-43 (military version: JRS-1) was found in Alaska by aircraft recovery specialist Gary Larkins. The wing was being used as a footbridge by the locals and the fuselage was off in the brush. Larkins recovered the historic seaplane and traded the Baby Clipper to the Marine Corps Museum. It has been cosmetically restored by volunteers at the Pima Air and Space Museum, Tucson, and is painted in the colors of VMJ-2 when based at San Diego, circa 1939.

the aircraft would need a complete rebuild, and that was often handled by a different set of specialists.

The needs of the air force base museums were filled by aircraft from the military storage yard adjacent to Davis-Monthan AFB in Tucson, Arizona. In the mid- to late 1970s, the military aircraft boneyard still held small supplies of Century Series fighters (F-100, F-101, F-102, F-104, and F-105), various helicopters, and transports.

A fleet of B-29s was recovered from the target ranges at the Naval Air Weapons Center in China Lake, California. The navy's ranges also yielded a couple of B-47 Stratojets, one of which was made airworthy and flown to Castle AFB, Atwater, California, for display. Trades were made with a number of air tanker companies to get their B-17 Flying Fortresses used as air tankers for museum displays.

The air force's Heritage Program horse-traded for other types missing from its collection. From South America came a B-17 and a B-24; another B-24 that had been abandoned at Tulsa, Oklahoma, was airlifted to Barksdale AFB, home to dozens of B-52s. The airlifted Liberator was reassembled and restored to commemorate one of the early bomber types flown from the field. Other aircraft for the Heritage Program came from civilian aircraft owners who swapped such rare aircraft as a P-38 and multiple B-25s to help round out the collections.

To complete their collections, nearly every major aviation museum has, or is, actively locating crash sites for potential exhibits or aircraft to restore. Who wreck-chases? Institutions ranging from the National Air and Space Museum, the Air Force Museum, the National Museum of Naval Aviation, to the Royal Air Force Museum and the Imperial War Museum have recovered aircraft from the wilds and either restored or displayed their finds.

The Planes of Fame Air Museum presents what was, at the time of its installation, one of the most unique displays in the country. By the early 1990s, the Mitsubishi G4M Betty bomber was extinct and no complete examples existed in museums or private collections. The

This combat veteran B-17 in New Guinea is ready to be recovered by someone with substantial financial backing. The B-17E, serial number 41-9234, was built as a lend-lease aircraft for the Royal Air Force and painted in RAF markings. The plane was diverted to the 19th Bomb Group in Hawaii in August 1942. The bomber then went to the 5th Air Force, 43rd Bomb Group, 65th Bomb Squadron at Port Moresby. Hit by Japanese anti-aircraft fire on January 9, 1943, pilot First Lt. Raymond S. Dau brought the plane back, but had to make a forced landing at Black Cat Pass where the aircraft's back was broken. The crew was rescued, although radio operator Robert Albright later died from his wounds. *Charles Darby*

museum acquired a nearly complete example and the twin-engine bomber is displayed in an as-found jungle diorama.

Along with the Betty bomber, the National Museum of Naval Aviation has recovered a steady stream of Grumman F4F Wildcats, F6F Hellcats, and Douglas SBD Dauntless dive bombers from Lake Michigan years after training crashes sent them to rest on the murky bottom. Once the museum rounded out its collection, many of the recovered aircraft have been farmed out to institutions across the United States for restoration and eventual display. The F4F Wildcat on display at Chicago's O'Hare International Airport, Terminal 2, is dedicated to the airport's namesake, Lt. Edward L. "Butch" O'Hare, and has been restored in the colors of his aircraft.

Other examples of aircraft recovered from the wild include the Sikorsky S-43 on display at the Pima Air and Space Museum,

Tucson, Arizona, that would not have survived had it not been for aircraft recovery pioneers such as Gary Larkins. Bill Klaers and Alan Wojciak, operators of WestPac Restorations in Colorado Springs, Colorado, are restoring a combat veteran P-38 known as "White 33," as well as a razorback P-47 Thunderbolt recovered from the South Pacific. Both of these aircraft will eventually become fliers. Another fine example of returning a wreck from the field and restoring it into a valuable museum display is the P-38 Lightning that is today on display at the Hill Air Force Base Museum, outside Salt Lake City, Utah. This beautiful display was built from parts of a number of different wrecked P-38s by Ed Kaletta of KalAero in San Diego, California.

Warbirds in the New Millennium

The technological revolution of the 1990s and the new millennium radically changed the cost of archive research and improved the way information is communicated. Gone are the days of a researcher sitting in some dusty archives looking at documents and images, finding something important, then having to photocopy it or send it out to be copied. Laptop computers and scanners have enabled documents and photos to be shared instantly with restorers thousands of miles away.

Greater levels of research and communication of those details to a wider audience has brought new, higher restoration standards—universally adopted by both the judges and the aircraft rebuilders. The details of how aircraft were built, what the correct paint color should be, and where items were located within the aircraft have drastically improved the authenticity of most recent restorations. With that comes aircraft owners who are willing to make the investment to have such beautifully detailed planes.

Another side benefit of increased authenticity standards is that a number of aircraft restored in the 1960s and 1970s are being re-restored. This process improves an aircraft's maintainability, extends its lifespan, and greatly enhances its safety.

In recent years, a number of collectors and museums have gone to great lengths to display their collections on a grand scale. The Air Museum-Planes of Fame has added hangars to get the majority of its collection in Chino under cover. Kermit Weeks's Fantasy of Flight has consolidated its collection at Polk City, Florida, with expanded facilities for both aircraft on public display and its storage/restoration shops. In Virginia, Jerry Yagen's collection of more than fifty flying warbirds is now housed at the Military Aviation Museum in Virginia

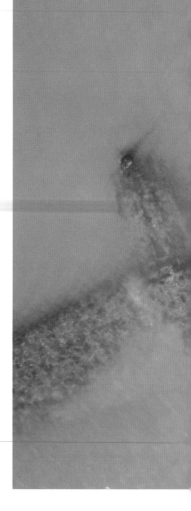

What is possibly the oldest Eighth Air Force P-38 Lightning emerged from the sands of the coast of Wales in the summer of 2007. The aircraft is thought to be P-38F 41-7677, which crash landed in 1942. Aviation historian Matt Rimmer has obtained a permit to recover the aircraft, and he requested assistance from the International Group for Historic Aircraft Recovery (TIGHAR), who sent a respected team of archaeologists to survey the wreck. Apparently the aircraft has been buried in sand and not exposed to the air/water interaction and reportedly has minimal corrosion. A recovery plan is currently being developed. Aviation archaeologist Craig Fuller used a camera on a kite to take this unique photo. *Courtesy TIGHAR, used with permission*

Beach. In spring 2012, the museum transported a 1936 German air force hangar from Cotbus, Germany, and reerected it to house the collection's Luftwaffe aircraft.

And there has been a lot of activity in Washington state: the Museum of Flight has built a new building and is now displaying its B-17F and B-29. Farther north of Seattle, the Flying Heritage Collection in Everett has announced plans for an addition to its facility, and the Historic Flight Foundation has moved into new quarters, also at Everett's Paine Field. North of Everett, Apollo 8 astronaut and retired U.S. Air Force Maj. Gen. William A. Anders and his flying family operate the Heritage Flight Museum at Bellingham International Airport.

In Europe, the Red Bull beverage-sponsored Flying Bulls operate the Hangar 7 Aircraft Museum at Salzburg, Austria. They regularly fly warbirds such as a PT-26, F4U-4 Corsair, B-25 Mitchell, and Lockheed P-38 at airshows across Europe. The facility opened in 2003 and is a beautiful blend of steel and glass housing both the aircraft collection and the maintenance hangar.

The Fighter Collection (TFC), located at Duxford Airfield in the United Kingdom, is by far the largest collection of flyable warbirds in Europe. TFC is also the host for the annual Flying Legends air display in July. Formed by Stephen Grey in 1981 with the purchase of

a Grumman F8F Bearcat, TFC has grown to more than fifteen warbirds ranging from prewar fighters such as the Curtiss P-36 Hawk and P-40B Warhawk, to carrier-based fighters from the Hellcat, Wildcat, and Corsair to a Hawker Sea Fury T20. In addition, restorations by the collection's team are of the highest quality and they are currently working on a Bristol Beaufighter, Fiat CR 42, and a pair of Spitfires.

These are just some of the collectors and museum programs throughout the world that are actively promoting, restoring, rebuilding, and searching for aircraft from the World War II era. They also demonstrate the health of the warbird movement and the global interest in preserving and flying former military planes. And as more collections are assembled, this has brought to the forefront the lack of certain historic aircraft types. To fill holes in these collections of flying aircraft or museum displays, they have to find *Hidden Warbirds*.

Part One

Up from
Under Water

Some amazing aircraft have come up from the depths in past two decades. Combat veterans, aircraft that are the last survivors of their type, and other, rare airplanes are now enjoying a resurgence because of advances in underwater detecting and salvage equipment. In recent years, recoveries from lakes in the United States and Canada have yielded everything from a single-seat Bell P-39 fighter, to a Curtiss SB2C Helldiver, to a North American B-25 Mitchell medium bomber, the front end of a Martin B-26 Marauder, and a four-engine Boeing B-17 Flying Fortress.

Warbird recovery is a worldwide phenomenon that's not just happening in the United States. The fall of the former Soviet Union has opened up hundreds of lakes and rivers that have yielded many different types—from lend-lease American P-39s to German Messerschmitt Bf-109s and Focke-Wulf Fw-190s, to a number of Ilyushin Il-2 Sturmoviks.

From a metallurgy standpoint, aircraft recovered from freshwater lakes hold the most promise as far as restoring the plane for flight, as the corrosion is minimal compared to aircraft sunk in shallow salt water. As a general rule, the salinity in seawater devours magnesium and is extremely harsh on aluminum. That's not to say an aircraft cannot be recovered from salt water and be restored to museum display standards or, given enough time and money, be returned to flight.

The majority of crashed navy aircraft are found underwater, and the sea service has a hands-off policy on aircraft recovery unless it is for an educational purpose or a museum. To secure a permit for the recovery of a navy aircraft more than fifty years old, potential salvors need to present a plan that details the recovery, conservation, restoration, and how and where the aircraft will be displayed, along with how its significance will be interpreted for the public.

The one aircraft missing from the National Museum of Naval Aviation's collection is the Douglas TBD Devastator torpedo bomber. Forty-one TBDs made attacks during the Battle of Midway, and only four returned. Historians and salvors have scoured the globe to find a salvageable TBD, considered by many the "Crown Jewel of Naval Aviation." Two aircraft were ditched in Jaluit Atoll, Marshall Islands (TBD-1 BuNo 0298 and TBD-1 BuNo 1515), one in the Atlantic off the coast of Florida (TBD-1 BuNo 0353) and TBD-1 BuNo 0377 was recently located off the Southern California Coast by A&T Recovery. Some day, one of the four will be recovered, restored, and displayed at the National Museum of Naval Aviation, and a second should also be restored for the National Air & Space Museum. *Courtesy TIGHAR, used with permission*

Using today's technology, finding a submerged airplane is not out of the question. The Naval Historical Center estimates that more than 12,000 aircraft could be potentially salvageable. Of those, an estimated 300 aircraft ditched into Lake Michigan. The Department of Defense Legacy Resource Management Program records "1,484 documented aircraft losses in the vicinity of the Hawaiian Islands"—and they estimate that number to be even higher. Thus starting a search in the right location makes all the difference and it's apparent that the numbers are in the searcher's favor.

Once a permit is obtained from the navy, there are a myriad of regulating agencies that need to be involved from the local, state, and federal levels. Freshwater recoveries will typically involve the Army Corps of Engineers, the Environmental Protection Agency, and representatives of the National Museum of Naval Aviation will need to be on hand. In addition, if the aircraft is carrying live bombs and ammunition, the local military explosive ordnance disposal unit will need to be close by, along with the Bureau of Alcohol, Tobacco, Firearms, and Explosives, as well as local police. All of this bureaucratic infrastructure must be in place before an aircraft can be raised to the surface.

On the other hand, the U.S. Air Force policy is 180-degrees from that of the U.S. Navy. Air force policy on the disposition of its former aircraft is quite clear as noted in the following excerpt from the USAF Supply Manual, AFMAN 23-110, Volume 6, Excess and Surplus Personal Property, Chapter 9, Processing Complete Aircraft and Missiles:

> Paragraph 9.10. Downed Aircraft. Aircraft that crashed before 19 November, 1961, when a fire destroyed the pertinent Air Force records, and that remain wholly or partially unrecovered, are considered formally abandoned. The Air Force neither maintains title to, nor has the property interest in, these aircraft. The authority for access to, and recovery of, these aircraft, as well as liability for damages associated with their recovery, are matters to be resolved between persons seeking recovery and landowners of the wreckage sites.
>
> 9.10.1. If any human remains are discovered at the site, recovery personnel should immediately contact the nearest

United States Embassy or the nearest United States military installation. To assist in proper identification of remains, recovery personnel should refrain from further operations at the site pending removal of the remains by United States experts.

Basically, if you find a former U.S. Army Air Forces or U.S. Air Force aircraft that went down before November 19, 1961, as long as you have the landowner's or body of water owner's permission, you are welcome to recover that aircraft.

One contributing factor to this policy is that the U.S. Air Force has an extensive museum program, with its flagship collection displayed at the National Museum of the United States Air Force in Dayton, Ohio. The museum program has also collected examples of historic aircraft at more than two dozen current and former air force base collections. Thus any wrecks of former air force aircraft would be surplus to the museum's needs, and the service recognizes that it does not have the funds to recover and conserve all of the potentially restorable crashed airplanes.

Oddly enough, the U.S. Air Force with its liberal aircraft crash recovery policy makes it difficult for researchers to obtain information about lost aircraft. The U.S. Navy, on the other hand, has the more restrictive policy on crashed aircraft recovery, yet its crash records are more readily available on microfilm. In theory, an entrepreneur could purchase all thirty-five of the navy's crash record microfilm reels for $30 each and be set for a career in aircraft recovery. The navy's policy has set out to avoid such a free-for-all by maintaining control and stewardship over what it considers are historical assets.

Agree or disagree, each service has set policy regarding how it manages its crashed historical aircraft. And it is important to make the distinction that aircraft with the remains of service members, especially those listed as missing in action, are a completely different discussion and deserve the respect and dignity accorded those who have given their lives in the service of our country.

Hidden warbirds *can* be recovered from underwater. It is just a matter of finding the right aircraft, obtaining the proper permissions, and having the financial backing to cover all of the bases, regardless if the plane is ex-navy or air force, or from the air arm of another nation.

Two of the Rarest
Side-by-Side Helldiver
and Dauntless Restorations

Naval aircraft of World War II did not find many uses after the war and most were scrapped shortly after the conclusion of hostilities. Those that did survive often became derelict and they too ended up at the smelters. There are a number of crashed examples of navy aircraft waiting to be discovered, most from under water, and the fresher the water the better.

Vulture's Row Aviation in Cameron Park, California, is rebuilding two U.S. Navy carrier planes from the Pacific War—at the same time. One is an extremely rare Curtiss SB2C-1A, BuNo 75552, the 825th of the 900 A-25A/SB2C-1A Helldivers built. The other is Douglas SBD-4, BuNo 10694, one of only twenty-four surviving army and navy Dauntless dive bombers.

Vulture's Row Aviation is owned and operated by Carol and Chuck Wahl. Chuck, a navy brat, grew up on naval air stations around the world while his jet pilot father was on deployment. He began

Found on the bottom of Lake Washington by two teenage scuba divers, SB2C-1A BuNo 75552 was raised and transported to the driveway of one of the divers. The navy sued to obtain the fuselage, but lost in court. The remains were acquired by Mike Rawson and today form the basis for the restoration at Vulture's Row Aviation. *Mike Rawson Collection*

taking flying lessons at the NAS Rota, Spain, flying club and soloed on his sixteenth birthday.

In 1999, Wahl purchased a derelict T-28 Trojan, BuNo 140068. After spending four years and ten thousand hours restoring the Trojan, he took the big navy trainer on the airshow circuit in 2003. Contest judges quickly recognized Wahl's meticulous level of craftsmanship and the T-28 was honored with the Grand Champion Warbird award at the 2003 Golden West Experimental Aircraft Association (EAA) Airshow in Marysville, California. That summer, Wahl's work was also recognized with the Silver Wrench restoration award, Best T-28, and a Judges' Appreciation award at the EAA AirVenture airshow in Oshkosh, Wisconsin. The following year, the T-28 was entered into the Rolls-Royce-sponsored National Aviation Heritage Invitational competition, held each year at the National Air Races in Reno, Nevada, where the aircraft received the Henry "Hap" Arnold Trophy for outstanding and authentic warbird restoration.

Restorer Mike Rawson examines the wreckage of one of two SB2Cs that crashed in a box canyon near Salt Lake City. Rawson rebuilt the A-25A version of the Helldiver that is now in the Air Force Museum's collection and is working on both the SB2C and the SBD at Vulture's Row Aviation. *Mike Rawson Collection*

In 2005, Wahl began work on a North American SNJ-5C, BuNo 90656, configured for shipboard operations. Once the restoration was finished, Wahl entered the rare, tail hook-equipped SNJ into the 2009 National Aviation Heritage Invitational competition. Here the plane was honored with the Grand Champion award, and Wahl's name was inscribed on the perpetual trophy that is housed at the Smithsonian Institute's National Air and Space Museum Steven F. Udvar-Hazy Center in Chantilly, Virginia.

Having established a solid reputation as a restorer of U.S. Naval aircraft, Wahl retired from his career in air traffic control and, with

Flight deck crewmen watch the pilot of a Douglas SBD Dauntless trying to handle his aircraft on either Sable (IX-81) or Wolverine (IX-64), circa 1944–1945. This image is from the scrapbook of PH Ulysses Pershing Buffington, who was a photographers' mate on both carriers. The aircraft under restoration by Vulture's Row Aviation was lost off the Sable.
San Diego Aero Space Museum via Tailhook Association

his wife, set up Vulture's Row Aviation at the Cameron Airpark in the Sierra Foothills east of Sacramento, California. The new restoration shop's first projects are a Curtiss SB2C Helldiver and a Douglas SBD Dauntless, two of the rarest World War II naval fighters being restored side-by-side.

Curtiss SB2C-1A Helldiver, BuNo 75552, is one of nine Helldivers surviving in United States with one additional aircraft in Thailand and one in Greece. Of those aircraft, only one, SB2C-5 BuNo 83589 owned by the Commemorative Air Force, is regularly flown. However, in the next few years, the number of flying Helldivers will double and possibly triple. In Granite Falls, Minnesota, Ron Fagen's SB2C-5 BuNo 83393 restoration is currently on hold, and Fagen also owns the remains of SB2C-1A BuNo 75448. When Fagen's and Wahl's restorations are complete, it will be possible to see a trio of Helldivers in formation. In addition, Wahl has another Helldiver that has combat history, BuNo 00020, which will be next in his company's restoration queue.

Helldiver Lost and Found

The Curtiss Helldiver suffered serious teething troubles when it was first introduced to the fleet. It gained a poor reputation, and a number of young ensigns lost their lives transitioning into the new dive bomber. Curtiss straightened out the aircraft's problems by replacing a number of systems, some as retrofits to aircraft in the fleet and other modifications were introduced on the production line. Mechanically, the SB2C is a new aircraft after the 250th plane built, and Curtiss eventually went on to build 7,140 Helldivers

Pilots who flew the new Helldivers thought highly of the plane, but its reputation of being a poor handling airplane was already set in the minds of naval aviators. The plane's reputation never recovered and the SB2C was commonly referred to as the "Son-of-a-Bitch, 2nd Class."

After the engineering modifications were made, Helldivers joined the fight on November 11, 1943, flying with carrier Bombing Squadron 17 (VB-17) aboard USS *Bunker Hill* (CV-17) attacking the bypassed fortress of Rabaul, New Britain. Subsequently, Helldivers were in every major naval engagement from the beginning of 1944 through the end of the war. They struck targets in the Marianas, the Philippines, Taiwan, and Okinawa. In addition, they participated in the sinking of the Japanese battleships *Musashi* (*Yamato* class), sunk in the Sibuyan Sea, Philippines, on October 24, 1944, and the *Yamato*, lost April 7, 1945, south of Okinawa.

Chuck Wahl of Vulture's Row Aviation holds the split cylinder head from SBD-4 BuNo 10694. The cylinder broke moments after takeoff from USS *Sable* causing a loss of power, forcing pilot Ensign Todaro to ditch the plane in Lake Michigan.

In addition to the navy, the U.S. Marines, Royal Australian Air Force, and the U.S. Army Air Forces (designated the A-25A Shrike) flew the Curtiss dive bomber. The Royal Navy Fleet Air Arm tested, but elected not to employ, the Helldiver. After the war, Helldivers saw service with the French Aeronavale, Royal Hellenic Air Force, Italian Air Force, and the Portuguese Navy and Air Force. The last of its type was phased out of service by the Portuguese in 1952.

The Helldiver under restoration at Vulture's Row Aviation, BuNo 75552, had a brief U.S. Navy career. It was the 825th of 900 Helldivers

The SBD's rear fuselage was damaged when USS Sable ran over the aircraft. The fuselage is loaded on the truck at an angle to keep the width within legal limits and avoid the need for pilot cars to escort the truck and trailer. *Chuck Wahl*

built and was delivered on June 30, 1944. The aircraft went straight to NAS Alameda on San Francisco Bay for paint and other small modifications. BuNo 75552 hung around Alameda for three months until it was transferred north to Seattle in November. Shortly after its arrival, the plane was involved in a nonflying accident, and BuNo 75552 was stricken from the inventory on January 31, 1945. The navy then stripped the plane of what it considered useable parts and used the hulk for fire training. When they were done with it, they took BuNo 75552, 76805, and 00020, and many other airframes over the years, out to the middle of Lake Washington and pushed them over the side. Out of sight, out of mind. And that's where the story should end.

In the early 1980s, two local teenage scuba divers and history buffs, Matt McCauley and Jeff Hummel, located the Helldivers in 150 feet of water off Juanita Point near the old Sand Point Naval Air

Station. After much effort, they were able to raise the remains of BuNo 75552 and drag it home. Shortly after the recovery made the papers and the TV news, the navy showed up and wanted its airplane back! The navy confiscated the aircraft and transported it to nearby NAS Sand Point and locked it in a hangar.

In 1984, the sea service filed suit against the young men in *United States of America v. Jeffrey Kenneth Hummel and Matthew William McCauley* (U.S. District Court, Western District of Washington at Seattle, Case No. C84-1058C), claiming that the Helldiver wreckage was still owned by the navy. One year later, after much wrangling, U.S.

The top of the SBD's restored wing center section showing seat mounts, radio racks, and control cable pulleys. The upper deck, cockpits, and rollover structure will be mated to this area.

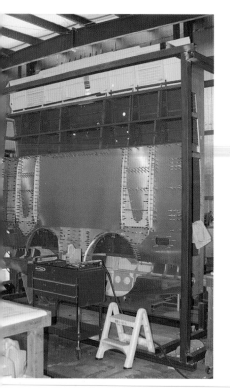

Under side of SBD-4 BuNo 10694's center section showing flap wells, top, and main landing gear wells, at bottom, demonstrates that the aircraft has been torn down to the last rivet and is being built up from there.

District Court Judge John C. Coughenour decided in the teens' favor, citing the navy's abandonment of this one specific aircraft in having stripped it of all useful parts, burning it in the fire dump, and sinking its remains in Lake Washington.

The teens and their friends later recovered the hulk of BuNos 76805 and 00020 and two F4F Wildcats without issue. The Wildcats went to collectors on the U.S. East Coast, and aircraft restorer Mike Rawson acquired the Helldiver wrecks. McCauley and Hummel went on to college and to raise families and, more than twenty-five years later, enjoy celebrity status in local Washington historical circles for their underwater exploits.

Mike Rawson has been in love with the Helldiver since he was a kid. His imagination was sparked when he heard his grandfather and uncle tell a story of a Helldiver crash they had stumbled upon while hunting in the mountains of Utah, on the west side of the Salt Lake Valley. It turned out that his uncle actually found the wreckage of two Marine Corps Helldivers that crashed in Black Rock Canyon, in the Oquirrh Mountains, in September 1944. Three planes were being ferried to MCAS El Toro, California, to enable a squadron to transition from Dauntlesses to Helldivers. The pilots left Hill Field, Utah, and were scud running, flying south in poor weather, when they entered a box canyon. Two crashed at the 7,500-foot level, and the third was able to return to Hill Field and report the accident. It still took searchers from Hill Field two days to find the crash sites. In 1999, with the help of crash recovery crew volunteers from the 419th Fighter Wing from nearby Hill AFB, Rawson was able to salvage the wings, aft fuselage, and tails from BuNo 75388 and the second aircraft. Parts from these aircraft became a source of patterns in Rawson's Helldiver restorations.

Around the same time, the hulk of Curtiss A-25A Shrike (BuNo 75448) and another SB2C-1A Helldiver were located

At one time there were only five SB2C Helldivers known to exist. Demand from collectors and museums have seen additional airframes recovered from various crash and dump sites, more than doubling the population. The Commemorative Air Force's SB2C-5 BuNo 83589 was recovered from a technical school in Helena, Montana, by Ed Maloney and the Planes of Fame Air Museum staff in 1962. Prior to the technical school, BuNo 83589 flew with the Navy Reserve out of NAS Glenview, Illinois. This Helldiver has been part of the CAF since 1971 and has been flying on the airshow circuit for many years. *Roger Cain*

Surviving SB2C Helldivers

BuNo/AAF serial no. Status	Model	Owner or location	
00020	SB2C-1	Chuck Wahl, Cameron Park, California	S
19075	SB2C-3	Yanks Air Museum, Chino, California	R
19866	SB2C-4	National Museum of Naval Aviation	R
75448	SB2C-1A	Fagen Fighters, Granite Falls, Minnesota	S
75552	SB2C-1A	Vultures Row Aviation, Cameron Park	R
76805/42-80449	A-25A	National Museum of U.S. Air Force	S
83321	SB2C-5	Hellenic Air Force Museum, Greece	PV
83393	SB2C-5	Fagen Fighters, Granite Falls, Minnesota	R
83410	SB2C-5	Royal Thai AF Museum, Thailand	PV
83479	SB2C-5	NASM, Chantilly, Virginia	R
83589	SB2C-5	Commemorative Air Force, Midland, Texas (N92879)	F

Status Key: F = Flyable; PV = available for Public Viewing; R = under Restoration; S = in Storage in the jungle surrounding MCAS Barbers Point, Hawaii. Rawson acquired both hulks and had the first one transported off the base to a storage site. When the truck was moving BuNo 75448, scrappers shredded the remaining airframe thinking it was just more discarded metal.

Unhappy over the loss of one rare aircraft, Rawson moved on to restoring the Shrike for the National Museum of the United States Air Force, at Dayton, Ohio.

After a multi-year restoration, Rawson delivered the restored Shrike to the Air Force Museum and moved on to other projects. He was wrapping up work on a Skyraider and a TBM when Chuck Wahl called. Wahl struck a deal for Rawson's Helldivers and the associated cache of parts, and trucks began to roll west. Wahl in turn marketed the BuNo 75552 project and the restoration services of Vulture's Row Aviation. Warbird collector Jim Slattery acquired the Helldiver and contracted with Vulture's Row Aviation to restore BuNo 75552 to authentic flying condition.

Vulture's Row Aviation has stripped the Helldiver down to its smallest components. The team uses a computer numeric controlled (CNC) milling machine, along with full heat-treating capabilities, to re-create parts that are missing or cannot be inspected, repaired, and returned to service.

Of note, Curtiss bought subassemblies from Chrysler and DeSoto for the Helldiver. Oddly enough, Chrysler built the right side of the center section and wing and DeSoto built the other. This mix and match of parts makes it extremely convoluted when rebuilding the aircraft. A part has to be checked against the manual to see if it is the most up-to-date version, and if not, it has to be crosschecked against the blueprints.

The early Helldivers had electrically controlled dive brakes and flaps. Two electric motors spun gears that went out to u-joints, which went

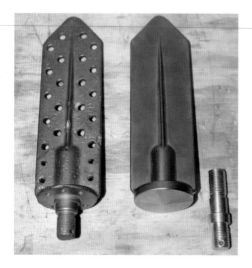

An original SBD engine mount on the left and newly milled engine mount components on the right awaiting heat treating and assembly. This is the level of restoration involved in returning these rare warbirds to the air.

down to drive shafts that twisted to move the flaps up and down. Early Helldivers had a lot of problems with this system, and people died because dissimilar flaps would deploy, causing asymmetric lift, one side up and one side down. Typically, there was not enough altitude for recovery when this occurred during a landing pattern.

"One of Curtiss's modification programs was to convert all of the electrical motors in the flap and dive brake systems to hydraulic motors, but leave all of the linkages. That was a band-aid, and was probably not a good idea," said Wahl. "So they stopped production to change the entire system to all-hydraulic cylinders. There's ten of them along the back side of the wing, and they used the same cylinder that raises and lowers the main gear for flap and dive brake extension.

The rear gunner's seat and gun mount for the SBD has already been restored and awaits installation in the fuselage.

"What we're doing on this airplane is incorporating all of Curtiss's later production line modifications for safety because this aircraft will fly. And because we're going through this aircraft from ground zero, we can take a system that was marginal and replace it with a better-designed and safer system from a later model Helldiver. It will not change the aircraft from a cosmetic standpoint, but it will be a more reliable, safe aircraft to fly. That makes it a real challenge to restore this airplane, but it is the only way to do it safely."

Currently the Helldiver's center section and horizontal stabilizer are in jigs and work is steadily progressing. Rollout of the Helldiver is expected in three years or so.

Dauntless under Rebuild

The center section of Douglas SBD-4 BuNo 10694 sits in a jig next to the Helldiver in the Vulture's Row Aviation shops. This scout bomber was built in El Segundo, adjacent to today's Los Angeles International Airport, and accepted by the navy on March 17, 1943. The plane was

Douglas Dauntless (A-24B 42-54532) of the Commemorative Air Force's Dixie Wing is one of twenty-four surviving A-24s and SBD dive bombers that exist to this day. Recoveries from Lake Michigan have added to the population of surviving airframes, some of which have been restored to flying condition. *Roger Cain*

flown the short distance south to NAS Roosevelt Base, a short strip surrounded by houses and part of the larger NAS Terminal Island complex in the Los Angeles Harbor. Here the West Coast Aircraft Delivery Unit (ADC) received newly built aircraft from Douglas, Lockheed, Vultee, and others.

SBD-4 BuNo 10694 departed for NAS Seattle on April 1, 1943, where she joined Composite Squadron 34 (VC-34). A little more than one month later, the dive bomber was at NAS Alameda for deployment to the Pacific. However, BuNo 10694 remained stateside, joining Bombing Squadron Five (VB-5) at NAS Alameda on May 14. On July 27, the plane was transferred to VB-18, where she remained for ten days before again heading to Terminal Island to join Scouting Squadron 52 (VS-52). Here BuNo 10694 was used in operational training to get pilots and radiomen/gunners ready for combat. BuNo 10694 flew in this role until January 23, 1944, when the SBD was transferred to NAS Jacksonville, Florida. Two days later, BuNo 10694 was assigned to the Naval Operational Training Command, and the aircraft's record card shows it was transferred to the Training Command Carrier Qualification Unit at NAS Glenview, Illinois, on May 29, 1944, and stricken from the inventory on June 26, 1944.

Surviving SBD Dauntless Dive Bombers

Model	BuNo or SN	Owner or location	Status
A-24A	42-60817	Tillamook Air Museum, Tillamook, Oregon	F
A-24B	42-54532	Commemorative Air Force, Midland, Texas (Dixie Wing)	F
A-24B	42-54582	National Museum of U.S. Air Force, Dayton, Ohio	PV
A-24B	42-54593	Kevin R. Smith, Fredericksburg, Virginia	R
A-24B	42-54643	Fantasy of Flight, Polk City, Florida	S
A-24B	42-54654	MAPS Air Museum, Akron, Ohio	R
A-24B	42-54682	Lone Star Flight Museum, Galveston, Texas	F
SBD-1	BuNo 01612	USS Midway Museum, San Diego, California	R
SBD-2	BuNo 02106	National Museum of Naval Aviation, Pensacola, Florida	PV
SBD-2	BuNo 02173	Pacific Aviation Museum, Pearl Harbor, Hawaii	R
SBD-3	BuNo 06508	National Museum of Naval Aviation, Pensacola, Florida	PV
SBD-3	BuNo 06583	National Museum of the Marine Corps, Quantico, Virginia	R
SBD-3	BuNo 06624	Air Zoo, Kalamazoo, Michigan	PV
SBD-3	BuNo 06626	National Museum of Naval Aviation, Pensacola, Florida	S
SBD-3	BuNo 06694	USS *Lexington* Museum, Corpus Christi, Texas	R
SBD-4	BuNo 06833	National Museum of Naval Aviation, Pensacola, Florida	PV
SBD-4	BuNo 06953	Royal New Zealand Air Force Museum, Christchurch, New Zealand (RNZAF serial NZ5037). Displayed as wreck.	PV
SBD-4	BuNo 06900	San Diego Aerospace Museum, San Diego, California	PV
SBD-4	BuNo 10508	Pima Air & Space Museum, Tucson, Arizona	S
SBD-4	BuNo 10518	Yanks Air Museum, Chino, California	PV
SBD-4	BuNo 10575	Midway Airport, Chicago, Illinois	PV
SBD-4	BuNo 10694	Vulture's Row Aviation, Cameron Park, California	R
SBD-5	BuNo 28536	Planes of Fame, Chino, California	F
SBD-5	BuNo 36173	Patriots Point Naval & Maritime Museum, Mount Pleasant, South Carolina	PV
SBD-5	BuNo 36175	Palm Springs Air Museum, Palm Springs, California	PV
SBD-5	BuNo 36177	National Museum of Naval Aviation, Pensacola, Florida	R
SBD-6	BuNo 54605	National Air & Space Museum, Washington, D.C.	PV

Status Key: F = Flyable; PV = available for Public Viewing; R = under Restoration; S = in Storage

Interestingly, one day prior to its paperwork transfer to Glenview, Ens. James Todaro was attempting to qualify on board USS *Sable*. Ensign Todaro had 120 hours in SBDs and 350 hours total time as a pilot. On his sixth takeoff of the day, BuNo 10694's Wright R-1820-52 radial engine coughed prior to takeoff. It was running smoothly, so Ensign Todaro was launched into the air. As the plane was clawing for altitude, the engine stopped completely, and Ensign Todaro was forced to ditch. Uninjured, he was recovered and went on to fly another day.

As Ensign Todaro was exiting the aircraft, USS *Sable* was bearing down upon him and the aircraft. The aircraft carrier struggled to turn to starboard to miss the floating SBD and split the dive bomber forward of the tail and aft of the rear cockpit. The plane

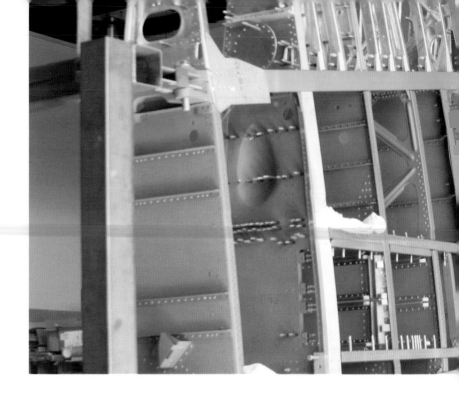

immediately sank beneath the waves of Lake Michigan at 10:45 a.m., on May 28, 1944.

Fifty years later, the National Museum of Naval Aviation was looking to recover additional aircraft from Lake Michigan. Unfortunately, they didn't have much of a budget. They contracted with A&T Recovery Inc. of Chicago to bring up a number of aircraft and in exchange, A&T could keep one of the planes, with the caveat that the museum had one year to raise the funds to pay for the recoveries or A&T would receive clear title to the aircraft.

A&T brought SBD BuNo 10694 to the surface in 1994. One year later, unable to raise the funds to reimburse A&T for recovery of BuNo 10694 and other aircraft, the Naval Museum authorized A&T to sell the plane, which was bought by a collector in Florida. It was subsequently acquired by Jim Slattery for his planned naval aircraft museum in San Diego, and then shipped to Vulture's Row Aviation for restoration, arriving in February 2011.

The aircraft has been disassembled, jigged, and restoration work has been underway for more than a year. The first assembly to come off the plane was the propeller. Only one blade was damaged in the ditching so the other two have been overhauled, a third added, and the assembly inspected, painted, and made ready for installation. As the engine came apart, it was quickly evident why Ensign Todaro

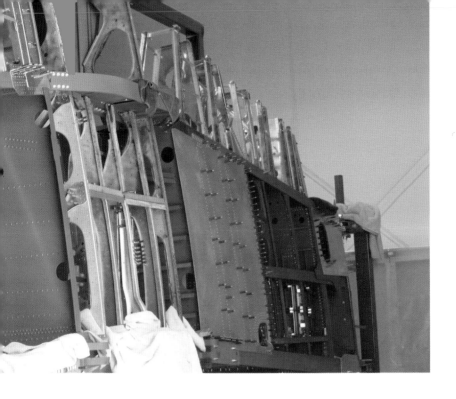

The wing and center section of the Helldiver is extremely complex. In addition to the main landing gear, this section holds the bomb bay. Bomb racks can be seen installed at the center of the wing structure.

ended up in the drink. One of the cylinders split in two, which immediately ended the aircraft's upward and forward motion.

The main wing spar was damaged in the accident and during the restoration the aircraft's center section was opened to enable the installation of a new upper spar cap. New wing attach angles were made in the CNC milling machine along with new landing gear supports. New wing leading edges have been made and the center section closed up with new upper wing skins. The center dive flap and spar have also been installed—this is the iconic perforated flap that is seen extended in all of the Dauntless dive photos from the Battle of Midway.

The aircraft is coming close to having the cockpit section of the fuselage installed, and then it will start to look like the dive bomber that it truly is. Plans call for both the Helldiver and the Dauntless to be finished in the same early war, tri-color blue scheme. Jim Slattery also owns the Brewster F3A-1 Corsair under restoration by Ezell Aviation in Texas, and it will wear the same paint scheme. It will be an amazing sight to see all three aircraft in the air.

The Last Vindicator
SB2U-2 up from Lake Michigan

The Vought SB2U Vindicator dive bomber is extremely important in the history of the U.S. Navy as it was one of the sea service's first low-wing monoplanes with folding wings and retractable landing gear. It was ordered at the same time as the Douglas TBD Devastator, and the low, folding-wing configuration set the standard for future carrier-based aircraft. In 1934, when the navy ordered prototypes of the SB2U be built, it was state-of-the-art. However, monoplane naval fighters were not widely trusted at the time, and the U.S. Navy followed up its order for Vindicators with an order for Vought's XSB3U-1, another biplane scout bomber, just in case the monoplane was unsuccessful. The prototype XSB2U-2 made its first flight on January 4, 1936, and was delivered to the navy for testing four months later.

The Vought SB2U Vindicator was the U.S. Navy's first low-wing monoplane fitted with folding wings and retractable landing gear. This aircraft entered service when biplanes were the sea service's design of choice. Shown is an SB2U-1, similar in appearance to SB2U-2 BuNo 1383, which was recovered from Lake Michigan and restored at the National Museum of Naval Aviation in Pensacola, Florida. *U.S. Navy*

USS *Wolverine* (IX81) at rest on Lake Michigan awaits the next round of naval aviators attempting to qualify for landing on an aircraft carrier. Originally the sidewheel steamer *Seeandbee*, she was acquired on March 12, 1942, and converted by removing her upper decks and replacing them with a 550-foot-long landing deck and island. *Wolverine* and her sister fresh-water carrier *Sable* were "unclassified miscellaneous" vessels and designated IX-64 and IX-81, respectively. SB2U-2 BuNo 1383 failed to land aboard *Wolverine* and ended up at the bottom of Lake Michigan. *U.S. Navy via Tailhook Association*

Shortly after being raised from the bottom of Lake Michigan, Vought SB2U-2 BuNo 1383 was towed into a safe harbor while suspended about forty feet underwater. Once in protected waters, the aircraft is boomed to prevent any oil or fuel from contaminating the lake. The plane is then lifted onto shore, processed to remove fuel and oil, and prepare it for transport. *A&T Recovery via NMNA*

Dismantled, the last SB2U awaits shipment from Illinois to Florida for restoration at the National Museum of Naval Aviation. Note the positioning of the oil cooler on top of the engine mount at the rear of the engine accessory section and the telescope gun/bombsight projecting through the windscreen. *NMNA*

The Vindicator's success in navy trials saw the sea service cancel its orders for the XSB3U-1 biplane scout bomber and purchase 54 SB2Us. Bombing Squadron Three (VB-3) accepted the first Vindicator on December 20, 1937, and the navy followed with an order for 58 SB2U-2s. Another order was placed on September 25, 1939, for 57 SB2U-3s. The plane was powered by an air-cooled, fourteen-cylinder (arranged in two rows of seven), 825-horsepower Pratt & Whitney R-1535 radial engine. And although lightly armed by World War II standards, the scout bomber was equipped with a pair of .50-caliber machine guns (one forward firing and one flexible gun fired by the radio operator/gunner in the rear seat). In addition, the SB2U could carry 1,000 pounds of bombs. A total of 260 of all Vindicator models were built by Vought, including aircraft built for the French (known as the V-156B) and British (V-156B-1).

When war with the Japanese broke out, Vindicators were on board USS *Lexington*, *Saratoga*, *Ranger*, and *Wasp*, and the U.S. Marine Corps scout bombing squadrons 131 and 241 were flying them as well. During the Japanese attack on Pearl Harbor, half a dozen VMSB-231 Vindicators were destroyed on the ground at MCAS Ewa. Sixteen days later, seventeen VMSB-231 Vindicators flew more than 1,100 miles to Midway with a PBY Catalina flying boat as escort. The flight took nine hours and forty-five minutes and stands today as the longest mass over-water flight by single-engine aircraft.

Once at the island outpost, the Vindicators were absorbed with Marine Fighter Squadron 221 (VMF-221) to form Marine Air Group 22 for the defense of Midway. Additional SBD Dauntless dive bombers were brought in by aircraft ferry to reinforce the Marine Air Group.

Both U.S. Navy and Marine Corps SB2Us fought the Japanese at Midway. On June 3, 1942, eleven Marine SB2Us, each carrying one 500-pound bomb on the centerline rack, proceeded to attack the incoming Japanese fleet. The SB2Us engaged the fleet from the side opposite the aircraft carriers and focused on the battleship *Haruna*. Although their bombs missed the ship, a 500-pounder dropped by Maj. Benjamin W. Norris was close enough to cause the battleship some damage. Four SB2Us failed to return to base, although two crews were rescued by marauding PT boats.

Later that day, six SBDs and six SB2Us were dispatched to finish off a Japanese carrier reported dead in the water and burning. By the time the dive bombers arrived in the target area, poor weather prevented them from locating the carrier. All planes returned to base, except for the one piloted by Major Norris, who, it appeared, became disoriented and flew into the undercast never to be seen or heard from again.

Shortly after day break on June 5, 1943, Marine Air Group 22's SBDs and SB2Us were sent after the cruisers *Mikuma* and *Mogami*.

After arrival at the National Museum of Naval Aviation's restoration shops, BuNo 1383 was stripped down to its smallest components. Here, reassembly has begun with the horizontal and vertical stabilizers having been reattached to the aircraft's tubular frame. *NMNA*

Test fitting of the SB2U's vertical and horizontal stabilizer fairings is underway. Notice the control cables have been rigged to the rudder and elevator, and the fabric-covered trussed fuselage construction. Newer aircraft, such as the SBD Dauntless, were built using stressed metal skin covering the fuselage frame. *NMNA*

Marine Capt. Richard E. Fleming led the second section of aircraft in for the attack on *Mikuma*. He scored a near-miss, but his aircraft was struck by anti-aircraft fire from the heavy cruiser. Fleming's aircraft was on fire and he was possibly incapacitated as his Vindicator failed to pull out of its dive, killing Fleming and his radio operator/gunner Private First Class George A. Toms. For his actions, Fleming was posthumously awarded the Medal of Honor. *Mikuma* was sent to the bottom later in the day by SBDs from USS *Enterprise*, and *Mogami* was set on fire but escaped to fight another day.

Vindicators also served in the Atlantic with Carrier Air Group 9 in 1942, and went on board USS *Essex* in January 1943. Less than a month later, the SB2Us were replaced with more advanced types and by the end of February nearly all of the Vindicators in the fleet had been transferred to the training command.

The Last Vindicator

The SB2U-2 model was equipped with the 825-horsepower Pratt & Whitney R-1535-96 engine, and the last of fifty-eight of the -2s, BuNo 1383, was delivered to the U.S. Navy on July 10, 1939, to Battleforce, NAS Norfolk, Virginia. On October 26, BuNo 1383 went aboard USS *Ranger* (CV-4) with VB-4 for patrols off the U.S. East Coast. It is interesting to note the *Ranger* was the first U.S. Navy ship designed from the outset as an aircraft carrier; all previous carriers had been converted from other types.

After nine months on the Ranger, BuNo 1383 was transferred to the USS *Wasp* (CV-7) on July 17, 1940. After *Wasp* completed its shakedown cruise, the carrier departed Norfolk in October for maneuvers en route to Guantanamo Bay, Cuba. The ship and its air wing trained in the Caribbean Sea until the end of November. Shortly after *Wasp* returned to Norfolk, BuNo 1383 was transferred to Scouting Squadron 41 (VS-41) back on board *Ranger*. Flying neutrality patrols from the ship in East Coast waters, BuNo 1383 was on board *Ranger* for a little more than nine months. On September 10, 1942, BuNo 1383 joined Bombing Squadron 9 (VB-9), which was forming the air wing for USS *Essex* (CV-9). From March to May 1943, BuNo 1383 underwent an overhaul at NAS Norfolk, prior to being assigned to the air station's Carrier Qualification Training Unit (CQTU) Atlantic.

On May 18, 1943, BuNo 1383 was transferred north to CQTU Glenview, a naval air station in the suburbs northeast of Chicago, Illinois. Fledgling naval aviators would practice carrier landings at one of Glenview's many outlying fields before attempting to land on board either USS *Sable* (IX 81) or USS *Wolverine* (IX 64). These were converted steamers that had plied the Great Lakes for years. Each ship

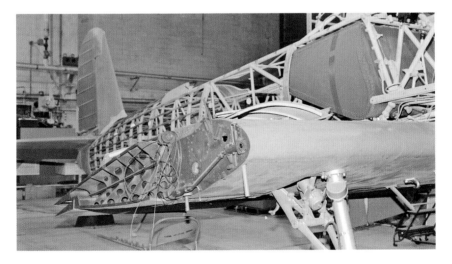

The SB2U's wing attach and fold points are readied to receive the outer wing panels. The fuselage fuel tank can be seen mounted between the two cockpits. *NMNA*

had its upper decks removed and an approximately 550-foot-long aircraft landing deck and navigation island installed. Neither ship was fitted with elevators, nor did they have hangar decks to enable aircraft to be taken below for maintenance or storage.

A little more than a month after BuNo 1383 arrived at Glenview, Marine Corps Second Lt. A.W. Lemmons took the aircraft out to qualify on board *Wolverine* sailing across Lake Michigan. As he approached, Lieutenant Lemmons was given the cut sign from the landing signal officer giving him permission to cut the throttle and touch down on the carrier deck. For some reason, Lieutenant Lemmons continued over the aft end of the ship under power, crossing over the arresting wires on the aft end of the deck. As he approached the crash barrier, Lieutenant Lemmons applied power trying to clear it. The barrier caught the SB2U's arresting hook, snapping it from the dive bomber and yanking it out of the sky. Lieutenant Lemmons and the SB2U struck the starboard side of the deck and inertia carried the young marine flier and his aircraft over the side. Lieutenant Lemmons was fished out of Lake Michigan, but BuNo 1383 sank to the bottom. Subsequently, on July 28, 1943, SB2U-2 BuNo 1383 was stricken from the navy's inventory.

Recovery and Restoration

Forty-seven years after Lieutenant Lemmons dumped SB2U-2 BuNo 1383 into Lake Michigan, childhood friends and divers Allan Olson and Taras Lyssenko of A&T Recovery in Chicago, Illinois, brought the Vindicator to the surface. Olson and Lyssenko spent nearly a decade surveying the bottom of the southern end of Lake Michigan, an area ripe with an estimated 150 naval aircraft and dozens of shipwrecks. The pair even discovered the final resting place of the World War I German submarine UC-97, a war prize that had been displayed in Chicago from 1919 to 1921. Due to treaty regulations, the U.S. Navy felt it was obligated to destroy the sub and towed it more than twenty-five miles out into Lake Michigan and used it for target practice. It sat on the bottom for more than seventy years before being relocated by Olson and Lyssenko.

Having worked to develop a database of under-lake wrecks, Olson and Lyssenko formed A&T Recovery and approached the National Museum of Naval Aviation in Pensacola, Florida, about the institution's interest in recovering some of the rarer and historic aircraft resting on the bottom of the lake. A&T Recovery offered to recover

Close-up view of the radio operator/gunner's cockpit showing the radio racks, mounted just behind the fuel tank. *NMNA*

SB2U-2 BuNo 1383, an SBD Dauntless, and a solid-wing Grumman F4F Wildcat for the museum in exchange for a pair of Wildcats and a Dauntless. A&T Recovery would take all of the risk, and the Naval Museum would obtain one previously extinct aircraft type, the SB2U Vindicator, along with two others it needed for its collection. At the time, the Naval Museum did not have a Dauntless in its collection, and over the years, through recoveries, it has added more than a dozen, many of which are on loan to other institutions.

"We were surveying the whole southern basin of Lake Michigan, so we started our search five miles from where the

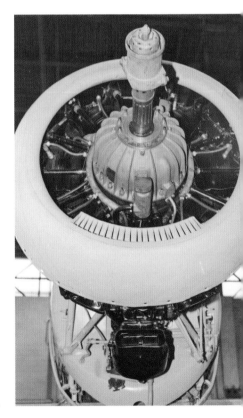

Components for the Pratt & Whitney R-1535 radial engine, from the firewall forward, have been installed onto the fuselage of BuNo 1383. The cowl nose bowl frames the engine. Notice the ignition wires connected to the spark plugs at the top of the cylinders. *NMNA*

Vindicator was reported to have crashed into the lake," said Lyssenko. "Keep in mind that coordinates from this time period are notoriously inaccurate; radar was poor, and if the location reported comes from dead-reckoning navigation, it could be miles off. What we did know was that there was a Vindicator somewhere in the vicinity."

"As soon as we dropped the sonar into the water, Allan [Olson] and I got into a friendly argument like we tend to do, and when we looked up, there was an airplane on the edge of the sonar paper," Lyssenko said. "We were about five miles off course, but there it was. So we turned around, went to a new corner point, and started the search again, and there it was. The exact same plane I had seen on the paper. It took us about one half hour. However, if we had started on the opposite side of the grid, it would have taken us three or four weeks to find it."

Although they had found the target, Olson and Lyssenko continued to scan the area to ensure that the aircraft they had located was indeed the target they were searching for. Nearing the end of the day, they returned to the site and sent divers over the side to visually inspect the plane. "We didn't tell our guys what we were after," said Lyssenko. "After descending 150 feet to the wreck, and returning, the divers asked, 'What the hell was that?' They'd never seen a Vindicator and because it was missing all of its fabric it looked like a skeleton."

Once delivered to the National Museum of Naval Aviation, volunteers began the task of carefully dismantling the Vindicator and cataloging the parts. Much of the aircraft could be refurbished; however, some of it would have to be re-created. And therein was the museum's biggest problem—very little documentation of how the SB2U was built existed.

Unbelievably, some small components were sourced from the navy's parts inventory, nearly fifty years after the type was phased out of service. Other bits and pieces came from aviation parts sellers and collectors, while still others were remanufactured in the museum's shops. The entire aircraft was disassembled cleaned, treated, preserved, painted, and reassembled. The museum estimates that between 90 and 95 percent of the aircraft is original—a testament to the craftsmanship of the volunteers.

After an eight-year restoration by volunteers who donated more than twenty thousand hours of their time, SB2U-2 BuNo 1383 was rolled out on February 5, 1999. The aircraft wears the colors of VB-9 on board the *Essex*.

Freshly restored and rolled out into the Florida sunshine, BuNo 1383 emerges from the shops at the National Museum of Naval Aviation. The eight-year restoration required more than twenty thousand volunteer work hours. *NMNA*

The restored SB2U is now on display in the National Museum of Naval Aviation's World War II aircraft gallery. A Pratt & Whitney R-1535 engine is displayed in front of the SB2U, and this view shows the Vindicator's bomb toss apparatus on the centerline 500-pound bomb, used to force the bomb down and away from the propeller arc during high-angle dive-bombing attacks.

Two Navy Crosses in SBD-2 BuNo 2106

Shortly after the Battle of Midway, SBD-2 BuNo 2106 is on the ramp, bullet holes visible on the wings and fuselage. Note the open life raft door and that the rear gunner's twin 0.30-cal. machine guns have been removed from the dive bomber. *NMNA*

Seeing Douglas SBD-2 BuNo 2106 completely restored, sitting on the carrier deck diorama at the National Museum of Naval Aviation in Pensacola, Florida, hides the bravery, skill, and sacrifice of the crews that flew this aircraft, and thousands more like it, in combat.

Imagine you're at 9,500 feet. It's a couple of minutes before 8 a.m. on June 4, 1942; the morning's golden sunlight gives the moment's events a surreal look. Sighting the Japanese fleet, you push the Dauntless's canopy closed. You can see Japanese Zero fighters on combat air patrol descending on your squadron from 20,000 feet. They've got the height advantage, but you'll only be sitting here for another couple of seconds.

Pulling the goggles down over your eyes, you then push the transmit button on the microphone, giving a heads-up to your radioman/gunner telling him that you are about to attack. He stows the twin, flexible 0.30-cal. machine guns, closes his canopy, and gets ready for one wild ride. He's counting on you to hit the target and bring him home safely . . . but you both know the odds are heavily stacked against you.

A Japanese Zero has just shot down your wingman, and below you, the carrier *Hiryu* and her escorts are furiously firing anti-aircraft shells that are bursting all around. They need to destroy you before you can deliver your cargo. You lower the dive flaps, set the controls, and push the stick forward.

Your wingman follows you down, and behind him the other planes in your squadron push over—separated by only seconds.

Diving down at a 70-degree angle, slight control inputs to the ailerons line up the carrier in your sights. Zeros are nipping at your tail. An occasional machine gun burst from behind fails to find its mark.

Twenty seconds pass as you're looking nearly straight down at the ocean below.

Thirty seconds. Two Zeros are closing on your tail, closing faster, hoping to get into range to kill you.

The starboard side of BuNo 2106 displays the battle damage inflicted by enemy gunners. It is amazing that the flight crew, Marine 1st Lt. Daniel Iverson and Marine Pfc. Wallace J. Reid, came through such intense anti-aircraft fire with only minor wounds. *NMNA*

Pulling back on the stick, you pass 4,000 feet and you put your eye up to the bombsight to select your aiming point. There's a rising sun emblem on each end of the carrier's deck.

Rolling the aircraft a few degrees clockwise, you've set the crosshairs in the center of the carrier's deck. It feels as if the ship is rushing up to greet you.

At 1,500 feet you release the 1,000-pound bomb from the centerline rack. The SBD jumps up from the loss of the weight of the bomb and you cob the power until the throttle hits the stops. You dive for the deck to avoid enemy fire. Clearing the carrier you use your momentum to carry you out of range and back up to altitude.

Looking back you see that your bomb has struck the carrier. Two other Japanese fighters, these with fixed landing gear, have joined to pursue you as you climb for the nearest cloud.

That's about how it went for Marine First Lt. Daniel Iverson and Marine Private First Class Wallace J. Reid flying SBD-2 BuNo 2106 in the Battle of Midway on June 4. When they got back to the island's airstrip, they were low on gas, their radio had been shot out, they had no airspeed indicator, the hydraulic fluid had long since leaked out after a line was pierced by an enemy bullet, and only one main landing gear would lock down—the other jammed in the retracted position by a Japanese anti-aircraft shell fragment.

Iverson successfully landed the plane with one wheel up, and through some miracle kept the SBD on the centerline of the runway, avoiding a number of parked B-17 Flying Fortresses. Iverson was wounded in the legs and face, and his radioman was shot in the foot by attacking Zeros. Both men were bandaged up and the following day sent in pursuit of the Japanese cruisers *Mogami* and *Mikuma*.

At Midway, BuNo 2106 was lifted up, its left landing gear lowered, towed off the runway, and then the counting began. When the final tally was in, 259 bullet holes were counted in the SBD. Many of the bullets had impacted the pilot's and gunner's armor plate. Both men were lucky to be alive.

For their actions, Iverson was awarded the navy's highest honor, the Navy Cross, and radioman/gunner Reid was awarded the Distinguished Flying Cross. As for BuNo 2106, the long process of patching the dive bomber's many holes began. The landing gear was repaired, and the plane made ready for flight again. Later in the war an aircraft with this much damage would be stripped of all usable parts and then pushed off into the jungle or over the side of the ship as

SBD-2 BuNo 2106 was at Pearl Harbor during the December 7, 1941, attack. SBD BuNo 2106 was flown by Lt. (j.g.) Mark Twain Whittier and radioman/gunner Forest G. Stanley in the counterattacks at Lae-Salamaua, New Guinea, in March 1942. Whittier was awarded the Navy Cross for his leadership and his attack on the light cruiser *Yubari* in the New Guinea action while flying BuNo 2106. *National Archives*

While approaching USS *Sable IX 81* in SBD-2 BuNo 2106 on June 11, 1943, 2nd Lt. Donald A. Douglas Jr. (USMCR) was waved off. Too low and too slow to abort the landing, the plane stalled and Douglas's right wing struck the water. The Dauntless cartwheeled into Lake Michigan and then sank. Douglas was quickly rescued. *U.S. Navy*

just so much scrap. However, at this stage in the war, on an island out in the middle of the Pacific, an SBD Dauntless was a prized fighting machine that could not be spared and the navy and marines did not have the luxury of drawing a replacement aircraft. BuNo 2106 was made flyable and would continue to soldier on.

Prior to and the Opening Months of the War

Built by the Douglas Aircraft Co. at the company's El Segundo factory on the west side of Los Angeles, BuNo 2106 was accepted by the U.S. Navy on December 28, 1940. Two days later the dive bomber was delivered to the fleet aircraft pool at NAS North Island, San Diego, California. The next day, BuNo 2106 was assigned to Bombing Squadron Two (VB-2) aboard USS *Lexington* (CV-2).

For the first half of 1940, BuNo 2106 and the *Lexington* air wing trained and trained hard. Patrols, field carrier landing practice, bombing, gunnery, squadron tactics, and anti-shipping and anti-submarine patrols occupied the pilots and gunners of VB-2. On September 9, 1941, VB-2 and other squadrons flew east to take part in the U.S. Army's General Headquarters maneuvers. Here the carrier-based planes were operating from unimproved, land-based strips that wreaked havoc on the aircraft. First it was mud, which then dried to a fine dust—something aircraft flying over the ocean are not equipped for. To remedy all of the environmental problems, all eighteen aircraft in VB-2 had to have their engines replaced upon returning to San Diego at the end of the month.

Recovered from 164 feet below the surface of Lake Michigan, SBD-2 BuNo 2106 is one of the most historic surviving U.S. Navy combat aircraft. Here A&T Recovery has towed the Dauntless from the lake into a safe harbor and begins the lift onto an environmentally secure work area that will prevent any fuel, oil, or hydraulic fluid from washing back into the water. *A&T Recovery via NMNA*

The dive bomber is in good condition considering it cartwheeled into the lake. Note that the underside of the wing was deformed during the crash and that all of the fabric on the control surfaces and the rubber on the tires are gone. Although the life raft compartment is open on the fuselage, it appears that the raft is still inside. *A&T Recovery via NMNA*

During the second week of October, *Lexington* left San Diego for Pearl Harbor. All of VB-2's aircraft were brought on the trip and some engines were replaced en route to Hawaii. On December 1, 1941, *Lexington*'s air group flew ashore and the ship steamed into the harbor later that day.

Two days later, *Lexington* was given the order to reinforce Midway Island with eighteen SB2U-3 Vindicators from VMSB-231. Sailing as Task Force 12 (TF-12) under the command of Rear Adm. John H. Newton, the heavy cruisers *Astoria* (CA-34), *Chicago* (CA-29), and *Portland* (CA-33), along with five destroyers, escorted *Lexington* on its transport mission. TF-12 steamed out of Pearl Harbor on December 5, 1941, leaving the SBDs of VB-2 behind at Ford Island. Sailing north, TF-12 was 500 miles south and east of Midway Island when the Japanese attacked Oahu. As the battle raged, TF-12 was recalled to Pearl Harbor and the SB2Us came home with the carrier. They would fly to Midway escorted by a PBY Catalina later in the month.

As Japanese dive, torpedo, and high-level bombers decimated the Pacific Fleet and the air bases that ringed the island of Oahu, the SBDs of *Lexington*'s scout and bombing squadrons escaped relatively unharmed. Scouting Two (VS-2) lost SBD-2 BuNo 2146 and SBD-3 BuNo 4639, and VB-2 lost SBD-2 BuNo 2112 primarily because

Once at the National Museum of Naval Aviation in Pensacola, Florida, volunteers begin the task of cleaning the plane before disassembly. The outer wing panels were removed before the dive bomber was trucked from Illinois to the museum. *NMNA*

the Japanese attacks were concentrated on the seaplane ramp area's hangars, sparing other hangars surrounding the Ford Island airfield. When *Lexington* returned to port, the SB2Us were off-loaded and its standard air group, including BuNo 2106, returned to the ship.

Second Navy Cross at Lae-Salamaua

On March 8, 1942, the Japanese landed troops at the town of Lae and the port of Salamaua on the north coast of New Guinea. Having patrolled the surrounding seas for any Allied warships, the Japanese were complacent that they faced no opposition. The following day, the invaders began bringing supplies ashore and reinforcing their beachheads.

SBD-2 BuNo 2106 undergoing restoration in the shadow of the sole surviving Consolidated PB2Y Coronado (PB2Y-5R BuNo 7099) at the National Museum of Naval Aviation. Notice that restoration technicians have left some of the SBD-2's original layers of paint exposed on the vertical tail. *NMNA*

Restoration workers have hung the Dauntless's 1,000-horsepower Wright R-1820-52 radial engine and are seen working in the accessory section. *NMNA*

Task Force 11, consisting of the carriers *Lexington* and *Yorktown*, escorted by eight cruisers and fourteen destroyers, had been steaming for a planned attack on the harbor and airfield complexes at Rabaul and Gasmata on New Britain Island, 400 miles north and east of Lae. With word of the Japanese landings, TF-11 diverted to the Gulf of Papua, north of Port Moresby, New Guinea, but on the south side of the island. Although TF-11 was riding at anchor only 150 miles from the invading Japanese, the American ships were shielded from detection by Japanese scout planes because the Owen Stanley Mountain Range formed a wall down the center of the island. The Owen Stanley's reach an average of 11,000 feet (3,350 meters) with the tallest point being Mount Victoria at 13,248 feet (4,038 meters). And when clouds obscured the mountain tops, they had a tendency to grab aircraft out of the sky.

After conferring with a number of local commercial pilots, the navy fliers were told where and how to safely navigate through a gap in the mountains to reach the north coast. Fifty-two aircraft from each carrier took off to attack targets in the Lae and Salamaua area on the morning of March 10.

SBD BuNo 2106 was flown by Lt. (j.g.) Mark Twain Whittier and radioman/gunner Forest G. Stanley. Whittier followed a squadron

Two views of the cockpit, as it was recovered and after restoration. Note the telescopic bombsight and the condition of the guns and gun charging handles in the as-recovered photo. *NMNA*

mate down to attack a cruiser. The leading aircraft's 1,000-pound bomb went into the water and, seeing this, Whittier was able to make corrections to his aim. Whittier dropped his bomb and pulled up, but could not get his dive flap to retract, which slowed him to about 110 mph as he tried to put distance between himself and the cruiser. Thinking fast, Whittier cycled his hydraulic system by lowering and raising his landing gear, which reset, enabling him to raise the dive flap, gain speed, and get out of the cruiser's gun range.

Upon returning to the carrier and debriefing, Whittier's squadron mates told him that his bomb struck the rear of the cruiser, raising the stern out of the water, and splitting the hull when it came down. It is assumed that Whittier struck the light cruiser *Yubari*, which was heavily damaged and had to be towed back to the Japanese home islands for extensive repairs. For his leadership and for pressing home his attack, Whittier was awarded the Navy Cross.

Lexington's and *Yorktown*'s aircraft returned from the attack with the loss of only one plane. The light cruiser *Yubari* and a pair of destroyers were heavily damaged, three transports were on fire, one was sinking and another was listing heavily and presumed to sink, and a seaplane tender was dead in the water.

Lexington returned to Pearl Harbor for a refit before its next engagement and BuNo 2106 was transferred to the base's aircraft pool. Here the SBD's engine was changed and the aircraft was made ready to fight again. On April 16, *Lexington* left for what was to become

Front quarter view of SBD-2 BuNo 2106 after restoration and on display in the carrier aircraft gallery of the National Museum of Naval Aviation. Note the centerline bomb drop crutch that tosses the bomb down and away from the propeller's arc.

the Battle of the Coral Sea, which occurred on May 7 and 8. Planes from *Lexington* and *Yorktown* heavily damaged the Japanese carrier *Shokaku*. In return, bombs and torpedoes from the enemy carrier's aircraft, and those of her sistership *Zuikaku*, caused fires that became uncontrollable on board *Lexington*. The *Lexington* was scuttled later in the afternoon of May 8.

While *Lexington* was fighting at Coral Sea, BuNo 2106 never left Pearl Harbor. From the base aircraft pool, BuNo 2106 was assigned to Bombing Three (VB-3) of the USS *Saratoga* (CV-3) air group. However, *Saratoga* was on the West Coast for overhaul having taken a torpedo from the Japanese submarine *I-6* on January 11, 1942. BuNo 2106 and VB-3 were then assigned to *Yorktown*. Subsequently, BuNo 2106 was administratively attached to Marine Aircraft Wing Two (MAW-2) and then, on May 23, was assigned to Marine Scout Bombing Squadron 241 (VMSB-241) based at Midway Island. Five days later, BuNo 2106 was on the island, and when the Japanese attack came, First Lt. Daniel Iverson and Marine Private First Class Wallace J. Reid took the plane into battle.

Into and Out of the Drink

After its engagement at Midway, BuNo 2106 was shipped to Pearl Harbor, arriving there on July 3, 1942. Two days later, the Dauntless left the Hawaiian Islands, coming dockside at NAS San Diego on July 22. Here she was put into the care of Air Base Group Two (ABG-2) for a well-deserved overhaul. Nearly six months later, on January 19, 1943, BuNo 2106 was transferred to the Carrier Qualification Training Unit (CQTU) at NAS Glenview, Illinois.

From CQTU Glenview, BuNo 2106 would enable fledgling naval aviators to gain experience landing aboard ship, specifically *Wolverine* (IX 64) or *Sable* (IX 81). Second Lt. Donald A. Douglas Jr. (USMCR) was at the controls of BuNo 2106 on June 11, 1943. Lieutenant Douglas had 377.7 total hours flight time, of which 83.4 were in SBDs. Lieutenant Douglas was approaching *Sable*, but he was low and slow. The landing signal officer waved Lieutenant Douglas off, and as he applied power and turned left to avoid the carrier, BuNo 2106's engine coughed. The engine caught again, but the aircraft was too low and the right wingtip hit the water. BuNo 2106 cartwheeled around its horizontal axis landing on its belly. Lieutenant Douglas was quickly fished out of the water by the Coast Guard cutter on plane guard duty as the Dauntless sank to the bottom.

Settling on the bottom of Lake Michigan, 164 feet down, BuNo 2106 lay there undisturbed for more than fifty years. The National Museum of Naval Aviation had contracted with A&T Recovery of Chicago to scout a number of aircraft wrecks to determine which planes had the most historical value and, of those, which were worth salvaging.

A&T's divers dove on what they determined to be BuNo 2106 and found that the Dauntless had lost its starboard outer wing panel and some of the engine cowling when it struck the water back in 1943. Other than that, it was sitting nose down in the sediment and everything else was intact. A&T brought the historic dive bomber to approximately forty feet beneath the surface of the lake and towed it into a harbor. Once in protected waters, the surface of the water is boomed to contain any oil or fluids that might leak from the aircraft. Once raised from the water, the aircraft is craned onto a "water treatment system"—also known as a blue tarp. The tarp is used to prevent any fluids, shellfish, or debris from reentering the lake. This also enables A&T Recovery's mechanics to prepare the aircraft to be moved to an area where the plane can be prepared for transport.

Once disassembled, the Dauntless was trucked to the National Museum of Naval Aviation for restoration. During the restoration, nearly a hundred skin patches were found where battle damage had been repaired. In addition, one fuel tank strap that had been hit by a Japanese projectile had not been repaired, and both cockpits showed evidence of incoming rounds.

When preparing this SBD for display, a portion of the vertical stabilizer's original paint was left exposed to show visitors its previous colors and markings. The aircraft that produced two Navy Crosses and participated in the opening salvos of World War II now sits in the National Museum of Naval Aviation's carrier aircraft gallery looking ready for battle.

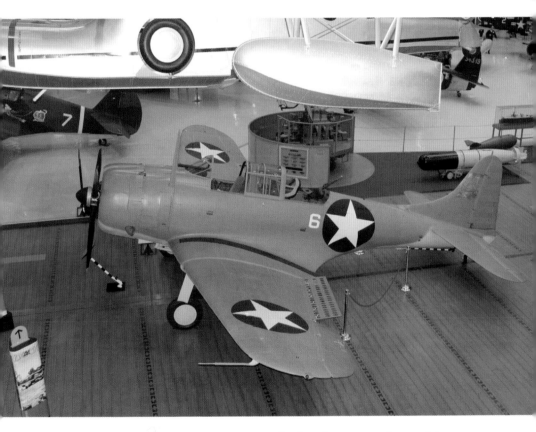

The original layers of paint on SBD-2 BuNo 2106's tail can be seen near the top of the vertical stabilizer. Two pilots were awarded the navy's highest honor, the Navy Cross, while flying against the enemy in this aircraft.

Part Two

In from the Jungle

Jungles, swamps, friendly natives, hostile natives, uncooperative governments, bribes-graft-payola, superstitious tribes, giant spiders, poisonous snakes, crocodiles, mosquitos, razor-sharp Kunai grass— you name it, recovering an aircraft from the jungle can be a dangerous business. Depending upon the island, there can be geological hazards as well—lava tubes and cracks that can swallow a person, and you don't dare venture out during monsoon season.

Then there's the cost of removing the aircraft. Depending upon the island, it would be best to employ as many of the native people as possible. Many believe deities reside in the crashed aircraft and they would prefer not to disturb them for fear of making the gods angry. Of course, if a salvor employs twenty indigenous people, they've got to house and feed them along with the recovery crew.

Another factor is whether or not to bring tools, generators, tents, carts, a-frames, come-alongs, insect repellant, and a myriad of other supplies from home or purchase it upon arrival in country. Will spending money on supplies in the destination country buy a salvor good will as well as the tools of the trade?

Plus there's the matter of transporting 6,000 to more than 10,000 pounds of aircraft out of the jungle. You cut a trail into the wreck with machetes, but a Wildcat or a Zero is not going to go back out on the same track. Will the same people you've employed as guides serve as porters to get the aircraft to the beach? During the David Tallichet/Military Aircraft Restoration Corp.–sponsored recoveries from New Guinea, many of the aircraft were put onto native-made rafts and floated down rivers to the coast. Other expeditions have used landing-craft type boats that can approach the beach, drop their bow doors, and front-load aircraft.

The jungles of New Guinea hold nearly every type of combat aircraft from World War II, including this B-17E, serial number 41-2627, *R.F.D. Tojo*. The plane took off from 14 Mile Drome near Port Moresby with fifteen aboard bound for a rest and recuperation period in Australia. Shortly after takeoff, the Flying Fortress crashed near the Laloki River. Its remains were fairly accessible and it was reportedly removed by the locals in the late 1970s. *Charles Darby*

Once the plane is off the island, it needs to get to a harbor where an intercoastal freighter can haul your prize to a larger port where it can be trans-shipped home. Then there are customs restrictions and duties that have to be paid before the aircraft can be shipped to a restoration shop or one's home hangar.

Recovering warbirds is a business fraught with danger, and the more remote the location, the higher the degree of difficulty. With today's restoration technologies, recovering warbirds from hot and humid climates is becoming an economical prospect, and the jungles of the Pacific are a storehouse of downed combat veteran aircraft. The question is how long does the warbird movement let its heritage sit in the jungles, swamps, and grass plains on islands in the Pacific?

B-17E *Swamp Ghost*
and Its Long Road Home

It is a legend. And it was a sight to behold.

An intact, early B-17E model Flying Fortress resting alone on a mat of tall, green Kunai grass in a Papua New Guinea swamp with nothing around for miles. The mountain tops in the distance are covered with clouds, and it is stifling hot. The bed of Kunai grass hides the fact that there is no solid ground here. There are saltwater crocodiles, poisonous snakes, spiders as big as a baseball mitt, and malarial mosquitoes constantly buzzing about. It is the *Swamp Ghost*.

The bomber that has become to be known as the *Swamp Ghost* was the fifty-fourth B-17E built at the company's Seattle factory. Boeing constructed 512 "E" models, of which the first 112 were fitted with a Bendix remotely operated belly turret that was aimed by a gunner looking through a periscope, rather than later B-17s that were equipped with ball turrets where the gunner sat inside and "rode" the turret. *Swamp Ghost* was assigned U.S. Army Air Forces serial number 41-2446 and delivered on December 6, 1941.

B-17E 41-2446 was assigned to the 7th Bomb Group's 22nd Bomb Squadron. This same unit, the 7th Bomb Group, was transiting eight new B-17Es from Hamilton Field, north of San Francisco, California, to Del Monte Field on the island of Mindanao in the Philippines. The flight of eight 7th Bomb Group B-17Es, plus four other B-17s destined for other bases, departed on December 6, 1941, and arrived over Pearl Harbor, Hawaii, at approximately 8 a.m. on December 7.

On December 8, B-17E 41-2446 arrived at the Sacramento Air Depot, California, where the bomber was armed and prepared for delivery to a combat unit. On December 17, 41-2446 departed for Del Monte Field; its first stop at war-ravaged Hickam Field, Hawaii. Arriving at Hickam Field, 41-2446's orders were changed and the aircraft was assigned to the 5th Bomb Group for the defense of the Hawaiian Islands. The commandeered Flying Fortresses flew sea search and reconnaissance missions through February 1942.

The permanent crew assigned to 41-2446 was led by Lt. Frederick C. "Fred" Eaton Jr., pilot; Lt. Henry M. Harlow, copilot; Lt. George B. Munroe Jr., navigator; Sgt. Richard E. Oliver, bombardier; Technical Sgt. Clarence A. LeMieux, flight engineer/top turret gunner; Sgt. Howard A. Sorensen, radio operator/gunner; Sgt. William E. Schwartz

The Royal Australian Air Force discovered B-17E 41-2446 in 1972, while flying over the area during maneuvers. The bomber's vertical stabilizer stuck up from the featureless Agaiambo Swamp and caught the attention of one of the flight crew. When the flight crew set down to investigate the bomber, they entered a time capsule. The guns were still loaded and the interior looked as if the crew had left only a few hours prior. *Charles Darby*

and Tech. Sgt. Russell Crawford, waist gunners; and Staff Sgt. John V. Hall, tail gunner.

On the morning of February 11, 1942, Lieutenant Eaton lifted off from Hickam Field en route to the aircraft and crew's new assignment with the 7th Bomb Group's 22nd Bomb Squadron in Australia. On the way, the B-17s transiting to Australia were to provide cover for Task Force 11 built around USS *Lexington* (CV-2), which was steaming for

The plane made a very soft landing in the swamp, aided by the fact that it was equipped with the Bendix remote control belly turret, minimizing protrusions under the fuselage. B-17s that bellylanded with later Sperry ball turrets typically broke their backs if the turret was not jettisoned before landing. *Charles Darby*

the Fiji Islands. Task Force 11 was on a mission to attack the harbor and airfield complex at Rabaul, New Britain Island. Eaton's first stop was Christmas Island, followed by Canton Island, arriving at Nandi, Fiji, on February 13.

Once at Nandi, the B-17s flew patrols for Task Force 11 and underwent routine maintenance between flights. On February 17 some of the B-17s left Fiji for New Caledonia. From New Caledonia the B-17s continued on to Townsville on the northwest coast of Australia in the state of Queensland. As soon as the flight of B-17s touched down from New Caledonia, they were being prepared for a raid on Rabaul, timed to follow Task Force 11's attack.

The Allies' First Attack on Rabaul, and 41-2446's Last

The navy's Task Force 11 had been discovered by the Japanese and attacked by land-based Mitsubishi G4M Betty bombers on February 20. The Americans lost two fighters but knocked down fifteen of the seventeen attacking Bettys. Having lost the element of surprise, Task Force 11 retired, electing to attack the target at another time. The army's air attack against Rabaul, however, was proceeding as planned—depart Townsville and fly directly to attack Rabaul, and land at Port Moresby, Papua New Guinea, on the way home. After refueling, the crews would head back to Townsville.

Nine of the twelve available Flying Fortresses were ready to depart at midnight on the evening of February 22. Two planes taxied into each other before takeoff and one aircraft could not get its engines started due to water in the fuel. That left six Flying Fortresses to head north and attack Rabaul. During the flight, a weather system broke up the formation, and the bombers proceeded on their own.

Upon arriving over Rabaul's harbor and airfields a little after sun up, at around 6:45 a.m., at 20,000 feet, the first two bombers found the target obscured by clouds and steam and smoke from a nearby volcano. The bombers circled for twenty minutes or so until a target presented itself. Finally a hole in the undercast enabled Lieutenant Eaton and another Flying Fortress to make a bombing run

View along the upper surfaces of the bomber taken from the area of the navigator's astrodome. Much of the upper glass was removed from the bomber to vent the tremendous heat that built up each day inside the fuselage. *Charles Darby*

Author Charles Darby visited *Swamp Ghost* in 1974, only two years after the bomber had been discovered. Darby stomped the Kunai grass down and away from the bomber's fuselage for better photos. Note the waterline up above the nose compartment windows. *Charles Darby*

on ships in the harbor. Eaton's bombs failed to drop and he circled around for another pass. He was met by heavy anti-aircraft fire, but Eaton was able to salvo his bombs; the results of which were not seen.

The loitering Flying Fortresses enabled the Japanese to launch half a dozen Zero fighters to assist the two Mitsubishi A5M Claude fighters on combat air patrol. Japanese anti-aircraft gunners quickly found the range of the Flying Fortresses, and 41-2446 took a shell in the right wing, outside of the number four engine. This was followed by the flight of Zeroes pushing home their attacks. Tail gunner Hall knocked down the first Zero as the bomber left the target area. Right waist gunner Crawford downed one Zero and claimed another as a probable. The remaining gunners all scored hits on the marauding Zeroes.

Eaton's B-17 was holed, but to the crew it did not seem severe, until they started looking at their fuel situation. One or more tanks were leaking, and it was rapidly becoming apparent that the bomber would not have enough fuel to clear the Owen Stanley Mountains and land at Port Moresby. Knowing this, the crew began to lighten the load and the now-empty bomb bay tank was jettisoned. Like the bombs, it hung up the first time it was released. One of the crew went into the bomb bay and helped the tank out of the bottom of the plane.

In 1974 the machine gun swivel mounts were still in place in the B-17E's Plexiglas nose windows. *Charles Darby*

Crossing the Papua New Guinea coast around 9 a.m. on the morning of February 23, Eaton and Harlow spotted a flat plain where the bomber could be bellylanded. As they reached the point of fuel starvation, the bomber set down on the tall Kunai grass as what looked like a flat plain turned into a swamp. The bomber stopped sliding in about four aircraft lengths. Lieutenant Monroe was cut on the head when he was thrown into the bomb bay during the rapid deceleration. He was bandaged up using one of the parachutes for a dressing.

The bomber began to settle into the swamp and the fuselage began to slowly fill with water. Radio Operator Sergeant Sorensen tried to send a message, but the batteries shorted out before a response could be heard. The crew took the bombsight out onto the wing and put a 0.45-cal. pistol round through it. They then dumped it in the swamp near the number four engine.

With Some Luck: Escape and Evasion

Deciding not to hang around to see if a Japanese scout party or a wandering Zero fighter would come investigate the downed B-17, the crew gathered the survival equipment they thought they'd need and packed it into a life raft. Unfortunately, the emergency rations in the plane had not been rotated and they were spoiled. Walking away from the plane, they did not get far dragging the life raft full of supplies. It was abandoned within sight of the bomber, and a couple of fishing knives, a fishing kit, and a machete were essentially all of the survival supplies they had when they left the bomber and the raft behind.

The Kunai grass was tall, ten-, twelve- and fifteen-feet high in places with four to six feet of water at the bases, and its edges were sharp. Moving forward was arduous at best. A rifle from the plane was used to push down the sharp blades of grass to make a path about the width of a man's shoulders. This helped, but it did nothing to repel the ravenous mosquitos. Fortunately the crew did not come face-to-face with any alligators, but they knew they were lurking close-by.

At night they collected rain water to replenish their canteens. They tried to sleep on piles of Kunai grass, but it sank under the men's weight. Their uniforms disintegrated as the mixture of Kunai grass tears, extreme heat, and constant dampness took its toll on the fabric. The tall grass did keep the sun off the men, which kept sunburns to a minimum.

After walking eight miles in four days through the Agaiambo Swamp, the crew reached the village of Gumbire. Here they were fed and then invited to sleep in the native's huts. The following day they were taken to another village where they were put into dugout canoes and floated downstream to the coast. They were met by Australian Resident Magistrate Alan Champion. He took the crew to Buna by motor launch. At Buna they rested and were waiting to be evacuated when word came that the Japanese were landing up the coast at Lae. On March 8 they left Buna with native guides, some of the crew too sick to walk. Nearly all of them had been stricken with malaria.

After walking or being carried into the mountains, the group stopped to rest at Higaturu. This rest was in its tenth day when a call for help was put out as the crewmen were getting worse, not better. They were told by radio to return to the coast where they would be picked up by boat and taken to Port Moresby.

Back down the group went, all being carried at this point, to the coast, which was thirty miles away. On March 15, the group arrived at Eroro on Oro Bay to wait for Magistrate Champion's launch, only to find it had been strafed by a Japanese plane and destroyed. On March 19, the crew was picked up and they set off for Port Moresby, which would require them to motor for more than three hundred miles in waters where the Japanese held the upper hand.

Floatation bags were used to raise the aircraft up out of the swamp to enable mechanics to begin disassembling the bomber. This scene is very early in the dismantling process as the propeller is still on the number four engine. A camera crew was brought along to record the recovery for a potential documentary. *Aero Archaeology*

A way down the coast, the boat the crew was on developed engine trouble. The captain let them off near Milne Bay on March 21. Four days later a schooner named *Matoma* picked the crew up and started off for Port Moresby. After traveling all night on March 26, the boat ran into a reef. Some of the crew rowed to shore, and when the tide came in, the *Matoma* floated off the reef and motored into the harbor at Abau. The following day the boat departed again, headed south. On March 30, the *Matoma* sailed into the harbor at Port Moresby. The following day the crew returned to Townsville by air after a thirty-six-day ordeal. After recuperating in Australia, the men returned to the fight against the Japanese.

Chance Discovery and Early Recovery Efforts

After resting on the Kunai grass for thirty years, a Royal Australian Air Force helicopter crew flew over the Agaiambo Swamp, its green grass broken up by the vertical stabilizer of B-17E 41-2446. The crew set down on the wing and explored the time capsule Flying Fortress. There was coffee still in the flasks and all the guns were loaded. The helicopter crew removed a couple of the machine guns and returned to their base camp with a great tale of discovery. That was in 1972, and the RAAF made a few more visits to the crash that year to remove the remaining machine guns and liberate a few other small souvenirs.

In 1979, author Charles Darby published a book of his photos detailing a number of Allied and Japanese aircraft crashes in the Solomon Islands, Papua New Guinea, and Irian Jaya regions. Titled *Pacific Aircraft Wrecks . . . and Where to Find Them*, the book caused a sensation within the warbird community. Many of the photos were taken by Darby during his time salvaging aircraft with David Tallichet in 1972. Darby first visited 41-2446 in October 1974 and his photos show rudder pedals, some instruments, the pilot's yoke and wheel, and the throttle stand, still in the cockpit.

Beginning in 1985, a group from the Travis Air Force Base Museum (now the Jimmy Doolittle Air & Space Museum) in Northern California, made an attempt to negotiate for the rights to recover the *Swamp Ghost*. Headed by Bob Gonzales, the museum group made a couple of scouting trips to Papua New Guinea, but were ultimately unsuccessful at making a deal with the government and raising enough money to make recovery a viable proposition. Their campaign to bring back the *Swamp Ghost* lasted until about 1993.

In 1995, the Internet became accessible to the general public. With this came a number of websites dealing with aircraft of World War II and their crash sites. The Internet became a vehicle for information about *Swamp Ghost*, and from this seemingly insatiable curiosity, a few years later, a couple of people began offering "niche tourism" trips to see the bomber in Agaiambo Swamp. The niche tourism guides were quickly at odds with potential salvors, and in the late 1990s David Tallichet and his partner Alfred "Fred" Hagen attempted to negotiate a recovery permit for the bomber. Tallichet was no stranger to aircraft recovery, at one time owning more than 120 ex–World War II aircraft (not all flyable or sitting on their gear—among them a B-29, a pair of B-17s, three B-26s, etc.) and having recovered more than two dozen aircraft from Papua New Guinea in 1972.

From the comfort of one's living room, these conditions do not look too bad. The photo does not convey the temperatures over 110 degrees Fahrenheit, constant attacks from malarial mosquitoes, saltwater crocodiles lurking in the distance, and the fact that a tool dropped is a tool lost. *Aero Archaeology*

Tallichet's friend and partner in the *Swamp Ghost* venture, Fred Hagen is a builder from Philadelphia, Pennsylvania, specializing in hospitals, high-rise buildings, and museums. Hagen's association with World War II aircraft began when he went in search of his great uncle, Maj. William G. "Bill" Benn, who perished on January 18, 1943, while piloting B-25C-NA 41-12485 named *Algernon*. Hagen located *Algernon*'s wreckage and produced a documentary *B-25 Down: Hunt for a Hero* (2003) for the Discovery Channel about his quest. Hagen also assisted Robert Greinert in the recovery of P-47D 42-22687 and details his exploits on the website aeroarchaeology.com. Hagen acquired the P-47's salvage rights from Tallichet around the year 2000, and proceeded with the recovery effort.

While Hagen was working behind the scenes to obtain permits to recover and export *Swamp Ghost*, explorer and webmaster of pacific ghosts.com and pacificwrecks.com Justin Taylan was visiting the crash site. Taylan produced a DVD about the Flying Fortress titled *Swamp Ghost B-17E 41-2446*, which covers its history from the bomber's construction to 2005.

Swamp Ghost's fuselage and port wing on the dock having been helicoptered out from its resting place in the Kunai grass. The early-style U.S. insignia of a white star with red center is still visible on the bomber's aft fuselage. *Aero Archaeology*

Successful Recovery

"That recovery was one of the most difficult salvage operations you could imagine. I know a couple of the guys that were up on the P-38 recovery in Greenland, where they went down 260 feet under the ice to get that airplane. I guess it wasn't as difficult as that; however, the logistics involved were nothing short of incredible," Hagen said. "The difficulty of accessing the site and bringing the salvage equipment to the plane were extraordinary. I shipped most of the salvage tools and equipment from the United States. They went over on sea freight and arrived in Port Moresby. They were supposed to be transferred to a coastal barge and shipped to the old PT Boat base at Tufi, which is now a dive resort. That never happened. When we arrived in New Guinea with a film crew and a salvage team, our equipment was stranded on a dock at Port Moresby. We had to jump through hoops to get it on a barge. We had all kinds of challenges.

"The next challenge was that we had arranged for a support helicopter, but that turned into a tragedy and set us back even further. We had chartered a Squirrel, which is a small helicopter that has lift capacity for small loads. We got that from Heavy Lift, a helicopter company in New Guinea. The helicopter we were going to use crashed several days or a week before we arrived. I think it killed everybody but the pilot, who was left a quadriplegic. We lost our helicopter and those people lost their lives.

"The problem in losing the Squirrel is that during the economic downturn in 2003–2005, most of the helicopter companies had reduced their fleets. The price of commodities had subsequently come back and there was quite a demand for these support birds. We were calling everybody in the country, but were unable to procure a small support helicopter within the time frame we needed.

"While we were scouring the country looking for a helicopter, I was trying to get my material moved up to Tufi. That became a huge ordeal. We got our material to Tufi and quickly reorganized it. Then we began ferrying it up the coast, a twelve-hour journey. We used a bunch of banana boats to trans-ship the salvage gear from the coast up the river to the village nearest the crash site. While we're doing this, one of the villages in between decided that they weren't being compensated for the plane and that they should be getting something. They blockaded the river at one point. We had quite a situation unfold there. It seemed it might be potentially violent, but we finally managed to quiet that down and make some accommodations.

"Ultimately, after this incredible, arduous ordeal, we managed to get our salvage equipment all moved up to the village, which was still a few miles from the site. We still had no support helicopter. We did have a satellite phone that the film crew brought in. They were filming for *Survivor*, and they loaned us a sat-phone. We were still calling out trying to organize the support bird when I finally gave up and phoned a friend of mine in Cannes, Australia, named Steve Spinozzi. I said, 'Steve, we're up here onsite.' I gave him my GPS coordinates. I said, 'I don't care what it takes, you've got to get here with your Squirrel. You've got to get a permit. You've got to fly it up here.' So it took him about three days to get a permit, and he flew up, across the Coral Sea. He refueled at Port Moresby and he flew to the GPS coordinates we gave him and landed at the village. Then we began our salvage."

The need for the helicopter was demonstrated when Hagen decided to walk from the village to the bomber. "I actually physically

The tail section of B-17E *Swamp Ghost* rests in the Military Aircraft Restoration Corporation's Chino restoration facility.

did it, and we filmed it. But it was incredibly arduous. You're going through water that varied from three-feet deep to six-feet deep and it's just trackless jungle. You couldn't possibly go in and out every day. You didn't want to sleep out there because there was no dry ground, and you couldn't carry your equipment back and forth. We needed a support helicopter based at the village to take us over to the site each morning and back and forth as often as necessary."

Hagen said conditions on the site were horrendous. "It was one of the most thankless places on earth to try to effect a salvage. You're in water with snakes and scorpions. I got hit by a scorpion once. Several other people did, too. We had snakes in the water. We had crocodiles in the water. Malarial mosquitoes were infesting the place. It would get so hot during the day, that by the afternoon, if you laid your bare hand on the top of the airplane it would burn your skin off. It was a very unpleasant atmosphere."

In planning the recovery, Hagen and his team had planned to disassemble the aircraft in a methodical manner where removing one part or section would, in theory, make the next step easier. For example, removing the engines would make the bomber lighter, thus it should float higher in the water giving better access to lower parts of the wings and fuselage. Hagen said, "We wanted to take the airplane completely apart, but we couldn't get it all the way out of the water for a variety of reasons. The bottom of the wing fittings never came clear of the water, so we basically had to burn them off. They were corroded anyway. If you were going to restore it, you would have had to have new wing attach fittings machined. We did manage to take the engines, wings, and the tail feathers off. We had all the pieces floating like oak. It wasn't a dry salvage and it wasn't a water salvage. It was kind of a hybrid, which made it even more tricky.

"Then the Heavy Lift helicopter came in and transported the pieces to a barge off-shore. We pulled the pieces out one by one. Sent them up to Lae where they were to be offloaded, and trans-shipped back to America."

After recovery, the forward fuselage of *Swamp Ghost* was displayed at The Air Museum/ Planes of Fame in Chino. The bomber was transported to the Pacific Air Museum at Ford Island, Pearl Harbor, Hawaii, where it is slated to be displayed in an "as-found" diorama. Many believe it is fitting that *Swamp Ghost*, one of the first U.S. Army Air Forces aircraft to attack the enemy, should be displayed at the place where the war began for the United States.

Defending the Salvage

"Many people in the warbird community had some comment to make about how we were reckless in the way we took the plane apart, but keep in mind they were not out there in the swamp, getting their flesh burned off, and getting eaten alive by malarial mosquitoes. Those same people were also saying that we shouldn't have salvaged it. We should have just left it there to rot in the swamp. None of it made any sense to me," Hagen said.

Hagen and his crew, guided by longtime Military Aircraft Restoration Corp. (a company owned by Tallichet) director Joe Krzeminski, successfully disassembled *Swamp Ghost* and transported it to the dock at Lae. Once the bomber was out in the open and ready to ship, that's when the trouble started. Accusations of bribery, the loss of a national treasure, the loss of an asset worth a claimed $28 million, the loss of a tourist destination, and claims of other dastardly deeds were leveled at Fred Hagen through the Papua New Guinea media.

The question on everyone's lips and crossing the airwaves in the South Pacific was how did a contractor from Philadelphia get the *Swamp Ghost* when so many august institutions failed?

"I had been boots on the ground year after year after year, getting to know the people in New Guinea, and dealing with them man-to-man on a personal level," Hagen said. "Once I got it, and we had the rights to it, then all hell broke loose. Everybody in the world who had any interest in warbirds had the fantasy that they were going to be the one to get it, or that someone else was more entitled to get it, than a contractor from Philadelphia. It became almost open warfare.

"Interestingly, through that whole process, the least vociferous opponents of my salvage were the people of New Guinea. They didn't really seem to care one way or the other. But they were reacting to all these external forces from the international warbird community.

"After I got it out, that question of value was brought up again, and of course all these ridiculous claims were put forth that the airplane was worth $28 million or $35 million dollars—whatever it was, it was some astronomical figure. The other side of that coin is that the most recent flyable B-17s that have been sold were all sold in the $2 million to $3.5 million range.

"My original hope was to restore it to flying condition. Due to the deterioration, we figured it would cost about $6 million to restore, at least. If we got it restored and had it flying, it might be worth $3.5 million, which is very true of most of these wrecked airplanes. You put more into restoring them than what they're ultimately worth. Just like restoring an old car, there was no monetary reward.

"The media was twisted into believing that the people of New Guinea were getting screwed out of this valuable artifact, and that we were going to walk away with millions and millions of dollars, which is absolutely absurd. The clear implication was that there must have been wholesale fraud. There wasn't any. The only thing these claims did was hold up the export of the plane for several years, which denied a couple of the last crewmembers the ability to see it return home. One of them had told me at one point that he truly hoped before he died that he had the opportunity to see the plane come back. Ironically, the last crewmember died virtually the same day the plane shipped out of New Guinea, so none of them saw it come back.

"At the time, because of the insinuation, that we were raping them out of this priceless treasure, and that there must have been corruption, the prime minister called for an investigation. They did have an investigation. There was no corruption. They never found any evidence of it, because there wasn't any. Ironically, I worked with the people, I made relationships, and I was able to translate that into an agreement to salvage and to bring back the *Swamp Ghost*, which I originally thought was a very worthy cause. At the end of the day, we won out. We brought it back."

Final Disposition

In early 2013, *Swamp Ghost* was transported to the Pacific Aviation Museum on Ford Island in Pearl Harbor, Hawaii. Here, Hagen hopes it will be displayed in an "as-found" diorama, showing the aircraft sitting in the Kunai grass and viewed from a walkway above.

People often referred to the *Swamp Ghost* as aviation's Holy Grail and for World War II aircraft enthusiasts it is a pretty apt descriptor. "It was," said Hagen. "Now the Grail's come home. It's probably a little less mysterious and exciting now that it's no longer sitting out there in this kind of mystical state in an almost inaccessible swamp. It still has a beauty and mystique that I think will translate well when it goes to Pearl Harbor."

Recovering the Mount Cyclops P-61 Black Widow

First Lt. Logan G. Southfield was flying a factory-new Northrop P-61B-1, serial number 42-39445, on the morning of January 10, 1945. The plane belonged to the 550th Night Fighter Squadron, and Southfield and his three passengers were on a local orientation flight having just buzzed the airstrip at Hollandia, New Guinea. After beating up the field, the Black Widow continued inland, leaving the coastal airstrip in its wake. Southfield had 74.30 hours in P-61s and 675 hours of total flight time.

It was a typical summer day in Hollandia with clear skies, and at this time of the morning visibility was unlimited. To observers at Hollandia, they could see Southfield pull 42-39445 straight up and could hear the engines whine as he applied full power in an attempt to climb over the top of Mount Cyclops. At 11:47 a.m., they lost sight of the aircraft as it mushed into the trees approximately two hundred feet below the summit of the mountain. There was no explosion or fire, but everyone was sure there would be no survivors.

Southfield later stated that the aileron and spoiler systems had frozen, making it impossible for him to turn away from the mountain. He gave the engines full rpm and manifold pressure and water injection to extract as much power as possible to carry him up and over the peak. Realizing that he was about to crash, he warned the passengers, ejected the pilot's escape hatch, and shut off fuel to the engines. As the plane mushed down through the trees, it lost the left wing and the tail booms were ripped off.

The plane's radar observer, Second Lt. Ben Goldstein, had a bad gash on his head and was complaining of back pains, while the two passengers, Second Lt. Floyd C. Lovey and Sgt. Ruth Hillman, had only minor cuts and bruises. After administering first aid to Lieutenant Goldstein, pilot Southfield started down the mountain for help. Southfield was picked up at the bottom of the mountain near a stream and immediately taken to a hospital. In the crash he had broken his ankle, had deep lacerations, and it was determined he had fractured his spine—before he hiked down the mountain for help. He would be hospitalized for six months and was soon shipped back to the United States to recuperate. A search party ascended the mountain and brought the others out. They all recovered and returned to their duties.

There were a number of groups interested in recovering the P-61 on Mount Cyclops near Hollandia, New Guinea. P-61B 42-39445 crashed into the trees on the side of the mountain on January 10, 1945, only two hundred feet from the summit. *Bruce Fenstermaker*

Southfield had violated the 13th Air Force's regulation 62-1 that prohibited flight under 500 feet above ground level. In his defense, aileron and spoiler locking was a known condition for Black Widows flying in New Guinea. The 419th Night Fighter Squadron had warned others, in a December 7, 1944, memo to all crew chiefs and mechanics, that pieces of coral had repeatedly entered the wing through the upper spoiler slot on top and wedged themselves between the spoiler and the bottom wing inspection plate. The fix was to remove the spoiler inspection plates and check for free movement of the surface.

Gene Strine stands near the tail gunner's compartment of P-61B 42-39445 during the aircraft's recovery. The jungle growth around the aircraft has been cleared and the tail booms have been and taken down the mountain. *Mid-Atlantic Air Museum*

This was to be done on a daily basis, but could not prevent coral pieces from entering the wing during taxi and takeoff.

A salvage party went up to the night fighter and recovered or destroyed all confidential or secret equipment. The U.S. Army Air Forces then wrote the plane off as completely destroyed. After the war, the aircraft became sort of a tourist attraction within New Guinea's missionary circles. Many people hiked to the plane, and later, when bush-walking became popular, the local people would earn money guiding tourists to the wreck. Numerous visitors scratched their initials into the Black Widow's fuselage, but nothing much was removed from the wreck. In warbird circles, this crash was virtually unknown until the late 1970s.

Did Ya Hear the One about the Crashed P-61?

"My father, Gene Strine, was copilot and crew chief on the B-25 *Briefing Time*. They were at the Cleveland air show along with the Commemorative Air Force's B-29 *FiFi*. It was after the show and all the warbird crews were sitting in the evening swapping stories, seeing who could top who," said Russ Strine, president of the Mid-Atlantic Air Museum in Reading, Pennsylvania. "One guy talked about knowing where a P-40 was, and it escalated in aircraft size and shape until one of the B-29 crewmen, Al Hocksey, said, 'Well I know where there's a crashed P-61.' My father's ears perked up and he asked for the information. Hocksey replied, 'You know I offered this to the CAF once before and they turned it down. In good conscience, let me offer the information to them one more time, and if they turn me down this time, it's yours.' A month or so later, all the information arrived in the mail to my dad's attention, which had some pictures of the airplane crashed on the mountain and exactly where it was. That was 1979, thirty-four years after the night fighter had crashed. It was just sitting there on Mount Cyclops."

The Black Widow landed on a rock outcropping that kept the fuselage up and out of the dirt, dirt that would have quickly corroded anything laying in it for more than forty years. The rock outcropping allowed all of the jungle's rain water to flow underneath the night fighter, thereby preserving it. *Mid-Atlantic Air Museum*

Helicopters lifted the heavy components off the mountain and down to Hollandia. From here the aircraft was crated for shipment back to the United States. *Mid-Atlantic Air Museum*

The disassembled Black Widow arrived at the Reading Airport in fifteen sea containers. It looked like a P-61 when removed from the containers, but everyone in attendance knew it was going to be a long, hard restoration. *Mid-Atlantic Air Museum*

Father and son Strine were proprietors of a fixed-base operation at the Harrisburg, Pennsylvania, airport, offering charter services, flight instruction, and a large maintenance operation. When Russ was growing up, Gene Strine owned an ex-navy Corsair, so aviation was in his blood. Russ soloed at sixteen and went on to get an aeronautical sciences degree from Embry-Riddle University with a major in aviation management. Russ flew corporate for a while before returning to help run the family FBO. He says he's a pilot at heart, but he loves history and maintenance, and has flown most everything owned by the Mid-Atlantic Air Museum, from the B-25 and P2V-7 Neptune to the Martin 404, C-119, Viscount, and Convair 580. However, all of this experience did not prepare him for the challenges of dealing with foreign governments and their way of doing business. It would be a learning process that Strine quickly mastered.

Having such strong backgrounds in aviation maintenance and management, the Strines believed they could recover the P-61 and restore it to fly. Their first task was to determine who owned the plane. "We went to the air force at the Pentagon and asked for permission to recover and take ownership of the P-61," said Russ Strine. "They sent us a letter back saying that the treaties that ended World War II considered this stuff as spoils of war and that the agreement between nations was that it belongs to whomever's soil it's resting on. That was the letter that we needed.

I used that letter to claim title to the airplane and we registered the aircraft with the FAA at Oklahoma City to protect our ownership claim once the word started to get out.

"Having the letter from the U.S. Air Force enabled us to go to the Indonesian Embassy in Washington. Here we presented the letter to the air attaché, who previously would not deal with us because they didn't know if it was their airplane or not, and they did not want to step on any toes. The letter made him very happy, doors started to open, and the process began. From the very beginning, what they wanted to do was have sort of a cultural exchange between our two countries through our museum and the Indonesian Air Force Museum.

Gene Strine (pictured) met Al Hocksey, a crewmember of the Commemorative Air Force's B-29 *Fifi*, at an airshow. The chance meeting led to the recovery of the P-61 in New Guinea. The Black Widow is one of World War II's rarest aircraft. *Mid-Atlantic Air Museum*

Unfortunately, the Indonesians at the time could not figure out what they wanted in exchange for the P-61."

To facilitate the exchange and give themselves some credibility with the Indonesian Air Attaché, the Strines started the Mid-Atlantic Air Museum. They printed business cards and letterhead, and opened a small facility, and soon after, the Indonesian government gave permission for an inspection trip to see the P-61. On the day after Thanksgiving 1984, Gene Strine, Jeff Ethel, Al Winger, and Paul Everly flew to Sentani, Indonesia. Here they arranged for some of the local people to act as guides to take them to the P-61 to see if it was recoverable and to determine if it could be made flyable again.

Ascending the mountain, the team from the then-new Mid-Atlantic Air Museum found a moss-encrusted airplane with air in the tires, hydraulic fluid in the lines, and very little corrosion. Fortuitously, when Lieutenant Southfield dropped the P-61 through the trees, it landed on a bed of rocks, which acted like a natural drain, moving the rain forest's daily deluge down and away from the aircraft. The aircraft had no contact with the soil, thus the underside was perfectly preserved. The P-61 was heavily damaged in the crash, but it was deemed recoverable and, with enough time and money, could be made flyable.

Once the team got back, they had to begin raising money for the recovery. "We're not rich people," Strine said. "We had just started this museum—on paper, literally—and we didn't have a membership to speak of, just a few people, friends and family mostly. Each trip to Indonesia ended up costing about $30,000 between the air fare and what it took once we were there. After arriving in Indonesia, we had to check in with security in Jakarta before we could venture out to Sentani to work on the plane. It usually took a week of sitting in a hotel before we would get our passes.

"With passes in hand, the military would meet us when we stepped off the airplane in Sentani, and we almost felt like prisoners. It was very laborious and very expensive. Finally, as years went on, those levels of security somewhat disappeared and made it a little easier for us. Eventually we didn't have to go through Jakarta every time to get the permission papers. However, we did need those papers. We had no clue what was written on the documents, but when one of these policemen stepped up and asked for our papers and we handed them over, their eyes got big and they backed away from us. It must have had some pretty strong language in it, supporting what we were doing."

During the recovery, the local people had built a hut up on the mountain using tree limbs and tarps for the American crew to sleep in. In addition, they hired a number of local people as runners. "They would bring parts down that been removed from the airplane," Strine said. "And then the next day they would take food back up to the camp. This went on day after day after day. I was the guy on the ground buying the food, buying the hacksaw blades, doing whatever I had to do to supply the men working on the plane. We had two-way

Mating the stub wings to the fuselage brought the project that much closer to flight. Note that the Black Widow's formidable cannon armament has been installed in the lower fuselage. *Mid-Atlantic Air Museum*

radio communications between me and the guys on the mountain, so I served as the facilitator during the recovery."

For the Mid-Atlantic Air Museum team, each trip to Mount Cyclops lasted two weeks and then the money would run out. Then they'd have to come home and raise more money. There were expeditions in 1985, 1987, 1988, and 1989, and they finally brought the P-61 home in April 1990. They'd spent more than $250,000 on the effort and that included helicopter time and $54,000 in sea freight for the fifteen containers needed to move the aircraft.

To honor the cultural exchange part of the deal, the Strines met an air marshal (the equivalent of a general officer in the United States) who had been instrumental in establishing the Indonesian Air Force Museum. He was one of the first cadets in the Indonesian Air Force when the island nation gained its independence, and he trained at the

U.S. Air Force Academy. The air marshal believed a Stearman would be a fitting display for the Air Force Museum at Yogyakarta, Java. The Strines acquired an airworthy Boeing Stearman for $28,000 and shipped the biplane trainer across the Pacific. Shortly thereafter, the export license was received and the P-61 was on its way back to the United States.

Generosity When You Least Expect It

While the Strines were negotiating with the Indonesians, Jim Ricketts, who ran an aircraft restoration business in Stockton, California, was on Mount Cyclops with a team of mechanics getting ready to take the rare night fighter apart and ship it home. Keep in mind that this was in the early days of the warbird movement and, essentially, if Ricketts could get the plane out—permit or not—it was his. An abandoned aircraft was fair game. The lead mechanic on Ricketts's crew had a heart attack, however, and that ended the operation.

Fast forward five years and the P-61 had just arrived at the Mid-Atlantic Air Museum. It was kept very quiet and few people outside of the museum's circle knew the night fighter had been recovered. One afternoon the phone rang; Russ Strine answered it, and it was Jim Ricketts on the other end of the line. Ricketts said, "Congratulations on getting your P-61. I've got a bunch of parts here that I collected when I was trying to get the airplane. Most of them came from Bob Bean who operated the last airworthy P-61 fire bomber. The parts are of no use to me. They're only of use to one person, and that's you. Are you interested in buying them?"

Strine thought to himself: "Hold on to your wallet!" Strine asked what he had and Ricketts responded with a list of 548 line items of parts, landing gear doors, tail booms, gun bay doors, engine mounts, couplings—everything a restorer would need if they were going to repair an aircraft that had landed on its belly. An entire tractor trailer load.

Strine asked how much, knowing that Ricketts could give a number anywhere from $100,000 to $500,000—he needed those parts and Ricketts had them. "Ricketts was in a position to take full advantage of us," Strine said. "After putting the question of money out there, Ricketts paused, thought about it, and came back with 'How's $15,000?'" The deal was quickly made and the parts were secured. Strine says there have been many other instances of generosity toward the project and the museum, but they're just too numerous to mention.

P-61B 42-39445 is now back on its landing gear for the first time since 1945. The tail gunner's copula is nearly complete, and the structure is held in place with Clecos prior to final riveting. Oxygen bottles are in the process of being installed in the starboard engine nacelle. *Mid-Atlantic Air Museum*

The Details

P-61B 42-39445 was built in Hawthorne, California, at the Northrop factory, and was delivered to the U.S. Army Air Forces on August 29, 1944, at Sacramento, California. The aircraft was transferred to Oakland, California, where it was put on a ship that sailed under the Golden Gate Bridge on November 16, headed for the Fifth Air Force at Brisbane, Australia. Once at Brisbane, the night fighter was trans-shipped to the aircraft depot on Biak Island. On January 6, 1945, Lieutenant Southfield picked up the plane and flew it to the 550th Night Fighter Squadron's base at Hollandia. The plane crashed four days later.

With this history in mind, it has been determined that when 42-39445 crashed, it was over-all black with red serial numbers, and the only markings were the star and bar insignias. The 550th Night

The P-61's SCR-720 nose radar antenna sits behind a fiberglass radome. The SCR-720 enabled the Black Widow to acquire targets at a distance of nearly five miles. The Mid-Atlantic Air Museum's P-61B is one of only four of the type to survive and will be the only flying example. *Mid-Atlantic Air Museum*

Fighter Squadron's unique colors of lime green on the wing tips, cowl flaps, and glare shield had probably not been applied when the aircraft was lost. Thus, the Mid-Atlantic Air Museum's current plans are to debut the aircraft and fly it in an over-all black scheme with red serials. Possibly in the second or third year they may add tail markings and some subdued nose art.

Eventually the museum would like to add the four-gun General Electric upper turret. This was not installed on this particular model of the Black Widow as the majority of GE's turret production was going to equip Boeing's B-29 Superfortress. The U.S. Army Air Forces had planned to retrofit the Black Widows when turret production exceeded the needs of the B-29 fleet.

Today the fuselage is done and both the inner wings are essentially done. The inner wings have been mated to the fuselage and the aircraft is now sitting on its landing gear. The tail booms are done and installed, the fins are installed, the stabilizer is done and installed. The elevator is now receiving attention, and its end caps are being formed out of aluminum.

There are still two rudders and both outer wing panels waiting to be rebuilt. The wings are fairly straightforward and one of the wings was recovered intact. The other wing was sheered in half during the crash, but the museum recovered all of it. The wings will have to come completely apart so that new spars can be installed.

All of the aircraft's original equipment, like radar and radios, is being wired as if it were going to be operational. In addition, the Mid-Atlantic Air Museum crew is installing all new circuit breakers along with the wiring. That adds a lot of extra time to the wiring task. "The wiring: It's like sitting and watching grass grow," Strine said. "It goes that slow."

The question on many people's minds is who will make the Black Widow's first, postrestoration flight. "I have flown our B-25 for thirty-four years. This airplane, even though it's got R-2800 engines, all the systems are virtually identical to the B-25's and I've got the qualifications to be able to do that," Strine said confidently.

"Although this project started out as my dad's dream, it has become so many other people's as well," Strine added. "Who would have thought that a crashed night fighter on a mountain in New Guinea would one day take to the skies again? We have a group of volunteers here that are the best, and their efforts, combined with the public's support, are making the return of a flying P-61 a reality."

Bringing Out a Betty, a Judy, a Tony, and a Zero

Almost every military aviation enthusiast has had the fantasy of exploring former jungle battlefields in search of lost combat planes. Imagine cutting away the vines with one swoop of a machete to expose a Brewster F3A Buffalo or a downed Mitsubishi A6M Zero fighter. That's what Bruce Fenstermaker did. The little boy who grew up near all the warbird activity at Chino Airport in Southern California lived out that dream—and then some.

World War II Japanese aircraft are rare—extremely rare. In the United States, the two best collections of the former enemy's aircraft can be found at the National Air and Space Museum (NASM) in Washington, D.C., and at The Air Museum/Planes of Fame in Chino. NASM's collection was assembled from army and navy intelligence specimens tested during the war as well as some aircraft, such as the Aichi M6A Seiran submarine-launched attack plane, that were used for war bond rallies and eventually pushed into the corner of a hangar and forgotten.

In addition to the Seiran, NASM's Steven F. Udvar-Hazy Center in Chantilly, Virginia, also displays a Kawanishi N1K2 George, a Kawasaki Ki-45 Nick, and a Nakajima J1N1 Irving. A Japanese copy of the German Messerschmitt 262 jet fighter, the Nakajima Kikka, is slated to undergo restoration, and the Hazy Center also has a Nakajima B6N2 Jill, a C6N1-S Myrt, and a Yokosuka P1Y1-S Francis in storage. The museum's downtown Washington, D.C., gallery displays a Mitsubishi A6M5 suspended in the air.

When Fenstermaker was a teenager in the 1960s, he hung around the Chino Airport at places like AeroSport—a P-51 Mustang overhaul and modification shop—and at Ed Maloney's Planes of Fame Air Museum. This museum boasts the largest private collection of Japanese aircraft, ranging from an Aichi D3A2 Val (under restoration to fly), a nearly complete Mitsubishi G4M1 Betty, a Mitsubishi J2M3 Raiden, a J8M1 Shusui, an A6M5 Zero flying with an original 14-cylinder Nakajima Sakae engine, a Yokosuka MXY-7 Ohka, and a Yokosuka D4Y4 Judy (under restoration to taxiable condition).

Fenstermaker saw the activities at Chino Airport and, like many others, was bitten by the warbird bug. At the time Fenstermaker was hanging around the Chino Airport, in addition to Planes of Fame, David Tallichet's Military Aircraft Restoration Corp. had a compound

Ki-61 Tony was located in a ravine at the end of the Babo Airfield in Indonesia. This hulk was recovered and brought back to the United States. The inline engine fighter is now in Russia awaiting restoration. *Bruce Fenstermaker*

The U.S. Army Air Forces caught a number of Japanese aircraft on the ground at the Babo Airfield. The Japanese pushed a number of unflyable aircraft into a ravine, and four decades after the end of the war a Ki-48 Lilly light bomber, the same type as seen to the left of the control tower; a Ki-43 Oscar; and Ki-51 Sonia were recovered by the Indonesian Air Force Museum. Bruce Fenstermaker subsequently brought out a G4M Betty, Ki-61 Tony, and A6M3 Model 22 Zero. The D4Y-1 Judy Fenstermaker recovered was located in the second revetment at the top of the photo. *U.S. Army Air Forces*

Fenstermaker's guide during the recovery was Paulus Manibuy (standing and wearing glasses), who recruited the native people who helped move the aircraft. The D4Y-2 Judy sits on a cart made from an abandoned truck frame and was powered by the men seen here. *Bruce Fenstermaker*

at Chino stuffed with P-39 fuselages stacked like cord wood, a couple of ex-Royal Canadian Air Force B-24 fuselages, the B-26 Marauders recovered from Canada, and a myriad of other rare aircraft.

Around this time, Fenstermaker saw a magazine with photos of discarded World War II aircraft in New Guinea, shot by an oil exploration company. "A decade or so later, in 1987, I was talking to J. D. 'Soup' Hosington at Aero Sport as he was clearing out his desk and closing the business. We talked about my hopes of going into the aircraft recovery business and he about his coming retirement," Fenstermaker said. "He offered to be my eyes and ears in Indonesia as I traveled between the islands and California. As surplus Indonesian Air Force equipment came up for bid, he would let me know by conference call with my agent in the area, and I'd figure out how to come up with the money and plan a quick trip to inspect the items for sale.

"Frank Taylor, later known for developing the highly modified racing P-51D *Dago Red*, joined the conversation and he became real excited about the prospects of recovering Japanese aircraft. So we set out for Guadalcanal, inspecting planes there, on Ballale Island and on Shortland Island. The national government prohibited the export of former World War II aircraft, so we came home empty handed."

Dejected, Fenstermaker set out on his own and spent the next four years doing his homework and talking with Indonesian government and military officials. In the interim, Hosington developed a fast moving cancer and died before he and Fenstermaker could survey the jungles of Irian Jaya as they had done in the Solomons.

This Mitsubishi G4M Model 11 landed at Babo with only one engine running. Upon touch down, the landing gear collapsed, driving the nose section into the ground. At some point during the war, Japanese aircraft mechanics began to disassemble the bomber, carefully removing both wings. *Bruce Fenstermaker*

Babo Airfield

Before World War II, the Dutch built an airfield at Babo, Western Papua (formerly Irian Jaya), Indonesia, which is located on the western end of the island of New Guinea, inland from Maccluer Gulf on the Vogelkop Peninsula. It was built in the 1930s as part of KLM's Dutch East Indies service (KNILM). Babo was attacked almost a month after war in the Pacific got underway, when, on December 30, 1941, a flight of Kwanishi H6K Emily flying boats bombed the airfield. Four months later, on April 2, 1942, the Japanese invaded the Maccluer Gulf area of New Guinea and took over the airfield. The Japanese added a second runway to the airfield, and from here army and navy units could defend the area and harass Allied operations in the area. From Babo, aircraft could attack shipping between Australia and the Philippines, and west to Ambon and other parts of the Molucca Islands.

Allied bombers began striking Babo in mid-1943, and one year later, the airfield was within range of B-24 and B-25 bombers from the Fifth Air Force. This area was bypassed by the Allies, and the Japanese in the area were trapped until the conclusion of the war. After the end of hostilities, Australian graves registration teams entered the region looking for their war dead. Australian pilot Flight Sgt. Peter F. Guster was lost on the August 23, 1944, attack on Babo while at the controls of P-40N A29-568 (ex-USAAF 42-106371). The Australian teams documented more than a hundred aircraft wrecks on and around Babo Airfield. Bruce Fenstermaker described the area, saying, "You couldn't go twenty-five yards without running into an airplane part."

From the end of the war until the 1970s, Babo sat, pretty much untouched. With the publication of Charles Darby's 1974 book *Pacific Aircraft Wrecks,* word quickly spread that there were abundant Japanese aircraft and components at Babo. The pictures were enough to give even the most jaded aviation enthusiast heart palpitations. There was a Zero sitting on its landing gear, a Mitsubishi Ki-51 Sonia, and a twin-engine Kawasaki Ki-48 Lilly light attack bomber, all ready for recovery. The Indonesian Air Force Museum at Yogyakarta Airport acquired and restored the Zero, Sonia, and an Oscar; all are on display today. The Lilly, a much more involved project, currently sits in storage.

Fenstermaker Recoveries: Take Two

Through his multi-year negotiations with the Indonesian government and representatives of its military, Fenstermaker was granted permission to enter the country and survey the aircraft at Babo. Under the auspices of various agreements to recover planes in exchange for aircraft types desirable to the Indonesians or for goods, Fenstermaker was able to obtain export permits, first for a Mitsubishi Zero fighter (serial number 3869), and later for a number of other aircraft.

"After discussions with the Indonesian Department of Defense, we came to an agreement that I'd deliver a PBY for the Indonesian Air Force Museum," Fenstermaker said. "I bought the PBY Gary Larkins was rebuilding in Northern California at the time. I had it trucked to the shipping line and hauled to Jakarta for the air force museum. My wife Linda made all of the shipping arrangements and handled the logistics from the States. Once there, I reassembled the flying boat, painted it, and built a shed to protect it from the elements. In exchange for the PBY, I got the rights to recover a Betty bomber and a Zero." Subsequently, for a stack of parts usable as patterns in the restorations, Fenstermaker moved a Lilly light, twin-engine bomber from Biak to Jakarta, and did some sheetmetal work to get it ready for display.

Having surveyed a Judy (serial number unknown) and a Tony (serial number 704), the Indonesian Air Force Museum would allow the aircraft to be exported if Fenstermaker moved a Tu-16B Badger from Malang to the Air Force Museum at Jakarta. "It's the size of a 727," he said. "I dismantled it, got it moved, reassembled it, and built a shed over it. That cost about $90,000 to complete that task." And that gave him permission to recover the dive bomber and the fighter from Babo.

Fenstermaker believed in treating the local people with respect and trying to improve their lives as much as he could. "I had brought medicine from the United States, but found a supplier in Jakarta that sold everything at wholesale prices, and I was able to supply many of the villages in the region with everything from Neosporin to anti-malarial tablets," he said. "I talked to the missionaries in the area as I wanted to hire as many locals as possible, but I didn't want to over-pay or under-pay for their labor. I hired twenty-five local people and received tremendous assistance from Susanto 'Tisan' Hartanto, Colonel Yum, General Suparman, and Paulus Manibuy. If it was not for them, I would not have been able to recover aircraft and survey additional wreck sites in Indonesia."

The tail section of the G4M stuffed with parts and crated for the sea voyage to California. *Bruce Fenstermaker*

Forward section of the G4M Betty loaded on a landing craft for transshipment to Sorong, then Biak, then onto a coastal freighter to Jakarta. From Jakarta the aircraft were loaded into open-top containers and shipped to Los Angeles (San Pedro) by way of Singapore and Tokyo. *Bruce Fenstermaker*

Babo is a paramount village that controls about ten or fifteen smaller, outlying villages, and has a small Catholic mission, a Protestant mission, and a mosque, plus a small school. Because it is so hot during the day, the kids would not go to school and people could not come to worship. To enable the local people to study and pray into the night, Fenstermaker arranged for a rebuilt generator to be delivered by the Indonesian Air Force along with wiring and light bulbs. Once installed and the lights strung, this lit up the village and allowed people to go to school or religious activities later in the day and early evening.

"I was continually told by people in the States that there was no way I was going to get anything out of Indonesia. They said I didn't have enough money for bribes, and I didn't have the clout. But everything was done above board, no bribes or kickbacks. Sure there were delays, but the military there was very business-like in the way they handled the trades. The Indonesian military was quite satisfied with what they were getting, and I was satisfied as well."

Once at Babo, with his small army of local workers, the group established a camp about 150 yards from the Betty bomber (serial number 1208). They put up tents, dug a fire pit, and pounded stakes for a laundry line. This kept travel time to the aircraft down to a minimum. The local people slept in open pup-tent-style shelters, while Fenstermaker brought a dome tent that was zipped shut to keep out marauding snakes. Apparently the locals were not frightened by the prospects of an encounter with a poisonous snake, but Fenstermaker was not taking any chances.

The first order of business was to survey the Betty to determine how to move it 2.5 miles to the river. It had bellylanded on the field and the bombardier section of the nose was crushed in. At some point near the end of the war, the Japanese removed the wings for possible use on another Betty and the engines were lying nearby. Fenstermaker had the local people cut down the grass around the aircraft to a height of about one-inch-tall. "That way we could see if any snakes were in the area," he said.

Determining that the Betty could be moved, Fenstermaker needed a way to do it. Locating an old mini-bus on Biak Island, he removed the axels and wheels, and, using angle iron, made a small trailer that could haul 1,500 pounds and still be pulled by a few local people. That worked out great for the lighter weight parts. "I found a Japanese tank where the top part had been blown off," he said. "I took the bogeys off that held down the tread, took the pivoting arms and used those to make a three-wheel trailer using hardwood. That would hold about 5,000 pounds." With a load on the trailer, if they encountered soil that was too soft, the local people would cut down trees about an inch and a half in diameter and make a three-rail railroad track to bridge the area.

The most sophisticated piece of machinery used to move the aircraft was a come-along. "We didn't use any tractors or helicopters. It was all done with high school physics—a fulcrum placed on the right spot on a log and you can move mountains with it. I had enough people around that if something got stuck, we could put a little grunt on it and move it."

Recovering the Ki-61 Tony fighter was more difficult because it was not on flat ground. It was sitting southwest of the old original

The G4M Betty bomber is now displayed at The Air Museum/Planes of Fame at the Chino, California, airport in an as-found diorama. Crushing of the nose section during the bomber's forced landing is evident in this view. Note that the tail section sits to the left in the background.

tower the Japanese had built during the war. The Tony was located down an embankment, which can be seen prominently in many wartime photos of the airfield. The first task was to clear all of the brush and vines away from the aircraft and make a path up the slope. Using 55-gallon barrels, teams of locals rolled the aircraft up the embankment to level ground. From there the fighter was rolled from the barrels onto the trailer and pulled down to the river.

Salvaging the Judy was not that difficult as it was closer to the original hard-packed runway. The first step was to clear the brush away from the aircraft to give a clear zone to protect against snakes. Then the Judy was loaded on the trailer and wheeled down to the river. The wings of the Judy and Tony were not removed for transport.

The Zero was disassembled where it sat. During the war it had been undergoing an engine change, and at the conclusion of hostilities, it was abandoned in place. Fenstermaker did not remove the wings for transport as the spar runs through the cockpit section. Maintaining the wings' integrity was done to aid in the aircraft's rebuild back in the United States.

All of the aircraft were towed to the village near the river, and the task of crating everything for transport began. "I had bought a chainsaw in Indonesia, and one of the villagers who had worked for one of the timber companies in the area cut some trees down for wood to make crates. I also bought some walls from some of the villagers huts to make the flat panels of the crates," Fenstermaker explained.

To get the aircraft shipped from Babo to the next largest port, Fenstermaker chartered a landing craft that had a ramp width of twenty-five feet and a cargo deck was approximately seventy-five feet long. The landing craft came in at high tide and was loaded the following day during low tide. When the tide rose again, the landing craft departed for the island of Biak. At Biak, the crates of Japanese aircraft were unloaded, and a few days later were put onto an inter-island ship going from Biak to Jakarta. Once at Jakarta the planes and parts were stored at the shipping agent's yard while containers were located. This was during the first Gulf War, and every container was in use to support the war effort. It took about three or four weeks to get enough containers to pack the planes in before they could be sent back to the United States.

The D4Y-2 Judy as found on the Babo Airfield, and as it nears restoration to taxiable condition at The Air Museum/Planes of Fame, May 2012. The D4Y-1 was originally delivered with an inline engine, which the museum has in its possession. Due to a lack of parts, however, the aircraft is being restored with a radial engine representing a D4Y-2 Model 33. *Bruce Fenstermaker (recovery); Roger Cain (restoration)*

Once in the United States, the Zero, Betty, Judy, and Tony were presented to the public at the Museum of Flying in Santa Monica, California. David Price and Alan Preston, principals of the museum, had acquired the Zero, and their first order of business was to trans-ship the Zero and the assorted pieces to Russia for restoration to flying condition.

After having recovered a number of aircraft, Fenstermaker became interested in searching for downed airmen and giving these MIAs the chance to come home. Fenstermaker located the crashed P-47D 42-75940 of Lt. Wynans E. Frankfort who was reported as Missing in Action on April 27, 1944, while chasing a Ki-43 Oscar away from the Allied beachhead during the invasion of Biak Island. In talking to the local people on the coast and working his way inland, Fenstermaker found Lieutenant Frankfort's Thunderbolt, crashed, lying inverted. The wreckage had not been disturbed for nearly fifty years, and the pilot's remains were still in the cockpit. The U.S. Army's Central Identification Laboratory in Hawaii sent a team to recover Lieutenant Frankfort and positively identify his remains. Lieutenant Frankfort's family received the Silver Star that had been awarded to him, but never received, and he was interned at Franklin, Virginia.

The A6M Zero, serial 3869, was returned to the United States where its restoration was completed and it flies today with the markings of "X-133" on its tail. This aircraft is operated by the Southern California Wing of the Commemorative Air Force at the Camarillo Airport, and is flown regularly. The Betty bomber was acquired by The Air Museum/Planes of Fame and is displayed in an "as-found" diorama at its facility at the Chino Airport. The Judy was also acquired by Planes of Fame and it has been restored as a radial engine configured D4Y3. The museum plans to bring this aircraft up to ground taxiable condition so it can be seen at special events and the annual Planes of Fame airshow, held each May.

The Ki-61 Tony recovered by Fenstermaker was also sent to Russia for restoration. Parts from other Ki-61 wrecks have been assembled, and this aircraft is now awaiting restoration in St. Petersburg.

The last words go to Fenstermaker as he reflects on his adventures in Indonesia: "I still have a lot of friends down there. Do I have regrets? Yes. Was it an incredible time? Yes. I learned how to research

Historians believe this A6M2 Model 21 Zero was built by Nakajima in the summer of 1943. At the time it was abandoned at Babo, it was undergoing an engine change and work on its landing gear as it was sitting on barrels. The plane was recovered by Bruce Fenstermaker and sold to the Museum of Flying. The museum shipped the fighter to Russia, where it was rebuilt to flying condition. Returned to the United States in 1997, museum personnel returned the aircraft to the air the following year. It is now owned by the Commemorative Air Force and based in Camarillo, California. *Roger Cain*

MIAs from World War II and I did a lot of surveys on crash sites there. A lot of good things came out of it. I was very proud to be able to do some of those things.

"There's probably seventy-five to a hundred aircraft that are recoverable in the region. Then there are a number of other aircraft that have been located but not surveyed, as well as other aircraft yet to be found. There's still some phenomenal stuff down there."

Big Island B-18 in Situ

If you blink, you'll miss it. But it is still out there.

Today, one of the six surviving B-18s, serial number 36-446, sits in almost the exact spot where it was crash-landed more than seventy years ago, on February 25, 1941. The pre–World War II Douglas B-18 is a twin-engine bomber, commonly referred to as the "Bolo." B-18 36-446, the last of the Bolos acquired with fiscal year 1936 funds, sits in the rain forest region on the northeast side of Hawaii's Big Island. It is sitting in a ravine at a nose-up attitude and has been seen by thousands of tourists who take helicopter tours of the Big Island of Hawaii.

Even though many have seen the aircraft, the bomber's crash site could not be more remote. It is located in Waimanu Valley, north and east of the Kohala Mountains, miles from the nearest road. The only practical way in is by helicopter, and the only way to land on the property is with advance permission, and a permit, from the landowners. There are times of the year that the northeast side of the island is shrouded in clouds most of the day, so an expedition to the site requires some planning. Then, of course, there's the walk out.

Guardian of the Hawaiian Islands

The Douglas B-18 was America's frontline bomber in the years leading up to World War II. The twin-engine, low-wing aircraft was considered a "heavy" at the time; however, many believed it was out-classed and obsolete in the face of Japan's new generation of frontline fighters. At the time, the B-18 was all the U.S. Army Air Forces had to work with and they had a fair number of the twin-engine bombers scouting the sea approaches to, and patrolling the skies over, the Hawaiian Islands.

The 11th Bombardment Group was activated in Hawaii on February 1, 1940, and was subsequently redesignated the 11th Bombardment Group (Heavy) in November 1940. Stationed at Hickam Field on the island of Oahu, 36-446 was assigned to the 11th Bomb Group's 50th Reconnaissance Squadron (Heavy), flying patrols around the islands in the months before the December 7, 1941, attack on Pearl Harbor.

On February 25, 1941, the first of four B-18s from the 50th Reconnaissance Squadron departed Hickam Field at 7 p.m., with the remaining three following at five-minute intervals. The mission was a night navigation training exercise to get new copilots familiar with flying in the islands and give them an opportunity to fly radio beams

The U.S. Army Air Forces frontline bomber and patrol aircraft in the Hawaiian Islands was the Douglas B-18. There were thirty-three B-18s in Hawaii on the morning of December 7, 1941, of which twelve were destroyed and another ten were heavily damaged. *U.S. Army Air Forces*

as well. All four bombers were to fly to Hilo, Hawaii, on their own and return to base. Each was to proceed at 3,000 feet, and the trip was expected to take approximately three hours.

The 50th Reconnaissance Squadron numbered its planes, and 36-466 wore the buzz number 50R81—for 50th Reconnaissance Squadron, aircraft in squadron 81. This was painted on the upper side of the port wing and the lower side of the starboard outer wing panel. In the cockpit of plane 80 was Capt. Boyd Hubbard Jr., pilot, and Second Lt. Francis R. Thompson, copilot, with Staff Sgt. Joseph S. Paulhamus serving as flight engineer, Pvt. William Cohn as radio operator, and Pvts. Fred C. Seeger and Robert R. Stephens as observers/gunners. Captain Hubbard, later a brigadier general, served as the squadron operations officer and had accumulated more than 2,900 hours flight time and had more than 870 hours at the controls of the B-18.

The mid-1930s Douglas B-18 owes some of its lines to the DC-1 and DC-2 commercial airliners. This type was the at the leading edge of bomber technology at the time it was introduced—all-metal construction, defensive machine guns in the nose and dorsal positions, 4,400-pound bomb load, and capable of a maximum speed of 216 mph. *U.S. Army Air Forces*

After lifting off at 7 p.m., Hubbard flew south to Lanai Island. Here he encountered scattered clouds and climbed to 5,000 feet to fly on top. At Maui, there was a cloud deck between 5,000 and 7,000 feet, so once again climbed to be on top of the clouds. Cruising at 7,000 feet, the bomber passed over the channel between Maui and the north end of the Big Island of Hawaii. The crew could make out Mauna Kea and Mauna Loa as they approached the Hamakua coast, although it was a very dark night.

Flying just off the coast of the Big Island and about even with the 13,796-foot tall volcano Mauna Kea, sometime between 8:15 and 8:20 p.m., an engine vibration captured the flight crew's attention. Thinking he might have run one of the bomb bay tanks dry, Hubbard switched tanks, then checked the fuel pressure. That was OK. It was definitely an engine problem, so Hubbard pulled back the throttle on the number one, or left engine, and moved the propeller into fine pitch to reduce drag. It is interesting to note that the B-18 was not equipped with fully feathering propellers, and a windmilling prop causes tremendous drag. With a dead engine, the propeller brake was engaged to minimize drag. Then the one good engine started to occasionally cough.

While the engine was being shut down, Hubbard recalled his weather briefing and remembered that weather at Hilo was iffy, covered with a cloud layer between 2,000 and 3,000 feet. Deciding to head for the airport at Maui, Hubbard reversed course 180 degrees by turning to the right, at which time he saw the red navigation lights of one of his squadron mates pass close-by. Descending, Hubbard had to fly on instruments as they entered the cloud deck. His only options

Two views of the Big Island B-18 as seen from one of the many aerial tour operators on the eastern side of Hawaii. Most tour operators know the location of the crash and, if the weather is right, will overfly the prewar bomber. The dorsal turret was removed in the mid-1980s and traded to the U.S. Air Force's museum program. The U.S. Army Air Forces removed both engines and most of the interior fittings during the war. *Lori Hahn*

at this point were to land at the Maui Airport, ditch in the ocean, or, if unable to make Maui, to land at Suiter Field at Upolu Point on the very northern shore of the island of Hawaii.

To lessen the aircraft's load, Hubbard instructed flight engineer Paulhamus to drop the bomb bay auxiliary fuel tanks. Hubbard then closed the bomb bay doors and trimmed the aircraft to fly on one

Surviving B-18 Bolos

Serial Number	Model	Location/Notes	Status
37-029	B-18	Castle Air Museum, Atwater, California	PV
37-469	B-18A	National Museum of the U.S. Air Force, Wright-Patterson AFB, Ohio	PV
37-505	B-18B	McChord Air Museum, Tacoma, Washington. Access is restricted due to the museum's location on base.	PV
38-593	B-18B	Pima Air & Space Museum, Tucson, Arizona	PV
39-025	B-18A	Wings Over the Rockies Air and Space Museum, Denver, Colorado	PV
36-446	B-18	Waimanu Valley, Hawaii. On private property.	in situ

Status Key: F = Flyable; PV = available for Public Viewing; R = under Restoration; S = in Storage

B-18A 37-469 ended its military career at the Reconstruction Finance Corp. storage facility at Ontario, which is today's Chino Airport. Note that the bomber has been parked with its bomb bay doors open, and that the national insignia has been painted out. During its civilian career, the bomber was used for spraying insecticide. It eventually ended up derelict at the Tucson Airport, Arizona, before being acquired for the National Museum of the Air Force's collection in 1971. *Emil Strasser via Gerry Liang Collection*

engine. The starboard engine was turning at 2,150 rpm, pulling thirty-three inches of manifold pressure, and the bomber was unable to hold its altitude, still losing one hundred to two hundred feet per minute. Thinking they were still over water, Hubbard was flying the bomber at about 90 mph, and descending through 3,200 feet when the aircraft hit. The various turns, drifting into the dead engine and then recovering, as well as a strong breeze from the north, had pushed the bomber three miles inland. The left wing caught a tree and the aircraft began a horizontal spin as it skipped across the treetops.

Once the aircraft came to rest, power and fuel were shut off as there was a strong odor of aviation gasoline in the main cabin. Hubbard's seat had torn loose during the crash, and copilot Lieutenant Thompson was knocked unconscious for a few minutes. Flight engineer Paulhamus opened the top hatch and shined a flashlight down the length of the wings to see where they were. The plane had skipped across the top of the jungle and through a sea of ferns before slipping down the face of a ravine, stopping only when its starboard wing dug into the ground. There were minor cuts and bruises among the crew—nothing that required immediate medical attention. With it raining outside, Hubbard ordered the crew to bed down inside the aircraft until daylight.

The landowners have left a rope attached to an engine mount to aid in climbing the ravine's walls for access to the nose section of the bomber. *Lori Hahn*

Once the sun came up and the low clouds burned off, around 8 a.m., Private Seeger climbed out of the top hatch, over the nose of the plane, and onto the top of the ravine. He was able to see the coast. Hubbard determined they were in the no-man's land somewhere between the point where the road north from Hilo and the road south from Upolu Point both end. Flares and a flare pistol were handed up to Private Seeger in case an aircraft flew by looking for them. Within forty-five minutes, another B-18 was cruising the north shore of the island looking for the downed airmen. As the bomber circled, three flares were fired in its direction, which the flight crew did indeed see. The pilot flew directly overhead, wagged his wings in recognition, and then flew off. Another plane returned and dropped food, coffee, and blankets and communicated to the downed airmen to sit tight until the rescue party arrived in a day or two.

The Rescue

At noon that day, a rescue party and pack mule train with supplies was dispatched from the Lohala Ditch Co., led by Fred C. Koelling. Following the ditch trail, the rescue party spent the night at Kaukini, a camp at the end of the ditch trail. The morning of the second day, the rescuers walked on a trail for three miles before it ended and they had to hack their way for another eight miles before reaching the crash site. Exhausted and a bit discouraged, the rescuers fired pistols into

Interior of the Big Island B-18 shows that the bomber has been stripped of most interior parts. This condition does not deter restorers as the original brackets exist and would make the replacement of military equipment that much easier.
Lori Hahn

the air in hopes of attracting the downed fliers' attention. This it did and the air crew shot flares into the air and let loose with a long burst from one of the machine guns. This was enough to get the rescuers headed in the right direction, and an hour later the two groups met. It took them six and a half hours by mule, followed by one hour on foot walking on the trail, and four and a half hours breaking a trail to the bomber, to make a total of twelve hours' travel time for the rescuers.

Koelling's rescue party retraced its steps, returning to the Kaukini camp, where they remained overnight. The following day, the survivors and rescuers made it back to Suiter Field. From here the downed fliers were flown back to Hickam Field. The return trip had taken five hours by foot and six hours by mule, a total of eleven hours, to get the fliers back to civilization.

Hubbard removed the bombsight stabilizer, and the radios were salvaged by the army in the days following the crash.

A second rescue team had left from the Waimea area on the western side of the Kohala Mountains at the same time as Fred Koelling's party. The Waimea group had to turn back because the terrain was too difficult to pass.

"The terrain is extremely rugged—unbelievably so to someone used to backcountry in the mainland United States," said Chris Rathbun of Laupahoehoe Nui LLC, which owns property in the area. "Every year hikers are lost attempting to cross the Kohala Mountains. It can take you days to go what looks like a mile on the map, if you manage to do it at all. The USGS maps are totally inaccurate, and unmapped gulches thirty feet wide and a hundred feet deep, hidden by vegetation, are a common hazard. Bottomless volcanic holes, five to fifty feet across and often hidden, are not uncommon. This is one of the wettest places in the world, and flash flooding can isolate you very quickly. There is a reason it took days to get a rescue crew to the site, and that the crew did not try to walk out themselves! And back then there was a trail system the Ditch companies maintained, but that is all overgrown now."

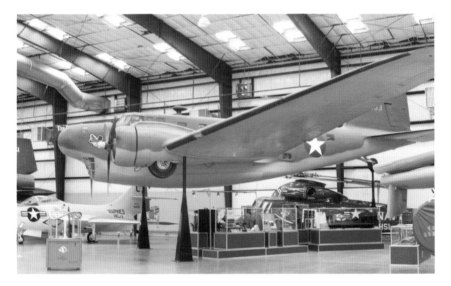

The top turret from the Big Island B-18, 36-446, is displayed at the Pima Air & Space Museum, Tucson, Arizona, underneath the museum's restored and elevated B-18B, 38-593.

Tourist Attraction

For a couple hundred dollars per person, most of the helicopter tour operators will fly by the Big Island B-18 during their aerial tours. Chartering a helicopter runs about $750 per hour, thus purposely chartered flights to photograph the bomber are out of the range of most people.

There was talk that this aircraft might be recovered by the Pearl Harbor Aviation Museum, which would then display the B-18 in an as-found diorama and that the Discovery Channel would produce a documentary showing the removal. This has not come to pass and the Big Island B-18 continues to rest in the Waimanu Valley.

The top turret from 36-466 was removed in the 1980s and traded to what is now the National Museum of the U.S. Air Force in Dayton, Ohio. The turret was subsequently placed on loan and restored by volunteers at the Pima Air and Space Museum in Tucson, Arizona. The turret can be seen displayed below the museum's B-18A, serial number 38-593.

With the *Swamp Ghost* recovered, is the Big Island B-18 the last, intact, World War II bomber sitting in the jungle?

Part Three

The Frozen North

Imagine every problem you would encounter when recovering a warbird and magnify it hundreds of times when retrieving a downed aircraft from the frigid north. Impact angle, temperature, weather, and weight of water are only four of the factors to consider when starting an aircraft search. Then there's the problem of transporting the aircraft across the terrain or flying it to the nearest road—daunting issues each one. Then there's caring for the recovery crew and the logistics needed to keep humans alive, healthy, and nourished in a land that most people avoid.

An aircraft's impact angle determines whether a relatively intact plane will be recovered or the crash will have predisassembled the plane before the warbird hunters arrive. Aircraft that have belly-landed on frozen terrain or iced-over lakes are prime candidates for restoration to flyable condition. If an aircraft landed on a frozen land and sank when the ice melted, there is the added difficulty of recovering the aircraft from under water with temperatures close to freezing. However, aircraft submerged or covered by ice are very well preserved, provided the ice has not shifted and crushed the plane. Smaller, more compact types like fighters have been shown to withstand the pressures of ice movement (for example the P-38 *Glacier Girl*), while larger bomber types, like the B-17E *Big Stoop* (41-9101) and the B-17G (44-83790) recovered from Dyke Lake, were heavily damaged by the weight of shifting ice and, in the case of 44-83790, strong underwater currents as well.

Aside from the technical and logistical hurdles, keeping a small army of aircraft recovery specialists fed, warm, and comfortable is another challenge. This means adding one or more cooks to the team who need to be as skilled as most highly trained chefs, to be able to vary the types of meals and to improvise with ingredients from the pantry at hand. There is no running to the local grocery to pick up potatoes—when you're out, you're out.

And there are other comforts that need to be attended to from the call of nature to insect repellant, to how to keep boredom from setting

The B-17E *My Gal Sal*, serial number 41-9032, flown by Ralph H. Stinson on June 27, 1942, ran low on fuel in bad weather and had to put down on the Greenland icecap. *My Gal Sal* had only 224 flying hours when she was lost. After ten days on the ice cap, the crew was rescued. In August 1995, Gary Larkins, from the Institute of Aeronautical Archaeological Research, recovered the aircraft on behalf of Jack Erickson and the Tillamook Air Museum in Oregon. In March 2000, the bomber was sold to Robert E. Ready, head of the Ultimate Sacrifice Memorial Foundation, who began the restoration and reconstruction of *My Gal Sal*. In August 2012, the bomber was acquired by the National World War II Museum in New Orleans, which displays the Flying Fortress suspended from ceiling of its air war gallery. *U.S. Army Air Forces*

in and how to keep everyone functioning as a team. A base camp must be established near the crash site to enable workers to access the aircraft without commuting long distances. For small teams the necessary infrastructure of a base camp is minimal, while larger efforts require a mini-city be established, with everything from residence tents, to a chow hall, engineering offices, communal spaces, as well as utilities such as electricity, sanitation, and communications with the outside world.

At higher latitudes, nearly all of the land is controlled by various governments. Being able to negotiate recovery permits and presenting how the recovery will impact the environment are two areas of expertise needed for these types of operations.

Once the subject aircraft has been located, disassembled, and prepared for transport, terrain will dictate how the plane is removed. Will it be moved by snowmobile and sled, flown out by helicopter or cargo plane, or if there is a body of water nearby, will it be loaded onto a barge or coastal freighter for shipping to the nearest major port?

The frozen north is not for amateurs, and those who venture there quickly become professionals.

P-38 *Glacier Girl*

Lockheed P-38F Lightning 41-7630 is now known as *Glacier Girl*. This Lightning was part of the initial cadre of combat aircraft sent to the European Theater of war; however, she never arrived and never fired a shot in anger.

Glacier Girl has been on an amazing journey, from the Lockheed factory in Burbank, California, to Maine, to Labrador, to the ice cap of Greenland and below. Today *Glacier Girl* is a pristine, immaculately restored example of a Lockheed Lightning and currently the only flying "F" model.

Operation Bolero

In late spring 1942, planners on the Combined Chiefs of Staff began developing a plan to turn England into a giant air base from which to launch attacks against Hitler's European fortress. During June and July 1942, Operation Bolero would move 386 aircraft from the 97th Bomb Group, the 1st (flying P-38s) and 31st (P-39s) Fighter Groups, and the 60th Transport Group from the United States to England. Planners estimated that 10 percent of the aircraft going east would be lost just getting to England.

A decision was made not to send the P-39s across the North Atlantic by air, and the 31st Fighter Group's aircraft and men were wisely loaded on ships for the journey to England. Less the P-39s, the planes from the other groups destined to see battle from bases in England began gathering in the northeastern United States. The plan was to have one B-17 lead six fighters across the Atlantic. On April 15, 1942, the P-38s and B-17s assembled at Grenier Field, New Hampshire, and at Dow Field, Maine, while the C-47s of the 60th Transport Group met at Westover Field, Maine.

The aircraft would rendezvous at Presque Isle, Maine, and fly the first leg, a distance of 560 miles, to Goose Bay, Labrador. From Goose Bay, the formations then flew to Narsarssuak, Greenland—code-named Bluie West 1 (on the south coast), or farther up the island's west coast to Sondre Stromfjord, known as Bluie West 8. The Goose Bay to Sondre Stromfjord leg was approximately 1,000 miles. From these bases in Greenland, the B-17s and P-38s would fly to Reykjavik, Iceland (approximately 760 miles), and then on to Prestwick, Scotland (833 miles). From Prestwick they would go their separate ways to bases in England.

Lieutenant Bradley McManus, left, was the first of the Tomcat Flight P-38s to land on the ice cap. McManus landed with his wheels down and the fighter immediately flipped on its back. Lieutenant Carl Rudder, leaning on engine nacelle, bellylanded his P-38 and joined Lieutenant Robert Wilson in making way over to check on McManus. At about that time, McManus dug himself out from under the overturned P-38. *Rajani Collection via Warren Bodie*

Eighteen B-17s made the inaugural Operation Bolero trip, departing Presque Isle on June 23, for Goose Bay. On the twenty-sixth, they continued on to Bluie West 1 and 8, but only half of them arrived at their destinations. Six returned to Goose Bay for weather or other reasons, and three went down on the Greenland ice cap. The crews of the three crashed bombers were rescued, all having survived.

Subsequent flights of B-17s and P-38s went off without a hitch, until July 15 when Tomcat Yellow and Tomcat Green (one B-17 leading three P-38s per flight) encountered severe weather over the Denmark Strait after crossing the coast of Greenland. The Tomcat flights on this day consisted of six First Fighter Group P-38s (all P-38Fs, serial numbers 41-7560, -7583, -7616, -7623, -7626, -7630) and two 97th Heavy Bomb Group B-17Es (41-9101 *Big Stoop* and 41-9105 *Do-Do*). It was

Lieutenant Dallas "Spider" Webb's P-38 lost its propellers upon touching down on the ice cap. Both propellers can be seen to the rear of the port vertical stabilizer, and one of the two B-17s has come to rest about one-half mile to the south. *Rajani Collection via Warren Bodie*

thought the flights also received false information from a German weather station pretending to be Allied forecasters. The Tomcat flights had departed from Bluie West 8 and, after encountering storms and based upon the information they received en route, elected to return to base. Flying west, the flights were buffeted by strong headwinds, and the P-38s were quickly running low on fuel.

Unable to make it to a military airfield, the flights were forced to set down on the ice cap. The chosen area was in the Ikersuak Fjord district, on the lower southeast side of the island. Lieutenant Bradley McManus in P-38F 41-7560 was first to land. McManus approached with his landing gear down while the remainder of the flight circled above. As McManus touched down, the P-38's landing gear broke through the crust of the ice and the nose gear dug in, flipping the fighter. Having suffered only a deep cut on his arm, McManus was able to dig his way out while the other aircraft continued to circle.

Lieutenant Robert H. Wilson landed next. He came in gear up, and as soon as his aircraft slid to a stop, he ran over to see if McManus was still alive. As he ran, as much as running is possible in knee-deep snow, McManus emerged from under his overturned Lightning. The remaining P-38s followed Wilson in, each landing wheels up, sliding across the snow and ice. Both of the B-17s continued to orbit above, sending distress signals and attempting to communicate with Bluie West 1 or 8. The navigators estimated the planes were down on the ice at 65 degrees 20 minutes North, 40 degrees 20 minutes West. As they, too, ran out of fuel, the Flying Fortresses set down on the ice.

The crews immediately went into survival mode turning the Flying Fortresses into barracks and gathering emergency rations. The food was rationed to last everyone fourteen days. All of the men bundled up and spent the first cold night on the ice cap. The second day came and went. The crews were able to start one or two engines on each bomber to keep the batteries charged, enabling the radios to be used. Late in the afternoon of the third day, a pair of C-47s was spotted. Using flares, the stranded airmen were able to catch their attention and the C-47s buzzed the makeshift camp dropping supplies to the downed airmen. The next day, a PBY Catalina flying boat dropped additional supplies and announced that a rescue party was making its way to the airmen.

Tomcat Yellow and Green had landed ten miles in from the coast. Six days after the squadron landed on the ice cap, the rescue party arrived to retrieve the downed airmen. And although the aircraft were ten miles inland, it would be a seventeen-mile walk to the coast with detours to avoid crevasses. Reaching the beach, the twenty-five-man party of airmen and rescuers were soon met by the U.S. Coast Guard cutter *Northland* (WPG-49). *Northland* took the men to Angmanssalik (Bluie East 2), from where they were flown to Bluie West 1. From Bluie West 1, the men were sent Stateside and were reassigned.

From June to July 1942, Operation Bolero moved 386 aircraft across the North Atlantic (164 P-38s, 119 B-17s, and 103 C-47s). By the end of the year, that number climbed to 882 planes safely making the journey. In all, thirty-eight aircraft were lost during the 1942 Operation Bolero movements, roughly 10 percent, just as U.S. Army Air Force planners had predicted.

In August 1942, the military sent a salvage team back to strip parts from the aircraft. When the salvors walked away from the planes of the Tomcat flights, no one ever gave them another thought. And that's where the story should end.

Initial Attempts at Finding the Lost Squadron

Warbird collector David Tallichet was aware of the downed B-17s and P-38s, and in 1974 he acquired a salvage permit for the aircraft. Busy with aircraft recoveries in other parts of the world, Tallichet never acted upon his permit.

Forty-one years after the crash, Roy Degan, Pat Epps, Russel Rajani, and Richard Taylor left Atlanta, Georgia, in search of the pair of B-17s and six P-38 flighters. Rajani and Degan, both commercial airline pilots, had researched the crash and lobbied the Danish government to cancel Tallichet's permit and transfer the salvage rights to their group. Rajani, a former navy A-7 Corsair II pilot with more than a hundred combat missions during Vietnam, and Roy Degan, a Korean and Vietnam War veteran air force pilot, were both pilots for Republic Airlines. Having obtained salvage rights, they brought Epps, operator of a large Atlanta flight school and fixed-base operation, and Taylor, an architect, into the partnership, known as Pursuits Unlimited, for the first exploration of Greenland in search of what would later become known as the Lost Squadron. Pursuits Unlimited was granted salvage rights in exchange for recovering and transferring one of the B-17s to the Danish government.

There were reports that the tails of the B-17s were visible on the ice cap as late as 1961, nineteen years after the crash. After determining where the squadron had crashed, Degan, Epps, Rajani, and Taylor arrived on the ice cap in August 1981. Having located the crash site, the intrepid explorers began using magnetometers to search for the planes. Buried layers of ice reflected the magnetometers' beams, which gave inconsistent readings, and although the Pursuits Unlimited team was in the right place when crash site photos were lined up with the terrain, they could not conclusively say they had found the aircraft. Returning home eight days later, the team took stock of their lessons learned and prepared for their next trip to the ice cap.

In discussions with researchers at the Georgia Institute of Technology, they learned that subsurface radar would be a much more productive tool for trying to locate an object below the ice. Using Epps's contacts through his aviation business, the team quickly raised $25,000 to fund a return trip to the ice cap two months later, in October 1981. After traveling to Greenland, the team was unable

The Greenland Expedition Society's iconic photo of the P-38 in its ice cavern more than 260 feet below the surface. Using hot water jets, the area around the Lightning was cleared, giving the team an opportunity to survey the fighter and its condition. Notice the toolboxes, electrical lines, sump pump discharge hoses, and the fact that the propellers are in the fully feathered position. *Lou Sapienza*

to reach the crash site due to poor weather. The October expedition was canceled, and Rajani, Degan, Epps, and Taylor's partnership was dissolved. Epps and Taylor formed the Greenland Expedition Society (GES) and began mounting a rival effort to find the aircraft. In late August 1982, Degan took geophysicist Bruce Bevan to the ice cap with his subsurface radar equipment to scan the terrain. High winds and bad weather forced the team to return without conclusive evidence of the aircraft's locations.

Later in 1982, Rajani and Degan met with Hollywood actor, restaurateur, and entrepreneur Jay Fiondella, who made introductions between Pursuits Unlimited and executives at the R. J. Reynolds, Co. Reynolds is a conglomerate of businesses, most notable for its cigarette brands such as Camel, Salem, and Winston, and the company was looking for ways to promote its cigarette brands. Sponsoring the expedition to locate and recover the World War II fighters and bombers was just the action event R. J. Reynolds was looking for.

Dubbed the "Winston Recovery Team" and outfitted in branded attire, the team had ambitious plans for summer 1983. Once on the ice, supply problems, weather, and radar issues kept success at bay. Frustrated, Rajani talked a P-3 crew stationed in Iceland to fly over the area with their magnetometer to confirm whether or not the search party was above the lost aircraft. The P-3s did indeed report something metal below the surface, but they could not tell the Winston Recovery Team how far down they were. Rajani then turned to Professor Helgi Björnsson from the University of Iceland. Björnsson traveled to the ice cap with his low frequency ice radar and by August 3, 1983, located both B-17s and all six P-38s.

In September 1985, Jay Fiondella mounted an expedition under the name of Historical Aircraft Recovery Team, or HART. Although they did not recover an aircraft, one of HART's engineers, Bill Thuma, upon his return to the United States, wrote a report estimating the aircraft was 258 feet below the ice.

Enter the Greenland Expedition Society

By the end of 1985, Rajani's and Fiondella's efforts had located the aircraft, but they were both out of benefactors willing to fund an expedition. In addition, it was one technological challenge to recover aircraft from under forty feet of ice, but it was another to face the hurdles presented by Bill Thuma's prediction of where the aircraft might actually sit.

The time was right for the GES to acquire salvage rights to the Lost Squadron. In April 1986, the Danish government transferred rights to GES and the group relaunched its efforts to locate and recover the aircraft. They were back on the ice in July 1986. And again, they were unable to locate the aircraft.

The 1987 season came and went as there was no money for an expedition. In 1988, nearly $200,000 was raised by selling shares in the as-yet-to-be-recovered P-38. Returning to the ice cap, the GES brought Professor Björnsson and his ice-penetrating radar in the hope that his equipment could finally reach deep enough to locate the aircraft. Having located a target with Professor Björnsson's radar, the task of drilling a hole down to the subsurface contact began. Soon the team had made contact with an object 250 feet below the surface. More holes were bored and each was marked with a flag. As hole after hole were sunk, the outline of a B-17 began to emerge.

GES's salvage rights were scheduled to expire in 1989 unless the group could produce tangible evidence that it had found the aircraft. Don Brooks and Richard Taylor developed a drill fitted to a unit that sprayed hot water to bore down to the B-17 and auger out a hole in order to capture a piece of metal from the aircraft. To the Danish government, retrieving a piece of the B-17 was essentially the same as arresting a wreck under maritime salvage laws, in that displaying a piece of the aircraft gave GES "possession" of the bomber. Seeing the evidence, the Danish government extended GES's permit and the group set about raising the money it would need to recover one or more aircraft.

For the 1990 expedition, GES worked with Ms. M. Bobbie Bailey, an investor in the recovery effort and founder of Our Way, Inc., an air-conditioning and compressor refurbishing company with more than 350 employees (sold to the Carrier Corp. in 2001), to develop an auger that could melt its way down to the aircraft. Dubbed the "Gopher," it was a four-foot-diameter cone with external pipes that circulated hot water to melt the ice it came in contact with. A series of PVC pipes were strung together and lowered down to the aircraft and this was used to guide the Gopher down to the wreck. The Gopher had a hollow center through which the PVC pipe passed, and the unit descended using this as its guide. The PVC pole enabled the Gopher to work unattended, boring a hole with minimal human supervision.

In addition to the Gopher, investors Angelo and Remo Pizzagalli brought a silo unloader to the ice cap to bore another, larger hole down to the bomber. At 40-feet down, the silo unloader began to break down, and at 120 feet, the inrushing glacial melt water was coming in faster than it could be pumped out. The silo unloader was moved over one of the P-38s and digging began. At 50 feet down, the unit quit working and time had run out in the 1990 season to repair it.

The Gopher reached the B-17 *Big Stoop* at 9 a.m., on June 6. After melting a cavern around the bomber, it was quickly evident that the Flying Fortress had been mangled by the weight of and the shifting of the ice cap. The roof of the cockpit had been pushed down below the tops of the pilots' armored seatbacks to give an indication of the aircraft's condition. Many parts were salvaged from the bomber, but it was clear that the aircraft's large open spaces could not withstand the forces of nature.

Determining that the P-38s with their smaller, more compact structure designed with a load factor of +7.33 g, would better withstand the weight and shifting of the ice, recovery of a Lockheed Lightning became GES's primary mission.

Shifting ice had broken the glass out of the windscreen, but everything else in the cockpit was intact, from the gunsight to a tobacco tin left by Lt. Harry Smith. *Lou Sapienza*

The GES found an investor in J. Roy Shoffner, an entrepreneur based in Middlesboro, Kentucky. Shoffner put up $350,000 to finance the 1992 expedition to the ice cap. Epps hired Bob Cardin, a Vietnam Huey helicopter pilot and retired army lieutenant colonel, to become project manager for the recovery.

Cardin began work on February 18, 1992, and the plan was to have three P-38s recovered and off the ice by July 15 of that year. "I started immediately working on the planning process along with Don Brooks," said Cardin. "Together, me and Don, in sixty-one days, came up with the concept of the operation. We designed, manufactured, assembled, and tested all of the equipment. We packaged it and put it on a big, flatbed truck and shipped it off to McGuire Air Force Base, New Jersey, for the first leg in the journey heading off to Greenland to recover the airplane.

"On April 21, 1992, I left Atlanta driving a truck carrying the melting unit to McGuire AFB. There I worked with the fellows that load the airplanes, and we put 38,000 pounds of equipment and 6,000 pounds of food on some C-141s, and we flew off to Greenland. We got to Sondrestrom Air Base, Greenland (Bluie West 8), around May 1, and I waited four days until the GES DC-3 showed up. We hung around 'Sonde' for a day waiting for some good weather, then we flew out to the glacier on May 6 and dropped off the crew that was going to relocate the P-38s under the ice."

The cargo sent by C-141 was dropped at Sondrestrom, and from there it was loaded onto New York Air National Guard ski-equipped C-130s and flown to Kulusuk on Greenland's east coast. At Kulusuk, the cargo was broken down into smaller loads and trans-shipped to the ice cap recovery site using the GES's D-Day veteran C-47, also

A single shaft was bored down to the Lightning to inspect the aircraft and begin the task of dismantling the fighter. Once the shaft had been enlarged, subassemblies from the fighter were hoisted to the surface of the ice cap. Here one of the Lightning's two Allison V-1710 engines is moved by a front loader and positioned so that it can be airlifted from the crash site. *Lou Sapienza*

fitted with skies. Once word that the aircraft had been relocated under the ice, the C-47 began making runs to the ice cap campsite.

"Once the camp was set up and the airplanes were located, we steamed a small probe hole, it was about six inches in diameter, down and touched the airplane," Cardin said. "Once the airplane was touched, that's how we confirmed that the aircraft was there. Then we set up our equipment to start to melt a four-foot diameter shaft. That process, setting the camp up, setting the tent up, and all that stuff, took about seven days."

Camp Life on the Ice Cap

"We had a twenty foot by forty foot Quonset hut made out of plastic for our communal area," said expedition photographer Lou Sapienza. It was Sapienza's photographs that captured the imaginations of warbird enthusiasts and the general public the world-over showing the intact P-38 more than twenty-five stories below the surface. "Other

The nose gun bay shortly after opening the door for the first time in more than fifty years. Some of the magnesium parts have corroded, but the guns were ready to fire. Once the nose section was disassembled and lifted to the surface, one of the guns was test fired on the ice cap. *Lou Sapienza*

than the communal tent, we had smaller Quonset-type little huts for living quarters. Nobody was really bored. If we weren't working, we were sleeping and getting ready for the next day. Everybody knew what they had to do because all of the planning was done before we ever got up there.

"The first time I went to the ice cap in 1989, I went up to photograph but they didn't really have a cook and I had been a line cook out in Eastern Long Island in a seafood restaurant so I just naturally took over. Once they found that out, they said, 'Well go for it, Lou, because we don't know what we're doing and we don't really want to do it anyway.' They had just brought up a mishmash of food. They had gone to the grocery store before they left with their wives or girlfriends, loaded up grocery carts, and trucked the stuff up there. I just tried to get creative with what I was doing.

"The second expedition in 1990, they brought the Pizzagalli group. There were two groups at the same time working side-by-side up there. They had supposedly brought a cook and I ended up doing a bit more cooking again, and then the third expedition, which we recovered *Glacier Girl*, the person who was supposed to cook bailed out, so I was told that in addition to my photographic duties, I would also be cooking. I'd have to plan the menus, order all the food and get it shipped up to Greenland, store it, cook it, and all that good stuff."

Going Down the Hole

Once the GES crew positioned the Gopher and started melting, it took about ten days to reach the Lightning. What they had found was 1st Lt. Harry L. Smith Jr.'s P-38F-1-LO 41-7630, and it was in remarkable condition, all things considered.

"We get on top of the P-38 and then, using hot water, we melted a room around the fighter. It was big enough to get to every piece of the airplane," Cardin said. "The wingspan on the P-38 is nearly fifty feet, and the length is thirty-seven feet, ten inches nose to tail, and the tail had been torn off by shifting ice, so that added another ten feet to the dimensions of the cavern around the aircraft. We had an area of about

After restoration, *Glacier Girl*, as 41-7630 had become to be known, was flown to the Experimental Aircraft Association's AirVenture annual fly-in at Oshkosh, Wisconsin. At Oshkosh 2005, the fighter was honored with the World War II Grand Champion award. Compare the "as-found" photo with this shot of the restored gun bay. Visible details include the 0.50-cal. gun firing solenoid and the 20mm ammunition drum.

50 feet by 50 feet melted out 265 feet inside the glacier in which we would start to disassemble the airplane."

As soon as the Gopher was up and out of the shaft, the GES team descended to see what condition the fighter was in. "We clipped onto a chain hoist that had a Bosun's chair that was just a flat piece of wood with a piece of strapping on it. You get in that and then you clip onto the chain as well with a [climbing] harness . . . in case you slip out of the seat," Sapienza said. "As you're going down there are two four-inch hoses as well as an intake and an outtake for exhaust for the Gopher's hot water for the unit. Also in the shaft was electrical cabling and another four- to six-inch fire hose that we used to pump water out. All of these lines and hoses were suspended on other chains, so it got a little crowded moving through the shaft and there was the constant danger of getting hung up on something.

"It was a long ride either direction and there really wasn't an emotional response to it all except you were thinking 'all this is cool' and you're just looking at the ice shaft as you're going up or down. It's got rings in it and it's melting in weird and wonderful ways that are quite beautiful.

"Nobody knew how the shaft would react—if there would be potential for a cave-in, or movement. It was actually quite stable and, as time went on, because of the warm air, the shaft expanded in size."

Lifting the Lightning

The GES team bored three holes down to the Lightning. Two holes were sunk next to each other, and the third was over about five feet. As the Gopher bored the third hole, team members were busy scraping ice to connect all of the bores. This made a slot approximately five feet by twenty feet, just large enough to lift the P-38's completely stripped center section.

At the top of the hole was an I-beam suspended on posts and strapped to keep it stabilized. Chain falls were suspended from the I-beam, and larger, heavier pieces like the engines were brought up, then chained to a front-end loader and hauled out. "Most of the individual pieces of the airplane are fairly light," Sapienza said. "Pieces like the tail booms and the radiators can be lifted by about three or four people. The parts are pretty light. I think four people could move a wing without any problem."

Aircraft salvors Gary Larkins and Thomas "T. K." Mohr were brought in to assist with the task of separating the Lightning into its component parts. It took the team about two weeks to dismantle the aircraft and haul the pieces to the surface with the exception of the center section. The center section weighed approximately 7,000 pounds, and once the shaft was enlarged, a cable was lowered, attached to the airframe, and the slow lifting process began. It took about four days to get the center section to the surface.

"We got the center section of the airplane on the surface and had a Sikorsky S-61 helicopter come in, and on August 21 we flew that the big piece off the glacier and over to Kulusuk," Cardin said. "And from there the rest of the trip was fairly easy. Not eventful. We put the center section on a barge and sent it out to a freighter that was waiting off the coast of Kulusuk, which then sailed for Denmark. From Denmark we had to ship it to Sweden, and then from Sweden it went on a container ship to Savannah, Georgia."

Some of the smaller parts had come out of the shaft earlier in July, and the most identifiable were flown on the DC-3 to the Experimental Aircraft Association's AirVenture fly-in for display. The remaining parts were either flown off the glacier by the helicopter and then transported on the reverse route from Kulusuk to Sondrestrom to McGuire AFB, where they were put on a truck and sent to Roy Shoffner's facility in Middlesboro, Kentucky, where the restoration was going to take place.

Restoration and Recognition

The entire airplane arrived in Middlesboro, on October 26, 1992. That was the day the recovery operation ended and the restoration process began. Roy Shoffner, who had staked the money for the recovery expedition, had acquired the aircraft and wanted to see it back in the air. Shoffner hired Cardin to oversee the restoration, and Cardin moved from Atlanta to Middlesboro for the job.

"Our plan was simple. What we wanted to do was fly the P-38, so we were going to take the broken stuff off, fix the broken pieces, put it back together, and go fly," Cardin said. "Well, after we took all the broken stuff off the airplane, there was nothing left. Every single piece of the airplane was broken."

When the GES team did its premission planning, it examined the photos and talked with Norman Vaughn who had led the salvage mission to the aircraft in August 1942. The aircraft selected for recovery was the only P-38 where the pilot feathered the propellers and shut down the engines before landing on the ice. The only damage to the propeller/engine system was one blade on each side was bent back when it impacted with the ice cap. Thus, 41-7630 was in the best overall condition of the six P-38s under the ice.

"We had the aircraft fully disassembled by mid-January 1993, and we started fixing the pieces one at a time. As far as the Lightning's condition, it was primarily crushing damage from the weight of the ice and the shifting of the glacier," Cardin said. "There was some corrosion damage on the magnesium pieces. Magnesium in a moist environment turns to a powder and dissipates. The aluminum was in perfect condition except it was crinkled and bent. As far as the damage goes, it was all from its stay in the glacier.

"We had a tremendous amount of bent metal that was good if we could straighten it out. So, we used a lot of heat-treating. We would anneal the aluminum pieces, straighten them out, and then harden them up again in the proper shape. We used a lot of what were then developing technologies that are commonplace today. For example, we were using computerized measuring machine technology that was just being developed to duplicate parts. And through a CAD, and using the CNC machine, we were actually able to whittle some of the castings out of a solid block of aluminum. Because this is a right side/left side airplane, we were able to push a button to mirror image that part and again make a second piece.

"We used cutting lasers to cut hinges. Not only did it save a lot of time, it gave us a perfect part, and it was very cost effective when you can program a computer to shoot a laser to cut a piece of stainless steel. This was done on the door hinges for the main landing gear and the nose gear. The door hinges are a whole bunch of very small, stainless steel pieces, like a popsicle stick with a hole at each end. Rather than try to manufacture those one at a time by cutting them out or stamping, we just went to a company in Knoxville that had a laser, and it was about $3 each to have them made where you couldn't have made it anyplace else. So, we were able to use the developing technology of the day to assist in speeding up and enhancing the quality of the restoration while keeping the expenses down.

"To get the airplane completely restored and repaired and into an airworthy condition took us about ten years, to the day, and Steve Hinton made its first postrestoration flight on October 26, 2002." The fighter was registered N17630 to reflect its wartime serial number.

Glacier Girl was flown to Dayton, Ohio, for the 2003 Rolls-Royce Aviation Heritage Trophy competition, sponsored by the National

Glacier Girl on the ramp at the National Championship Air Races, which is also home to the National Aviation Hall of Fame's Neil A. Armstrong Aviation Heritage Trophy competition. In 2003, the competition was held in Dayton, Ohio, and *Glacier Girl* was honored with the Aviation Heritage Trophy as well as the People's Choice Award.

Aviation Hall of Fame. (In 2012, the Rolls-Royce trophy was renamed in honor of Neil A. Armstrong.) At Dayton, *Glacier Girl* took the Rolls-Royce Aviation Heritage Trophy and was also selected for the People's Choice Award. The Aviation Heritage Trophy is a perpetual award and is displayed year-round at the National Air and Space Museum's Steven F. Udvar-Hazy Center outside of Washington, D.C.

In 2005, *Glacier Girl* was flown to what is certainly the largest airshow in the world—the Experimental Aircraft Association's AirVenture at Oshkosh, Wisconsin. This event attracts more than ten thousand aircraft and anywhere from 750,000 to 1,000,000 visitors during the show week. There is a separate area for warbirds, and in 2005, *Glacier Girl* was the star. The Lightning was judged by a panel of restoration experts to be worthy of the prestigious Grand Champion World War II award. The fighter has returned to Oshkosh a number of times and always attracts large crowds.

Where are they now? Pat Epps continues to run his fixed-base operation at the Peachtree-DeKalb Airport. Bob Cardin is flight director for the Lewis Air Legends collection of warbirds, and Lou Sapienza continues his photography work. Having served on a number of expeditions to both the north and south pole, Sapienza has formed North South Polar Inc. to find American MIAs in the polar

In 2006, Rod Lewis acquired *Glacier Girl* for the Lewis Air Legends warbird collection. Considered the crown jewel of Lewis's collection, her journey has been long and arduous, from under the ice to a Kentucky restoration shop, and here with Steve Hinton at the controls in the skies over Nevada's Pyramid Lake. *Glacer Girl* looks best in flight. *A. Kevin Grantham*

regions. He is now working to recover the three-man crew of a U.S. Coast Guard J2F-4 Duck (Lt. John Pritchard, radioman first class Benjamin Bottoms, and Army Cpl. Loren Howarth) that crashed in Greenland on November 29, 1942. It is interesting how the recovery of an unmanned P-38 has led to the search for other downed airmen in such a hostile environment.

Glacier Girl **Today**

The driving force behind *Glacier Girl's* recovery and restoration, J. Roy Shoffner, passed away on September 24, 2005. He would be pleased to know that *Glacier Girl* continues to be exhibited at airshows around the country. He wanted her to fly, and she does.

In 2006, *Glacier Girl* was acquired by Rod Lewis and the rare P-38 fighter became part of the Lewis Air Legends Collection based near San Antonio, Texas. The Lewis Air Legends collection now numbers more than two-dozen rare warbirds ranging from an F4F Wildcat, to a couple of F8F Bearcats, a P-47 Thunderbolt, a Mk Vb Spitfire, and the P-38. Lewis shares his collection at airshows throughout the year.

Million Dollar Valley
Marauders

The Martin B-26 Marauder's reputation of "One a Day in Tampa Bay" and the "Widow Maker" apparently did not motivate anyone to save many examples after the end of World War II. In 1970, there were only four Martin B-26 Marauders known to exist. There was *Flak Bait* in the Smithsonian's collection, an example in the French national collection (Musée de l'Air, Paris), another former French example at the National Museum of the United States Air Force, and the Commemorative Air Force (then the Confederate Air Force) had the only flying example, the former *Valley Turtle* air racer that competed in the 1949 Bendix Trophy race from Rosamond Dry Lake, California, to Cleveland, Ohio, and later flew as a corporate aircraft.

If any museum or private collector wanted a B-26 Marauder it was going to have to be recovered from one of the former World War II battlefields around the globe. There were one or two known examples

B-26 40-1464 was flown by Second Lt. William J. Dancer and copilot Second Lt. Howard F. Smiley. They landed wheels down not knowing the snow was five feet deep. At more than 140 mph, the left main gear caught a bush beneath the snow, which drove the nose down, collapsing the nose gear and crushing the cockpit. Shortly after the crash, some of the airmen can be seen covering the port wing to make a shelter while the crew awaits rescue. *Howard Smiley via Dik Shepherd*

The three aircraft sat in Million Dollar Valley for more than thirty years. The valley looks like an area that can be easily worked until one realizes that the ground is muskeg, having a consistency similar to a wet sponge during the warmer months. *Dik Shepherd*

that could be recovered, but at what cost? There was a well-known, fairly intact B-26 wreck on the island of Kiriwina that had crashed after attacking Rabaul, but it lay inverted and its nose section was completely crushed. A good candidate for recovery, but most museums and warbird collectors were looking for a more complete aircraft.

In September 1941, a group of new Martin Marauders was sent to the Sacramento Air Depot, California, to be winterized. Once that was accomplished, the planes were transferred to the Fourth Air Force, a subordinate unit to the Western Defense Command, which also controlled the Alaska Defense Command. These were factory-fresh B-26s having been delivered to the U.S. Army Air Forces in May through July 1941.

Less than a month after America's entry into World War II, the U.S. Army Air Forces were sending men and equipment west to fight the Japanese. Just before Christmas, crews from the 42nd Bomb Group, 77th Bomb Squadron were ordered to the Sacramento Air Depot, California, to pick up fourteen winterized B-26s and ferry them to Elmendorf Field, near Anchorage, Alaska. On January 5, 1942, the bombers departed Sacramento for Portland, Oregon, then east to Spokane, Washington, and on January 14, flew north across the border to Edmonton, Alberta, Canada.

From Edmonton, the Marauders were to fly 1,000 miles to Whitehorse in the Yukon Territory. There were no navigational maps,

Unable to get their army-surplus wrecker to the aircraft crash site, each of the medium bombers had to be disassembled by hand. *Dik Shepherd*

so the pilots made sketches on paper for the flight. Three of the fourteen Elmendorf-bound B-26s departed Edmonton on the morning of January 16 en route to Whitehorse. These Marauders were from the initial production order of 201 aircraft built at Martin's Middle River, Maryland, factory. B-26 40-1501 was flown by First Lt. Glenn A. Doolittle, B-26 40-1459 had Second Lt. Edward S. Avery in command, and B-26 40-1464 was being flown by Second Lt. William J. Dancer and copilot Second Lt. Howard F. Smiley. Lieutenants Dancer and Smiley were typical of the flight crews in the opening stages of the war—Dancer having only 356 hours of flight time and Smiley just 10.

Passing Fort Nelson, British Columbia, the flight encountered a snowstorm in the area. The three Marauders descended below the clouds to fly under the scud, and somehow managed to keep each other in sight through the rain and snow. Scud-running in unfamiliar territory only got the planes lost, and they were fortunate not to fly into any tall peaks. Lost and on low fuel, the pilots discussed their options over the radio. It was 4:15 p.m., and at that latitude in January it was rapidly becoming dark. The three pilots elected to land on a snow-covered meadow in a valley below.

First in was Lieutenant Avery in 40-1459. As he made his approach and moments before touching down, he lost one engine to fuel starvation. Avery was committed and his only option now was to bellyland the bomber. Lieutenant Doolittle in 40-1501 followed, landing the bomber on its belly and sliding across the relatively flat terrain. The bottoms of the bombers were torn up fairly well, but none of the crews were injured in the landing.

Last to touch down were Lieutenants Dancer and Smiley in 40-1464. They lowered their landing gear to slow the bomber down during the approach, as the short wing (66-foot span) Marauders usually approached their landings at speeds between 140 and 150 mph. The short-wing B-26's stall speed was 125 mph, so there was not much margin for error. Approaching the meadow with everything hanging out to slow the bomber down, the snow appeared flat with only a few blades of grass sticking up. Dancer set the main gear down in the snow, and the aircraft immediately sank five feet going 130-plus mph. The left gear caught a huge bush, which spun the bomber to the left, and as the front of the aircraft came down during the deceleration, the nose gear collapsed, crumpling the forward fuselage. Lieutenant Dancer was thrown from the cockpit, suffering cuts to his head, and Lieutenant Smiley was knocked unconscious, his legs were wrapped under the rudder pedals, and he was pinned in his seat. The rest of the passengers were unharmed.

After attending to the pilot and copilot's injuries, the aircraft crews started to set up shelters while others determined their position (the U.S. Army Air Forces crash report put them at 59.52 degrees N 126.03 degrees W). The radio operators of all three aircraft tried, unsuccessfully, to get word of the crash landings to the base at Whitehorse and Watson Lake. The good news was that there were enough supplies for each man for two weeks, along with arctic survival gear, including sleeping bags and plenty of water.

Search planes took off from Fort Nelson looking for the trio of downed Marauders on January 17. After searching all day, they found nothing. Then, midday, on January 18, a flight of Curtiss P-40 fighters escorted by a Curtiss C-46 Commando en route from Fort Nelson to Watson Lake passed close-by. The men on the ground lit fires, shot flares, and fired the turret machine guns to attract attention. This worked, and the flight of fighters and its escort circled the downed Marauders before flying on the Watson Lake.

A ski-equipped bush plane landed at the crash site the following morning. Lieutenants Dancer and Smiley, the two injured men in the group, were flown to Watson Lake. They were then transported to a hospital at Ladd Field, Alaska, for further examination. Smiley was back in the war the next day and Dancer was left to recuperate. The

The wings, horizontal, and vertical surfaces were separated from the fuselages and prepared for transport by helicopter. Note the large yellow "X" on the upper surface of the wing. This was painted by the army to advise pilots flying over the area in the future that these were known wrecks. *Dik Shepherd*

remaining men were guided to a nearby lake where float planes came and shuttled them to Fort Nelson so they could return to the 77th Bomb Squadron and their war duties.

The U.S. Army Air Forces sent a crew of mechanics back to the crash scene to strip the Marauders of all useable parts. These formed the basis of the B-26 spare parts inventory for the region at a time in the war when they were hard to come by.

Each of the aircraft cost exactly $120,586 when new, but many believed they cost more or were worth more. Pilots flying over the crash site guessed they would be worth a ton of money if the three B-26s were ever brought out and restored to flying condition. Thus, the area became known as the "Million Dollar Valley" and the story of the bombers made its way through the warbird community. However, even with a name that foretold certain riches, the trio of Marauders sat for thirty years.

Bringing the Marauders Home

Warbird collector David Tallichet had gone north to look for a downed P-39 near Watson Lake, and he, too, had heard the rumors of the Million Dollar Valley Marauders. In September 1971, Tallichet organized a team of men to head north and retrieve the aircraft. The recovery crew was led by Al Redick, with warbird mechanics Jim Maloney, Dik Shepherd, Leo Gay, Bernie Burger, John Watkins, and Tallichet rounding out the team.

Driving a war-surplus M-135 army truck loaded with tools and supplies, Redick, Maloney, and Shepherd left Phoenix, Arizona, on September 16, 1971, heading to Fort Nelson, British Columbia, to begin the recovery operation. Arriving five days later, the trio investigated an abandoned P-39 and located a set of P-40 wings, both of which were recovered and sent to Tallichet's base of operations in Southern California. From Fort Nelson, the truck was driven to the Smith River Airfield with the intention of driving the truck and its tools and equipment to the crash site. After scouting the way from the airfield to the crash site and determining it was impassible, the group left the truck at the Smith River Airfield and the men and their equipment were ferried in by helicopter. Gay, Burger, Watkins, and Tallichet met the truck and Redick, Maloney, and Shepherd at Smith River, which would become the team's base of operations once the aircraft were recovered from the bush.

"I went in on the second helicopter trip," said Dik Shepherd. "I jumped in and the other guys loaded the cargo nets. As we got airborne, I looked around and the view was absolutely beautiful. The whole area was a mass of colors and everything seemed so unreal.

"When we reached the area of the crash site, it was as if we had traveled back into time for on the ground just ahead of us was an aircraft of another era. Ahead was an aircraft that had been built in the 1940s and that had been sitting in the same spot for the past thirty years. The area was so desolate that it hardly seemed possible that a change would have happened in that thirty-year span. As we flew over the bomber, we could see a second one off to the right, about a mile and a half from the first. After passing over it, we circled back and headed for the campsite, which was on a hill, about a mile and a half behind the first Marauder."

Shepherd makes a point to relate the distances between the aircraft and the campsite because every step was on a type of terrain known as "muskeg." He described it by saying, "Having never walked on the stuff before, I didn't know what to expect. Muskeg looks like a thick moss growing on the top of a lake, and when you step on it you tend to sink. It's a lot like walking on a field of wet sponges." Being wet didn't help, as the temperature was below freezing throughout the entire operation.

After hauling their tools and supplies from the helicopter landing zone to the campsite, the team set out to inspect the bombers that evening. The visit was brief, and then there was the mile and a half trek back to the campsite. The following morning, the team headed for the bombers. "We reached the first aircraft and noticed that it was sitting on a natural pedestal of permafrost. We hadn't noticed it the night before because of the darkness," Shepherd said. "As soon as everyone had finished taking a few pictures of the aircraft, we began the job of disassembling it. One group started to work at disconnecting the wings, starting with the right side, while the rest of us worked at removing the tail section. The first pieces to come off, after about three hours, were the horizontal stabilizers. Six hours later we removed the aft section of the fuselage. The following day, the left wing was removed, then we began to gather up all of the small pieces and stuffed them into the tail section."

The second aircraft wasn't in as good shape as the first. It was sitting on the side of a hill without its horizontal and vertical stabilizers, and the bomb bay section was pretty well torn up. The wings and nose section were removed from this aircraft before the team headed to the third Marauder.

"The third aircraft was in the worst shape of the three because the pilot chose to land with his landing gear down, rather than wheels-up as the other two had done," said Shepherd. "From the looks of the nose and cockpit section, it was apparent that the nose wheel had collapsed when it touched down, causing the nose section to slide along the ground and disintegrate. After examining the cockpit, I could only imagine how bad the pilot and copilot must have been injured. Fortunately for us, because the pilot had chosen to land with the gear down, even though it ended up with a very bent nose, this was the only one of the three aircraft to have a set of main landing gear. It seems that after the military had rescued the crews, they sent a crew of mechanics into the crash site to remove the engines, armament, radio gear, instruments, and other assorted odds and ends from all three aircraft. They also removed the main landing gear from the first and second aircraft, while leaving the nose gears; however, they removed the nose gear from the third aircraft while leaving the main gear." Using the main landing gear as pivot points, the right wing was removed first, followed by the left. This left the fuselage precariously

Once at Fort Smith, the fuselages were split at the production breaks and mounted onto pallets that would enable the sections to be loaded onto flatbed railcars for the journey to David Tallichet's base at the Chino Airport in Southern California. *Dik Shepherd*

perched on a mound of permafrost. The now-wingless fuselage was braced so it wouldn't roll down hill in order to separate the tail section from the forward fuselage.

The next order of business for the team was to prepare the aircraft sections to be flown out by helicopter to the Smith River Airfield and break camp. A turbine-powered Sikorsky S-58T was used to lift the Marauder sections from the crash site to the airfield at Smith River. From Smith River, the aircraft sections were trucked to Fort Nelson where they were loaded onto pallets, then onto railcars for the long journey to Southern California. The recovery operation took nearly three months to complete.

Restoration, Flight, and Current Status

After hauling the disassembled bombers to Chino, the long task of making one out of three began. In the process, Tallichet picked up the majority of another B-26 from one of the Hollywood studios. This Marauder was used as a studio stand-in for Japanese Betty bombers and may have appeared in the 1943 Warner Brothers film *Air Force*.

When the U.S. Army Air Forces salvaged the Marauders, they removed the main landing gear from the two planes that bellylanded, but 40-1464, sitting on its mains with its tail in the air, was left alone. The Tallichet crew removed the crushed nose from 40-1464 and bolted on the intact nose from 40-1459. They now had one complete fuselage with empennage and wings from which to start the restoration.

Progress was slow as Tallichet's massive collection demanded attention. Some of his aircraft were moved between locations around the United States, and during this time B-17G 44-83546 underwent a massive transformation. Tallichet's crew, led by Joe Krezminski, converted the G model Flying Fortress into a B-17F to play the lead role in the remake of the movie *Memphis Belle*. The chin turret was removed and the area reskinned, the Sperry upper turret was made functional, the waist gunner's windows were unstaggered, and the G model's Cheyenne tail turret was converted into an F model Stinger tail.

It took nineteen years to complete the Marauder's restoration. Once it was ready for flight, David Tallichet and Roscoe Diehl flew the aircraft for the first time on April 18, 1992. The plane was flown from the Chino Airport to the March Air Force Base in Riverside, California, where it was on display for about a year. Diehl and George Rivera flew the bomber for photographer John Harjo on August 5, 1993, when the aircraft returned from March Air Force Base back to Chino.

When Tallichet ran into temporary financial difficulties in the mid-1990s, he sold a number of aircraft to raise money. His ex-Indian Air Force B-24J and B-26 40-1464 were acquired by Kermit Weeks for his Fantasy of Flight Museum in Polk City, southwest of Orlando, Florida. He asked Tony Ritzman and Carl Scholl of Aero Trader at Chino Airport to check over the bomber before flying it across country to its new home.

"Tallichet's crew had spent a number of years working on that airplane, and when Weeks bought it, he asked us to go through the bomber," said Carl Scholl of Aero Trader. "The aircraft has only flown a couple of times, and then it sat again for a couple of years. We didn't do any cosmetic work to speak of, other than make and install a new turret dome.

"Mechanically, we had some work to do. The hydraulic system turned out to be an absolute nightmare. We not only had to completely rebuild the hydraulics, we also had to repair the fuel system to make sure it was functioning properly. We also installed an effective fire extinguisher system and rebuilt the landing gear. During retraction tests, another nightmare came up in aligning all the gear doors and making sure the whole system worked properly. One of the tubes supporting the landing gear was bent and we made a new unit.

"We overhauled all the instruments and radios, redid the center console, and replaced all of the rubber hoses that had gone out of date. We recovered the control surfaces and built new spinners for the engines." The Tallichet crew had converted this early Marauder from a 12-volt system to the standard aircraft 24-volt configuration. This made maintaining the aircraft easier.

"We got the plane pretty sound, and made the first postoverhaul flight on March 25, 1997. Tony Ritzman and I flew the plane. We obtained FAA authorization to fly it. No one was rated in the airplane at time, of course, and there was no one current in it. We flew it maybe five or ten hours, or something, around here locally. It has short wings, a short rudder, and engines that just quite didn't have enough power.

"I wasn't particularly fond of the airplane. It had some unusual flying characteristics. When you would stand on the rudder, then take your foot off the pedals, the rudder would stay where you put it. It wouldn't streamline back to neutral on its own. I'm thinking a gap-seal was missing, which the later airplanes did have; maybe the early ones didn't have it or maybe this one was just missing. I don't know. That was a little bit weird.

"The other thing that was strange about it is that the single-engine performance on takeoff was in the toilet. If you lost an engine on takeoff, the aircraft just wouldn't climb. Even at minimum controllable airspeed, it was real sluggish with the gear down because all the doors were out. It was just a real draggy airplane. Losing an engine on takeoff was definitely a problem. I think a lot of guys found that out during the war or in training."

Once satisfied with its performance, Kermit Weeks and Tony Ritzman flew the Marauder back to Florida. Weeks flew the bomber a couple of times in the local area, and then north to the Experimental Aircraft Association's annual AirVenture fly-in. "They had an engine problem with it at Oshkosh when they were leaving, and returned to the field," Scholl said. "They pulled the engine off and took it down to engine builder Rudy Blakey and he fixed it. Some counterweight came loose or something like that, and they took it back up to Oshkosh, hung the engine, and then flew it back to Florida. To my knowledge, it hasn't flown since."

B-26 40-1464 can be seen at Kermit Weeks's Fantasy of Flight in Polk City, Florida.

A year after the aircraft had been transported to Chino, 40-1464 gained a new forward fuselage and was reassembled. The restoration process took nineteen years. The bomber made its first postrestoration flight on April 18, 1992. *Tom Piedmonte*

Other Surviving B-26 Marauders

In late 1946 or early 1947, Charles "Pat" Patterson of Pacific Palisades drove out to the Reconstruction Finance Corporation's sales yard at the Chino Airport and bought the nose sections of two Marauders (B-26B-25-MA 41-31856 and B-26C-20-MO 41-35075). Patterson, an engineer at North American Aviation, was planning on building a travel trailer out of the two cockpits, bolted together at the fuselage production break behind the navigator's station. This travel trailer idea did not come to pass and the dual Marauder cockpits were hidden in his backyard in Pacific Palisades for nearly forty years. David Tallichet bought both cockpits in the early 1980s and they were later incorporated into two Marauder restorations. B-26B-MA 41-31856 is the nose section used by the Pima Air & Space Museum, Tucson, Arizona, for its restoration. This also incorporates the wings from Million Dollar Valley B-26 40-1501. The second Pacific Palisades Marauder nose section, B-26C 41-35075, is owned by Kermit Weeks and is held in storage by Aero Traders of Chino, California.

The Hill Aerospace Museum, Hill AFB, Utah, acquired a B-26 nose section that Tallichet recovered from one of the movie studios. The nose section will be incorporated into the museum's restoration of B-26 40-1370, which crashed at King Salmon, Alaska, on August

David Tallichet sold 40-1464 to warbird collector and Fantasy of Flight operator Kermit Weeks in the mid-1990s. Weeks asked Carl Scholl and Tony Ritzman of Aero Trader at Chino to go through the airplane prior to its cross-country flight to Fantasy of Flight near Orlando, Florida. When the aircraft was ready, Scholl and Ritzman flew the aircraft for ten hours testing the new hydraulic and brake systems. *Michael O'Leary*

16, 1942, while assigned to the 11th Air Force, 73rd Bomb Squadron. Currently the parts have been gathered, but restoration is yet to begin.

There are two other substantial Marauder components. The nose of B-26 40-1453 was recovered from Watson Lake in July 2009, by John Jasman and his family. This aircraft originally landed short at Waton Lake on January 16, 1942. The aircraft was damaged beyond economical repair and the plane scrapped. The U.S. Army Air Forces retained the cockpit section for use as a trainer. After the end of the war, it was dumped in the lake where it sat for more than sixty years.

In the United Kingdom, the tail section of B-26C-25-MO 41-35253 has gone on show at the Boxted Airfield Museum in Colchester, Essex. This aft fuselage section was found in a scrapyard in the 1970s and has been variously displayed at museums or in storage with a private collector until recently. This Marauder served with the 45th Bomb Group's 323rd Bomb Squadron.

The third Million Dollar Valley Marauder, 40-1459, is being grafted to the nose section of 40-1501 at the Military Aviation Preservation Society Air Museum at the Akron-Canton, Ohio, airport. Restoration of this aircraft is moving rapidly, and in 2011 and 2012, the wings were attached, the vertical fin and rudder have been installed, and it is moving toward standing on its landing gear for the first time since 1942.

Two former French Air Force Marauders survive today. B-26G-10-MA 43-34581 was donated in 1965 to the National Museum of the United States Air Force in Dayton, Ohio, by Air France, who had been using the bomber as a ground instructional airframe. The second former Air France Marauder, B-26G-25-MA 44-68219, belongs to the French national collection (Musée de l'Air, Le Bourget, France), who have painted the aircraft in D-Day markings and are displaying the bomber at the Utah Beach D-Day Museum in the Normandy town of Sainte-Marie-du-Mont. The B-26G is pained to represent a B model flown by the 9th Air Force's 386th Bomb Group

The World War II combat veteran *Flak Bait* has been on display at the Smithsonian Institute's National Air and Space Museum on the Capital Mall in Washington, D.C., since its opening in 1976. This Marauder is a B-26B-25-MA 41-31173, which flew 207 missions with the 332nd Bomb Group's 449th Bomb Squadron and was flown by Lt. James J. Farrell of Greenwich, Connecticut, more than any other pilot. There was talk that this Marauder would be reassembled and displayed at the museum's Steven F. Udvar-Hazy Center in Chantilly, Virginia.

At the beginning of 2013, there are four complete Marauders, three in the United States and one in France, and two more under restoration to static display standards using components that were recovered from an eccentric travel trailer maker and airframes brought back from the frozen north.

Alaskan Liberators
One in Place, One Recovered

Although sixteen Consolidated B-24 Liberators survive today along with the substantial remains of another eight, one aircraft has been virtually forgotten. This Liberator currently rests on a remote island in the Aleutian chain, part of the state of Alaska. Its career against the Japanese was brief, but its significance is extremely important to military aviation history.

During the opening days of World War II, the 21st Bomb Squadron flew anti-submarine patrols off the west coast of the United States. On January 9, 1942, the 21st Bomb Squadron was loaned to the

B-24D-CO 40-2367, the nineteenth B-24D built at Consolidated San Diego, crashed in bad weather on Atka Island in the Aleutian Islands on December 9, 1942. The crew was rescued the following morning. *Ted Spencer*

Known as the Atka B-24, this combat veteran Liberator remains where it crashed more than seventy years after its final flight. The aircraft is on the National Register of Historic Places and will likely stay in the Aleutians. Notice the nose art remains to this day in spite of the harsh winters on the island. *Ted Spencer*

11th Air Force's 28th Composite Group, serving as part of the region's offensive strike capability. In March, a new B-24D-CO, serial number 40-2367, the nineteenth B-24D built at Consolidated San Diego, arrived to begin operations with the 28th Composite Group. This aircraft was equipped with ASV surface-search radar, identifiable by the antenna hanging under the port wing. Being a very early "D" model, the nose compartment had two distinguishing features—it lacked an astrodome and had a small observation window in the port side.

On June 11, 1942, aircraft of the 21st Bomb Squadron were deployed to Umnak, Alaska, to counter the Japanese landings on Kiska and Attu in the Aleutian Islands. Liberators, including 40-2367, began flying bombing missions against Dutch Harbor, Kiska, and Attu. The Japanese abandoned Dutch Harbor near the end of June, but were entrenched at Kiska until they evacuated in August 1943. Shortly after the Japanese pulled out of the region, 40-2367 was assigned to weather reconnaissance duties.

On December 9, 40-2367 departed for a weather reconnaissance mission over Kiska, Attu, and Agattu Islands with Capt. John Andrews, pilot, at the controls. The *11th Air Force History 1941–1945* describes the December 9 flight in detail:

> "After the death of Colonel Everett S. Davis (in 1942), Col. John V. Hart was named chief of staff of the Eleventh Air Force and remained in this capacity until the conclusion

When the B-24D bellylanded on the tundra, the aft fuselage tore off as the bomber crossed a small creek. Brig. Gen. William E. Lynd, who was an observer on the flight, suffered a broken collarbone in the crash. Aside from bumps and bruises, he was the most injured. *Ted Spencer*

of the Attu-Kiska campaign. Col. Hart's beginning as chief of staff was marred by one slight mishap, which, without exceptional skill on the part of one of the Eleventh Air Force's bomber pilots might have ended in tragedy.

"On December 9, 1942, Col. Hart and Brig. Gen. William E. Lynd of General Buckner's staff, took off from Adak in a B-24 piloted by Captain John Andrews. The two officers wished to accompany the weather plane to make personal observations around Kiska and Attu. The plane reached Attu, circled over Holtz Bay, and then returned to Adak. Arriving back at Adak at 1600, the pilot found his base socked in by weather. He notified the tower that he planned to fly to the far end of Atka Island and attempt a crash landing.

"Atka, too, was closed in, and the plane crash-landed about halfway to the eastern end of Atka.

"There was only one casualty. General Lynd sustained a fractured collar bone, and the flight crew and Col. Hart spent an uncomfortable night on the beach while the personnel of Eleventh Air Force Headquarters spent the night wondering what had happened to them. The next day they were sighted by a Navy PBY which landed and put a rubber boat ashore.

Consolidated LB-30, Royal Air Force serial AL557, was delivered on October 13, 1941. This aircraft operated in India and the Mediterranean before returning to England in April 1945, where it was converted to carry passengers and cargo. It was later acquired by the Morrison-Knudson Co. Note the external ladder behind the cockpit and ahead of the leading edge of the wing to enable the crew to enter the cockpit when the cabin is full of oversized cargo. *Dave Menard via Brian Baker*

The men had adequate food and were able to gather enough driftwood to build a fire — a difficult problem in the treeless Aleutians. The castaways were picked-up on December 11 by the Navy seaplane tender USS *Gillis*, chilly and tired, but otherwise unharmed."

After the war, the aircraft's remote crash site and changing world events saw its location fade from memory.

Survivor In-Situ

The site, virtually untouched since the December 1942 crash, was visited once in 1975, by a navy helicopter crew who removed the machine guns and occasionally by native fishermen. The early to mid-1970s saw the warbird restoration movement picking up steam, and a number of "snatch-and-grab" aircraft recoveries had taken place in Alaska. In an attempt to keep 40-2367 from being illegally recovered, Ted Spencer, at the time a director for the Alaska Aviation Heritage Museum in Anchorage, campaigned hard to preserve this aircraft in-place.

Although its tail was torn off in the bellylanding and the forward fuselage is slowly sinking into the tundra, 40-2367 is in excellent shape. The separated rear fuselage retains the tail turret and the horizontal

Morrison-Knudson registered the Liberator as N92MK and flew it for almost eight years in the 1950s. In 1958, N92MK landed short at Kalikat Creek, Alaska, and the abandoned bomber was pushed off to the side of the airport. Here she sat for more than thirty years. *Milo Peltzer*

stabilizer, with the verticals lying nearby. One set of the four propellers is bent and a number of cowling panels are missing, but the wings are in great condition with the gear still tucked underneath. The ASV radar antenna remains under the port wing to this day. The forward fuselage is buckled slightly and the lower portion of the bombardier's greenhouse was destroyed in the landing; otherwise the fuselage is in a restorable state.

Spencer's efforts led to 40-2367 being designated as site ATK-036 on the Alaska Heritage Resource Survey, and its subsequent listing on the National Register of Historic Places on July 26, 1979. On August 12, 1983, more than forty years after the end of the Aleutian campaign, Ted Spencer accompanied 40-2367's pilot John Andrews and, a few days later copilot Louis Blau, to the wreck site. The Alaskan Historical Aviation Society produced a video titled *The Forgotten Front—Veterans Remember*, in which pilot Andrews described the crash: "The weather, of course, pretty rapidly became all bad. There were five separate fronts over the Aleutians at that particular time. Time was then running out because we only had fifteen to twenty minutes of daylight left, and maybe half an hour or so of fuel. So it was time to make a decision. The question was: Land on the water, land on the beach, or land going up the mountainside?

"The hills were all surrounded by fog and bad weather. This [the crash site] was the only land we could see. We came in off the ocean, into the bay, crossed the ridge of shingle on the edge of the beach, and dropped down in here [on the tundra].

"There was one hell of a racket as the airplane bounced along the tundra, and then came to a stop. Then there was a great deal of silence. It was broken by someone saying, 'Let's get the hell outta here before it burns!' Then we all piled out of the pilot's and co-pilot's windows."

Located on the west end of Atka Island at Bechevin Bay, the plane rests two hundred yards from the beach with its fuselage perpendicular to the shoreline and the nose of the aircraft headed into the box canyon at the land side of the bay. The fuselage is crumpled behind the pilot's seats from the weight of the upper Martin turret. The rear half of the fuselage separated aft of the wing's trailing edge and rests across a small creek inverted. (Note that 40-2367 has often been mistaken for the Liberator that crashed intact and is seen in a photograph on Page 121 of Steve Birdsall's *Log of the Liberators*.)

The crash site is now on property under the jurisdiction of the Aleutian Islands National Wildlife Refuge. Access to the site is restricted and often impossible due to weather and surf conditions. The U.S. Department of Interior's Fish and Wildlife Service, who in turn supervises the Aleutian Islands National Wildlife Refuge, intends to preserve and maintain the aircraft in place.

Since the *Lady Be Good* (B-24D-CO 41-24301) was recently removed from its resting place in the Libyan desert, 40-2367 is the only nearly intact, combat veteran B-24 preserved at its war-time crash site.

Combat Veteran Ready for Restoration

Another B-24 type lost and found in Alaska is an LB-30B Liberator. The LB-30s were ordered by the British before the United States entered the war. They were, essentially, short-nosed B-24As that were delivered in an armed configuration—with a greenhouse nose, flexible tail guns fitted into a window at the very back of the aircraft in lieu of the turrets seen on later models, and a Boulton-Paul mid-upper

In 1990, the Alaska Aviation Heritage Museum dismantled the Liberator and had another aviation antique transport it the hulk from Kalikat Creek to Anchorage. LB-30 N92MK took its last flight in the cargo hold of Cargomaster Corporation's C-133A N199AB. *George Radovich via Cal Taylor*

turret mounted on top of the fuselage in line with the trailing edge of the wing—and an unarmed version used for multi-engine training and as a long-range transport.

The fifty-fifth Liberator built was an LB-30B that was delivered to the Royal Air Force (RAF) with serial number AL557 on October 13, 1941. The bomber was accepted at Dorval, outside of Montreal, Quebec, Canada. After acceptance flights, this LB-30 was flown from Dorval to Gander, Newfoundland, then on to Prestwick, Scotland. At Prestwick, the bomber was turned over to Scottish Aviation Limited on November 23, 1941, where it was modified for duty with RAF Coastal Command. From there the Liberator went to No. 120 Squadron at Nutts Corner, Northern Ireland, where it may have seen combat against enemy shipping as part of Coastal Command. The plane was returned to No. 22 Maintenance Unit at Silloth, England, and back to No. 120 Squadron in July and August 1942, before being transferred to 1445 Flight at RAF Lyneham in Wiltshire, England. Here the bomber was prepared for operations in India.

After making the transit, AL557 arrived at Salbani, India (west of Calcutta), on July 10, 1943, where it was assigned to No. 159 Squadron, Air Command South East Asia. Here the Liberator served

Surviving B-24 Liberators

The Flyers

LB-30	AM927	Confederate Air Force, Midland, Texas	*Diamond Lil*
B-24J-85-CF	44-44052	Collings Foundation, Stowe, Massachusetts	*Witchcraft*
B-24J-95-CF	44-44272	Kermit Weeks, Polk City, Florida	*Joe*

Static Display

B-24D-CO	40-2367	Aleutian Islands National Wildlife Refuge, Atka, Alaska	
B-24D-10-CO	41-23908	Hill AFB, Ogden, Utah (Restoration using substantial parts of wrecked 41-23908 and the fuselage of PB4Y-2 59932.)	
B-24D-CO	41-24301	Tripoli, Libya	*Lady Be Good*
B-24D-160-CO	42-72843	Air Force Museum, Wright-Patterson AFB, Ohio	*Strawberry Bitch*
B-24M-5-CO	44-41916	Castle Air Museum, Atwater, California	*Shady Lady*
B-24M-10-CO	44-41956	The B-24 Liberator Memorial Fund, Melbourne, Australia	
B-24J-95-CF	44-44175	Pima Air Museum, Tucson, Arizona	*Shoot You're Covered*
B-24J-90-CF	44-44213	Indian Air Force Museum, Palem, New Dehli	
B-24J-20-FO	44-48781	8th Air Force Museum, Barksdale, Louisiana	*Laiden Maiden*
B-24L-20-FO	44-50154	Canadian National Aeronautical Collection, Ottawa, Canada	
B-24L-20-FO	44-50206	Imperial War Museum, Duxford, England	
B-24M-21-FO	44-51228	American Air Museum, Duxford, England	*Dugan*

Substantial Sections/Restorations

LB-30B	AL557	World Jet Inc., Fort Lauderdale, Florida	
RB-24A	40-2369	Yankee Air Force Museum (bombardier's compartment)	
B-24D-25-CO	41-23311	Rahni M Koc Museum, Istanbul, Turkey (nose section displayed)	*Hadley's Harem*
B-24D-70-CO	42-40461	Virginia Air & Space Museum (nose section), ex-RCAF 599	*Grumpy*
B-24D-60-CO	42-40526	North Atlantic Aviation Museum/Avalon Historical Aircraft Recovery Association, Gander, Newfoundland, RCAF 586 (nose section)	
B-24D-70-CO	42-40557	Fantasy of Flight, Polk City, Florida (nose section), ex-RCAF 600	*Hail Columbia*
B-24J-5-FO	42-51457	Mighty Eighth Air Force Museum, Pooler, Georgia	*Fightin' Sam*
B-24L-1-FO	44-49112	Michigan History Museum, Lansing, Michigan (nose section)	
B-24L-20-FO	44-50022	Pony Maples, Memphis, Tennessee (nose section)	

as a long-range transport for nearly a year. On May 23, 1944, AL557 departed India for the Mediterranean Allied Forces. In April 1945, AL557 was flown from the Mediterranean to Scottish Aviation for conversion to a passenger carrier.

When the company had completed the conversion, AL557 took on the civil identity of G-AGZI, and in 1946 Scottish Aviation retained the Liberator for charter flights to Iceland. Converted B-24 Liberators, and in 1947 C-47s, replaced Consolidated PBY Catalinas on the route from Prestwick, Scotland, to Reykjavik, Iceland. The ex-military aircraft flew the route for the next two years until a DC-4 was acquired.

In February 1948, G-AGZI was sold to the Greek carrier Hellenic Airlines. Once back in the Mediterranean, the aircraft was reregistered

SX-DAA and christened *Maid of Athens*. SX-DAA transported passengers and light cargo around Greece in the intervening years. On January 3, 1951, *Maid of Athens* tangled with a fuel truck at Athens's Hassani Airport. Quickly repaired, the bomber-turned-airliner re-entered service, and following a four-year career flying passengers in Greece, AL557 was sold to Morrison-Knudsen, Inc., in November 1951, and reregistered N9981F. After acquiring the Liberator, Morrison-Knudson upgraded the engines; replaced the existing birdhouse canopy with a newer, high-visibility windscreen; overhauled the instruments; installed new radios; and added a modern aircraft galley. N9981F had great short-field performance, perfect for landing in the tight, recently cleared airstrips above the Arctic Circle. Most of the runways that N9981F operated from were 2,500-feet long. No more.

Morrison-Knudsen Co. was a large infrastructure construction company headquartered in Boise, Idaho. The company built the San Francisco–Oakland Bay Bridge, the Hoover Dam on the Nevada/Arizona border, and numerous airfields during World War II. It used the LB-30 during the construction of the Distant Early Warning (DEW) Line in the 1950s. The DEW line is a chain of radar stations that stretched from the Aleutian Islands in Alaska across the Arctic to Iceland to warn of approaching Soviet bombers should they attempt to attack North America by flying over the North Pole.

The majority of the DEW line stations were only accessible by air, and everything from nails and screws to radar antennas, building siding, and food had to be flown in. LB-30 AL557 was part of this fleet of flying transports, and its cabin floor, low to the ground, did not require a lot of ground handling equipment for loading and unloading cargo. In December 1951, Morrison-Knudsen changed the former bomber's registration to N68735.

Flying in the Arctic is fraught with danger, and the pilots of AL557 certainly encountered their share. On June 1, 1953, N68735 landed on the ice-covered runway at Wales, Alaska, on the westernmost point of the United States at Cape Prince of Wales on the Seward Peninsula. Wales is approximately a hundred miles northwest of Nome. After touching down, N68735 was unable to stop and slid off the end of the runway into a drainage ditch. After flying in replacement parts, N68735 was flown out and repaired. Before returning to fly again, the Liberator's registration was changed to N92MK.

In 1958, after more than five years of safe operations in support of the DEW line construction efforts, N92MK was approaching the small

Combat veteran LB-30 AL557 was later sold to World Jet Inc., of Fort Lauderdale, Florida, and has been in outside storage at Fort Collins, Colorado, since 1991.

airport at Kalikat Creek, about thirty miles south of Galena, Alaska, when the aircraft landed short. Here it sat for more than thirty years, covered over annually by snow, and then exposed in spring. In July 1990, the Alaska Aviation Heritage Museum in Anchorage recovered the ex–World War II bomber and put it up for sale. In 1996, the fairly intact bomber project was bought by the Lone Star Flight Museum of Galveston, Texas. The museum already owned a Consolidated PB4Y-2 Privateer project (Bureau of Aeronautics serial number 59819), and the Liberator would have made a perfect companion on the airshow circuit. Lone Star had the aircraft transported to Vintage Aircraft Ltd. at Fort Collins, Colorado, where it has remained in outside storage. In 2001, Lone Star sold the bomber to Don Whittington's World Jet in Fort Lauderdale, Florida.

Whittington and World Jet have been buying and selling warbirds since the mid-1960s and were responsible for recovering Boeing B-17E 41-9210 from Bolivia in the late 1990s. World Jet restored the Flying Fortress to airworthy condition and then sold the plane to the Flying Heritage Collection in Everett, Washington. Many had hoped that N92MK would be far on its way to flying today, but a buyer with extremely deep pockets has not come along at this point. It's in the lower forty-eight states, it has combat history, and it is ready for restoration.

Part Four

Lucky Finds
Rare Warbirds in Unusual Places

Some people don't believe in luck, while others think that luck is what you make of it. Those who believe they can influence their luck know that this superpower is made up of five components: Many believe it's all in who you know. Then there's being in the right place at the right time, being willing to take a chance, and being ready, and knowing when, to act.

And then there's the ability to read people, especially the story-tellers. One needs to be able to separate fact from fiction and do so quickly. The inability to separate fact from fiction can, at the very least, be a big waste of time, and on the other end can endanger one's wallet or at the extreme one's life and limb.

Once a hidden warbird story is told, it certainly bears repeating. The question is, how far from the original source are you? Stories have a way of changing with each retelling. One has to wonder if the P-38 in the barn story is not actually two BT-13s sitting side-by-side?

That P-38 in the barn story many heard was actually true, except it was *two* P-38s, not one! P-38L 44-26969 and 44-27083 had been operated by Mark Hurd Aerial Surveys in Santa Barbara, California. The company put all four of its P-38s up for sale in 1967, and electrical engineer Bruce Pruitt bought two of them. He dismantled the twin engine fighters and hauled them to his parents' barn outside of Sacramento, California, for storage. Rumors of the P-38 in a barn gained traction as the warbird movement picked up momentum in the mid-1980s.

After the fiftieth anniversary of the P-38s first flight in 1989, there was a huge push to track down these airplanes. It was Pruitt's intention to rebuild them as a retirement project and he had spent the better

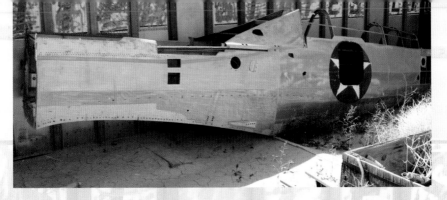

Imagine walking around a yard full of sea containers and discovering a Curtiss P-40N fuselage. A major assembly like this would form the basis of an excellent rebuild project. Others have started with much less and have assembled flying aircraft. A restored, flying P-40 is a $2 million aircraft.

part of twenty years gathering as many P-38 spare parts as possible. Warbird hunters hounded him until he was made an offer he couldn't refuse—both aircraft would be rebuilt to flying condition, and the restorers would keep one in exchange for their work and investment in making the planes fly. Unfortunately, Pruitt's P-38 was destroyed in a crash on June 6, 1997, near Tillamook, Oregon. Although he was devastated after the loss of the P-38 that had been such a big part of his life, Pruitt acquired a Bell P-63 project to occupy his interest in World War II aircraft restoration.

For every story that's told, some people, probably not intentionally, spread misinformation. For example, there is a B-17F near Leech Lake in Northern California that yielded a number of rare parts used to restore other Flying Fortresses. Even the guns were located, but they were buried on the site. Many people told stories of how "hippies" had gone into the site in the 1960s and scrapped out the bomber for its metal content. Yes, people did go into the foothills and mountains to recover metal from crash sites, but after having hiked to the Leech Lake B-17F, there's no way anyone made that trek and certainly not to haul in all of the equipment needed to reduce a bomber to molten metal. Thus not every story about a crashed or abandoned warbird is factual.

There's always been the story of the biplane or the Cub in a barn, but a hidden warbird like a P-51D Mustang in a guy's garage? Not likely . . . Or the story of a B-17 four-engine bomber in a forest? Possible, but highly unlikely as well. How about an ex–U.S. Navy patrol bomber, a type that saw combat in World War II, sitting on a grass strip sunk up to its axels in mud? All you have to do is fly it out before the land used as a runway becomes houses. Sounds like tall tales, each and every one of them.

Mustang in a Garage
P-51D (F-6D) *Lil' Margaret*

"Mustang Mike" Coutches of American Aircraft Sales in Hayward, California, was on the hunt for P-51H parts in the late 1950s and early 1960s. Coutches was selling licensed, ready-to-fly P-51Ds for $3,995 at the time, but his interest was in the P-51H. The 194th Fighter Squadron of the California Air National Guard operated P-51Ds and -51Hs from the Hayward Airport, and it was a sad day when the unit moved to Fresno, California, and transitioned to the F-86A. About a hundred miles northeast of Hayward, the U.S. Air Force depot at McClellan Air Force Base, near Sacramento, California, had seen hundreds of Mustangs pass through its overhaul lines and dozens were sold surplus from here as well. In addition, thousands of pounds of Mustang parts were auctioned off as they were no longer needed in an all-jet air force.

In the late 1940s, someone had purchased a Mustang at a surplus sale (possibly at McClellan), and then attempted to sell it to Israel or one of the Latin American countries looking for aircraft in the late

Here it is, every warbird enthusiast's dream: a P-51 Mustang in a garage. Butch Schroeder had heard stories of the garage Mustang, but never could confirm its existence. Finally tracking down the story, he found this photo reconnaissance version of the P-51D in Missouri. Schroeder approached the owner, who had worked on the Mustang for years. It was the right time and a deal was struck. *Butch Schroeder*

Parts, spare parts, and the engine came out of the garage as well. The F-6D photo reconnaissance Mustang had never been civilianized, which made it an easy decision to restore the plane to as close to original as possible. *Butch Schroeder*

1940s or early 1950s. The plane was reportedly disassembled, crated, sitting on the dock, about to be loaded on a ship, when U.S. Customs stepped in and seized the Mustang. The aircraft did not leave the country and was later sold at auction and then purchased by a scrap dealer.

Coutches was going into one particular Sacrameto-area salvage yard that was rich in H model Mustang parts—parts that only Mustang Mike needed and wanted. Every time he would go in, the scrap dealer would bug him to buy a disassembled D model Mustang sitting in a corner of the yard, but they could never reach an agreement as Mustang Mike didn't want a disassembled P-51D when he could buy flying aircraft for not much more of a premium.

Coutches returned once again, and the scrapman finally told him if he wanted any more H model parts, he was going to have to buy the disassembled P-51D Mustang. The aircraft was ready for transport, so Mustang Mike hauled it home and put it in his backyard. The story has it that the Coutches's kids played on it for years.

In 1961, William "Bill" Myers of St. Charles, Missouri, bought the disassembled P-51D from Coutches. Hauled east, the fighter plane project took over Myers's house, basement, and garage. And slowly word got around the neighborhood that there was a plane in a garage. The rumor gained legs as people would see it when the door was up, and by the mid-1970s as the warbird movement picked up steam, the rumor had grown and was beginning to spread to pilots in neighboring states.

Mustang owner and restorer John Dilley from the Fort Wayne Air Service, Fort Wayne, Indiana, and Butch Schroeder of Danville,

It was decided not to separate the wing halves, which were transported in one piece. Notice the six 0.50-cal. gun ports in the leading edge of the wing. *Butch Schroeder*

Illinois—who at the time owned former El Salvadorean Air Force Cavalier conversion P-51D FAS 409, ex 45-11559, *North American Maid*—had heard the rumor, too. "I kind of beat Dilley to it," said Schroeder. "I had the opportunity to go to St. Louis on business and I was always looking in the phone book trying to find who I thought was the owner at the time, but I always ended up empty handed.

"A short time later, a friend of mine who owned a Hawker Sea Fury asked me to take *North American Maid* to an airshow in St. Charles, Missouri. I asked if the airshow was going to pay for fuel and said I wasn't interested in going without it. After turning him down, we got to talking about this mystery Mustang, which was thought to be in the same area. My friend said the hosts of the airshow knew where the Mustang was, and I'm thinking 'Yeah, right.' I told my friend that if the show hosts would take me to see the plane, then I'd fly down.

"I went to the airshow and one evening they took me to see the Mustang, and on the way over they said they were not interested in buying it. So I tried and made a deal to buy the plane." Butch Schroeder had found the elusive P-51D Mustang in a garage, and bought it!

Restoring an F-6D Mustang
Upon closer inspection, Schroeder determined that the Mustang was a rare photoreconnaissance version of the P-51D known as an F-6D, and later an RF-51D, serial number 44-84786. "When we researched the history of the airplane, we knew exactly what we were looking at. It still had the original data plate showing it was designated an F-6D. It was kind of ironic; most of your airplanes have a metal data tag with the information stamped in it. This was all done on phenolic and it was handwritten using something like a paintbrush," Schroeder said.

The F-6D was built at North American Aviation's Dallas, Texas, factory and delivered on June 8, 1945, after the war in Europe had ended, but still three months before the Japanese surrendered. The photoreconn fighter was assigned to U.S. Army Air Force bases at Andrews, Washington, D.C.; Stuttgart, Arkansas; Brooks Field, Texas; Topeka, Kansas; Hobbs Field, New Mexico; Spokane, Washington; Kelly Field, Texas; Pope Field, North Carolina; and finally to McClellan Air Force Base, part of the Air Material Command, for storage in June 1949. The F-6D was stricken from the air force's inventory on November 25, 1949.

As the now proud-owner of a Mustang project, Schroeder had to get the fighter from the St. Louis area home to Danville, Illinois, a distance of 215 miles. First he had to call his friends with pickup trucks, then find enough additional friends to help load the project. "Bill Myers's wife was real glad to see the Mustang go because, in essence, I had to clean their garage to get the plane out," Schroeder said. "I think it took us six pickup trucks and five trailers and we went down early one morning, loaded up, and we and had it back home that afternoon." Myers had about 95 percent of the airplane, and what he didn't have Schroeder would use his extensive contacts in the warbird community to locate.

Once home, the P-51D was stored in Schroeder's hangar while he worked with Mike VadeBonCoeur to return his AT-6 to full, stock military configuration. "I had become friends with Mike when he was still in high school," Schroeder said. "He came and started

New owner Butch Schroeder takes a seat in the Mustang's cockpit after loading it on a trailer for the trip to Illinois. *Butch Schroeder*

just helping me and I would pay him flying time in exchange so he could work on getting his pilot's license. So in essence, to start out with, he worked for me, and then years later, he went off on his own and started Midwest Aero." VadeBonCoeur had worked with Schroeder on his warbirds before leaving to attend Spartan School of Aeronautics in Tulsa, Oklahoma. When he returned, VadeBonCoeur and Schroeder finished the restoration of U.S. Air Force T-6G serial number 49-3144 in 1990. The aircraft was awarded the Experimental Aircraft Association's Warbird Reserve Grand Champion Award, and VadeBonCoeur was recognized with the Golden Wrench Award for his work. Today, VadeBonCoeur's Midwest Aero has been recognized for its highly detailed, award-winning P-51D Mustang restorations, such as *Cripes A' Mighty*, *Daddy's Girl*, *Happy Jack's Go Buggy*, *Live Bait*, and *Red Dog*.

"I was doing most of that early work on the T-6 and the Mustang part time, as I had a really nice job at the University of Illinois," said VadeBonCoeur. "I left the University of Illinois to come work for Butch full time on the T-6. I kind of always had it in the back of my mind that if I was going to leave a good, solid university position that my hope and goal was to be able to eventually start my own business."

Once the T-6G was out of the hangar, Schroeder and VadeBonCoeur began the restoration of the photoreconnaissance Mustang full time. The project would take three more years of hard work. "This airplane had never been a surveying airplane or a warbird. When we got it, it still had the markings on the wings and was pretty much the way it had come out of the factory. So early on, it was decided that the goal was to make it look just like the day that it rolled out of the factory and keep it stock—single seat, guns, cameras, the whole deal," Schroeder said. "For some reason, guns had never been put in that airplane even though a lot of the equipment was in there. We had to go out and I made about three different trips to California scrounging around. Back then, the rare, original fittings were pretty easy to find because nobody wanted them. Now, everybody wants those detail parts, so they're much harder to find. There's an armor plate that sits right behind the propeller to protect the fuel tank that's back there. I found it in California at a Mustang shop and they were using it just to prop the door open. The armor plating that goes behind the seat . . . somebody was using it as a barbecue grill.

"I had a list of everything that I was looking for, and I left copies with people, and again, at the time, this was stuff that nobody

A fifth-wheel trailer was used to transport the wings, which span more than thirty-five feet with the tips removed. The restoration of *Lil' Margaret* took more than twelve years to complete. *Butch Schroeder*

wanted. I can't remember if it was *Strega* or *Stiletto*, but one of the racing Mustangs had been an F-6D and some original, cool stuff came out of one of them. Later I was out in Fort Collins, Colorado, and I went and talked to Darrel Skurich [known for rebuilding the XP-51 on display at the Experimental Aircraft Association Museum]. He had the camera mount I needed for my aircraft. Dennis Schoenfelder had the camera ports, but they needed some repair work, which was done by John Neel of Low Pass Inc. in Griffin, Georgia. I also had the good fortune to become friends with Brian O'Farrell. He's the guy that bought all the Dominican Mustangs and their spares, and he had a warehouse full of brand-new parts. I had the chance to pick through O'Farrell's inventory of new parts for my airplane."

Mike VadeBonCoeur said, "We did everything except the engine, propeller, the radiator, and instruments. I probably built most of the systems. I did all of the hydraulic systems, all the electrical wiring, most of all of the installation of the interior components, and basically all of the assembly work. Butch had already restored certain components and had those sitting aside and ready to go in."

Try as he might, Schroeder could never locate any factory blueprints for the F-6D conversion. None of the P-51D Mustang microfilm showed any of the photoreconnaissance modifications, and many parts had to be made from photos, or from original parts that were duplicated. Schroeder's Cavalier Mustang was used as a template for the interior installations, but when it came to the F-6 modifications, the restoration crew was on its own. "There are no diagrams for cable

If you're going to recover an aircraft project, its good to have friends with trucks and trailers. The Mustang kit must have been a sight to see going down the freeway. It took five truckloads to get the F-6D home. *Butch Schroeder*

links, for instance, for the trim cables or the elevator cables, and are all modified in the rear fuselage to avoid the cameras. It's different than a standard P-51D in the oxygen bay area as well, so we kind of had to experiment trying to come up with proper cable links," said VadeBonCoeur. "I remember that being a challenge for me at the time, but we ended up making it all happen. I think we had samples of elevator cables, but we didn't have samples of any of the trim cables. Those had disappeared from the fuselage years ago, so I didn't really have anything to go off of. We kind of had to back-blueprint it and sort it all out. We just followed the original routing, which in an F-6D the elevator and trim cables are all routed differently than they are in a stock D. There's just not data available that we've been able to come up with that I've ever seen. The manuals show illustrations of how the cables were routed, but no specifics for cable links and things like that."

Mating the wing to the fuselage was a first for VadeBonCoeur. "We had called a crane out to do the heavy lifting, and we looked at the weather radar before we got started. Of course, back in 1990, the weather radar wasn't as good and no one had a smartphone to give one last peek to see how conditions had changed. We decided to go ahead and do it, and as soon as we got the airplane up, got the wing put in position, and were ready to lift the fuselage up, a thunderstorm hit," VadeBonCoeur said. "We ended up putting that thing together in a pouring rainstorm, and of course, once we were done and the crane was ready to leave, it was beautiful. Fuselage to wing was in the middle of a rainstorm, the engine we did the same day and it went just fine."

Inside the F-6D, the oxygen bottle arrangement is different from the standard P-51D. The -51D has two long and two short bottles in the aft fuselage while the F-6D uses large, bomber-size oxygen bottles. In addition, the ribs on the left side of the fuselage were changed to accommodate the camera installations. To access the cameras, an access panel was fitted to the starboard side of the fuselage, forward of the fuselage/tail production break.

"In comparison to what we do today, there's really no comparison. A lot of it is just learning over the years. I think that we knew that the interior color that it is today wasn't what it was, but Butch had already started that and it wasn't in his best interest, or desire at that point, to go backwards and change it all," said VadeBonCoeur. "We left it with interior Imron green that he had picked."

Putting Her Back in the Air

When the restoration was nearly complete, Schroeder settled on a suitable paint scheme for the F-6D. He chose to replicate the markings of *Lil' Margaret* flown by Capt. Clyde B. East, who, at age nineteen, joined the Royal Canadian Air Force and entered the European war flying P-51As against targets along the enemy coast. He transferred to the U.S. Army Air Forces and was assigned to the Ninth Air Force's 15th Tactical Reconnaissance Squadron flying Supermarine Spitfires. The squadron transitioned into the P-51B, and then into the F-6D.

East participated in the June 6, 1944, D-Day invasion, downing an Fw-190; the December 1944 Battle of the Bulge (one Bf-109); and in March and April 1945 downed another eleven enemy aircraft. By war's end, East had thirteen confirmed aerial victories. After the war, he remained in the service, and later flew reconnaissance Mustangs and RF-80s during the Korean War. East retired from the U.S. Air Force as a lieutenant colonel in February 1965.

Lil' Margaret's first postrestoration flight was done by John Dilley on June 18, 1993. "I was the second person to fly the airplane," Schroeder said. "I guess it had this kind of an eerie feeling like somebody's looking over your shoulder, which comes from the armor plating sitting right behind you, and trying to get used to looking through the gunsight. Originally the gunsight had kind of a gold-colored lens in it and you had to look around it as you couldn't look

Side profile of *Lil' Margaret* being marshaled into the Mustang corral in the warbird parking area at EAA AirVenture fly-in at Oshkosh, Wisconsin. The K-24 aerial camera was fitted into the lower facing port or a K-24, K-17, or K-22 could be installed in the upper, larger window. Access to the camera bay is from the starboard side of the aft fuselage.

through it. We ended up changing that and putting in regular glass and that took care of the vision problem.

"I had quite a bit of time in the Mustang, having owned *North American Maid* before flying *Lil' Margaret*. When flying the plane, the first thing I noticed was that *Lil' Margaret* was heavier than the Cavalier P-51D because we had installed guns and ammunition, armor plating, and all that detail equipment. It probably adds up to a couple of hundred pounds."

Schroeder has united East with the aircraft resplendent in his colors many times, and East and *Lil' Margaret* have always drawn a big crowd when the two have been featured at the EAA's Warbirds In Review at the annual airshow in Oshkosh. At EAA AirVenture 1993, Butch Schroeder's *Lil' Margaret* was recognized with the EAA Warbirds Grand Champion Award, and Mike VadeBonCoeur was given the Golden Wrench in recognition of his restoration work on the F-6D.

Reflecting on the restoration, VadeBonCoeur said, "I think the thing that most people probably appreciated about *Lil' Margaret* was all the original details that went into this restoration," said VadeBonCoeur. "I say original details meaning things like guns and the camera that was installed, and we put decals on. We made vinyl decals instead of what we do today, which uses water transfer materials like they did during the war, so in terms of authenticity it really is not anywhere close . . . I'd like to get another shot at it.

"At the time, *Lil' Margaret* was certainly heralded as a really authentic airplane; however, today it is not anywhere close to the standards we do, or even other people do in a Mustang restoration. For instance, we made one North American Aviation inspection stamp during the F-6D rebuild. Today I've got a box full of them so every time I find a new one, we try to replicate it and use it in the rebuild. That's one difference between what we do today and what we did back then, but at the time that level of detail had not been seen yet. When people did see *Lil' Margaret*, they thought that attention to detail was really a nice touch. On top of that, it was an F-6D, and nobody had seen one with the camera, fuselage gas tank, the armor plating, all the wing guns installed, bomb racks that worked, and basically a stock instrument panel. Most Mustangs at the time were restored with gray interiors and modern avionics everywhere, leather interiors, and that was the standard. I think *Lil' Margaret* was one of the first airplanes, if not *the* first, with so much original equipment. I think what we've done was really nice, but it was just something different—something people hadn't seen before."

In December 2012, Schroeder is doing *Lil' Margaret*'s annual inspection and the airplane has 158 hours on it. With pride, Schroeder said, "I've probably flown half of that."

For Butch Schroeder the tale of a Mustang in a garage is true and he's got flying proof!

John Lane is seen at the controls of *Lil' Margaret*. Pilot/owner Butch Schroeder chose to restore his F-6D in the markings of twelve-victory ace Capt. Clyde B. East, who flew with the Ninth Air Force's 15th Tactical Reconnaissance Squadron, 10th Photographic Reconnaissance Group. This restoration was recognized with the World War II Grand Champion award at EAA AirVenture 1993. *David Leininger*

Navy Harpoon
on a Grass Strip

Lockheed's PV-2 Harpoon has to be the most underappreciated of all the World War II U.S. Navy warbirds. The type entered service very late in the Pacific war with Patrol Bombing Squadron 139 (VPB-139) in the Aleutians. Harpoons flew long, over-water missions from their base at Attu to bomb and strafe Japanese targets more than 650 miles away in the Kuril Islands. The Kuril Island chain forms a boundary between the Sea of Okhotsk, which lies between Russia and Japan, and the Pacific Ocean. Lockheed's Harpoon also saw service in the South Pacific as well.

Shipping and radar sites in and around Paramushiro and Shimushu Islands were favorite targets of the PV-2s of VPB-139. Harpoons could lock their dorsal turrets to face forward, increasing their firepower by two additional .50-cal. machine guns, making them ideal straffers. As combat veteran aircraft seeing action late in the war, Harpoons rarely came face-to-face with Japanese fighters, but they did, however, take a beating from Japanese anti-aircraft fire.

Lockheed built 535 PV-2s, of which 35 were "D" models that featured eight .50-cal. guns in the nose, two in the aforementioned dorsal turret, and provisions for a twin .50-cal. gun pod under each wing. After the war ended, nearly all of the 35 PV-2D Harpoons constructed were parked at the navy's storage facility at Litchfield Park, Arizona, outside Phoenix. The "D" models were, typically, factory-fresh aircraft with just ferry time in their log books, most delivered to the navy too late to see service.

When offered for sale in the late-1950s, Harpoons were quickly snapped up for a variety of aerial applications, from fire bomber to bug sprayer to insect bait disperser. Harpoons used as fire bombers were typically modified by removing all of the military equipment and installing a retardant tank in the bomb bay, while the bug sprayers were fitted with a bait tank in the fuselage and dispersal booms on the trailing edges of the wings. The insect bait dispersers had loading holes cut in the top of the fuselage, hoppers made from sheet metal installed in the fuselage, and augers pushing the bait pellets out to chutes along the trailing edge of the wing.

PV-2D BuNo 84062 was the third from the last PV-2D built by Lockheed at its Burbank, California, factory. This gun nose Harpoon was accepted by the navy on September 21, 1945, and, after

PV-2D BuNo 84060 is seen at Litchfield Park in the late 1950s. BuNo 84060 is only two serial numbers from the Harpoon recovered by Taigh Ramey's Vintage Aircraft (BuNo 84062). To ensure the accuracy of the markings on Ramey's Harpoon, details from this photo were scaled up and applied to the fuselage during restoration. *Brian Baker*

Rare color photo of BuNo 84062, which was registered N6657D, prior to 1960 when the Harpoon had its borate tank installed. *Milo Peltzer via Rick Turner*

modifications, delivered three months later on December 11 to the aircraft acceptance group at NAS Terminal Island in the Los Angeles Harbor. BuNo 84062 was then transferred to the Naval Auxiliary Air Station Holtville, California, before reporting to its final station in February 1946 at the aircraft storage pool at NAS Litchfield Park. Here it was sealed and held in storage in the navy's reserve aircraft pool should there come a day when the service might need additional patrol aircraft. That day never came. The navy's fleet of more modern Grumman S-2 Trackers and P2V Neptunes was fulfilling the service's needs, and by 1956, the Harpoons were no longer needed. On December 17, 1956, BuNo 84062 was stricken from the navy's inventory, having accumulated only seven hours of total time flight time.

A nice PV-2 Harpoon could be bought at one of the Litchfield Park surplus sales for between $2,000 and $4,000—depending upon who was bidding. A gentleman named Ralph Johnson acquired a number of Harpoons to service the agricultural market, and he bought BuNo 84062 on August 12, 1959, for $3,678.89. Most of Johnson's aircraft were flown as bug sprayers, although four were modified with a 1,200-gallon tank to fight fires. BuNo 84062 was one such aircraft; its bomb bay doors were removed and the tank hung in their place. The tank was then given an aerodynamic fairing, and the plane painted overall white with red trim. Johnson soon sold the plane and it flew many seasons as Tanker 101 dropping fire retardant. When the U.S. government ceased twin-engine air tanker operations, BuNo 84062 was used to spray insecticide to combat a grasshopper infestation in Wyoming.

In 1988, a different Ralph Johnson purchased the aircraft with the intention of putting it back in warbird configuration. This Johnson and his son Stephen owned a number of warbirds, including the B-29 *Fertile Myrtle,* a dozen or so PV-2s, and in the late 1970s Stephen brought back a number of P-51s that were being surplused by the Indonesian Air Force. Six years after acquiring BuNo 84062, Johnson had the Harpoon flown to his ranch in Northern California.

Johnson's plans for BuNo 84062 never materialized, and the aircraft and some spare engines were later sold to Everts Air Cargo of Fairbanks, Alaska. The company wanted the Harpoon and its spares primarily for the R-2800 engines, which it needed for its fleet of Curtiss C-46 Commandos. The Commando can haul 12,000 pounds into and out of runways as short as 3,500 feet; thus the aircraft is extremely versatile in the wilds of Alaska. Everts Air Cargo immediately took possession of the spare engines and moved those items to Alaska, leaving the Harpoon on Johnson's property with the promise to come get it . . . soon.

Becoming a Lucky Find

And there it sat. Day in, day out. Month in, month out. Before anyone realized, sixteen years had passed. Finding a former navy patrol bomber sitting on a dirt strip nearly seventy years after the war is truly

Lockheed PV-2D BuNo 84062 flies eighty-two miles from its hidden location on a ranch in Northern California to Stockton Airport. One of the first tasks was to remove the belly tank and reinstall the bomb bay doors. *Roger Cain*

a lucky find. Many local pilots knew of the old, twin-engine, former air tanker because they had caught a glimpse of it from the air. It was, however, parked on the far end of Johnson's strip so it was not visible from the road. Its location protected it as no one got inside and the aircraft had not been vandalized during its enforced stay on the dirt strip. To illustrate how secure this aircraft had been, the navy eight-day clock was still in the instrument panel, and the clocks are the first things souvenir hunters grab.

When the Johnson family decided to sell the ranch in late 2009, Everts Air Cargo was told it had to move the plane or it would be scrapped on site. The distance between Everts Air Cargo's operation in Fairbanks and the plane's location north of California's Napa Valley made recovering the Harpoon an uneconomical prospect. However, well aware of the historic value of the former navy patrol bomber, Cliff Everts and Marty Hall began looking for a museum that could recover the Harpoon and give it a good home.

At the end of July 2010, the Stockton Field Aviation Museum, Stockton, California, was approached about accepting the aircraft as a donation on the condition that it would have it off the property by October 9, 2010. That same offer had been made to a couple of other aviation heritage groups, but none had the funding, expertise, or the infrastructure to get the plane flying in such a short amount of time.

Before and after restoration comparison of the BuNo 84062's cockpit. Gone are the nonstandard World War II gauges and radio stack and back is the stock military panel and instruments. *Roger Cain (as-found)*

The Stockton Field Aviation Museum's founder, Taigh Ramey, is also the proprietor of Vintage Aircraft, a maintenance and restoration shop specializing in the Beech 18/C-45 and warbirds. Vintage Aircraft holds the supplemental type certificate for the Aerospace wing spar strap kit and also performs kit installations, maintenance, and restoration, so there's always a corral of Twin Beeches on the company's ramp at Stockton Airport. To recover the Harpoon, the Stockton Field Aviation Museum would draw upon Vintage Aircraft's wealth of radial engine, sheet metal, and warbird experience that would be needed to recover the Harpoon from a remote location.

"I went to take a look at the Harpoon, and as ugly as she was, she still looked beautiful to me," said Taigh Ramey. "She had sunk into the ground so far that she was resting on her belly tank. Amazingly enough, the tires held air and we rolled her out of the rut she was sitting in. Several aviation folks looked at the Harpoon and they all said it was too far gone to save. They said that the corrosion was too great and that the control cables were all rusted. When I looked at Tanker 101, I saw a different aircraft all together. No corrosion at all and the rusted cables were actually covered in peralketone, which is the preservative that was used at the factory. The cables are about as good as they day they were manufactured. She had not been cut up and heavily modified like almost all of the other surviving Harpoons and she still retained many of the original small fittings, floor structure, and bulkheads. I remember thinking how she could easily be returned to her wartime configuration." After inspecting the patrol bomber/air tanker, Ramey, the museum, and the staff of Vintage Aircraft agreed to the challenge of flying the plane out. They had seven months and nine days to do it in.

"We flew up in the Twin Beech to work on the Harpoon, which was about eighty-four miles as the Beech flies each way," Ramey said. "The Twin Beech was great for this job as a sky truck hauling all of us and our tools, parts, fuel, and oil. We made about a dozen trips in the Beech and one in the van/trailer hauling the big wing jacks for the gear swing."

The crew's first order of business was to send a family of ground squirrels packing. Along with the furry-tailed nut-gatherers, their home and pantry had to be removed from the right wing. Opening all of the inspection panels, the Vintage Aircraft crew found that there was very little corrosion on the aircraft. This was credited to the navy and Lockheed's liberal use of anti-corrosion sealants and the aircraft's inland, dry location. Most of the exposed steel parts had "California rust" (surface rust, as opposed to the deep rust seen in the northeastern part of the country), but those parts could be easily cleaned or replaced.

The engines were next to receive attention. The oil screens were pulled and only small amounts of carbon were present. No metal in the screens was a very good sign. Ramey said the left fuel system was in decent shape. The boost pump came alive and pumped new fuel into the carburetor, which started soaking the diaphragms and seals. "Later that day, we were able to start the left engine," he said. "She didn't fight us much at all." The right side fuel pump was a different story. Water had gotten into the tank and rusted the pump. The second day, the right pump was replaced and the engine fired right up.

"Both engines ran okay, but the right didn't like going much above 1,600 rpm," Ramey said. "Both of the carburetors were overhauled just before the Harpoon was flown to California in 1994, so overhauling

Interior of the aft fuselage in "as-found" condition showing many of the original brackets and mounting holes. The fact that the interior was unmodified, other than being stripped of its military equipment, enabled all of the original World War II–era gear to be reinstalled. The interior paint was in good condition and was not sprayed over. *Roger Cain*

the carbs was likely going to be mandatory, and the corrosion found in the right carb screen made the decision pretty easy. Off to Aero Accessories they went. The fresh overhauled carbs sure looked pretty, especially next to the crusty-looking engines."

The Vintage Aircraft crew found new wheels, brakes, tubes, and tires for the Harpoon. These were built up, then flown to the Johnson Ranch for installation. The hydraulic system was in good shape as well. There were a few weeping seals, but nothing that would prevent the aircraft from being ferried back to Stockton. The seals would be addressed after the bomber was moved.

"With the new carbs, wheels, and brakes it was time to drive her around, and that was a lot of fun," Ramey said. "She sure kicked up some dust. One of our runs was done with the leading edges between the fuselage and engines removed. While scooting down the runway at a good clip, all of the dust and dirt that was kicked up by the props went right in the open leading edges, which ported right under the pilot's and copilot's seat. While pulling forty-two inches of manifold pressure rolling down the runway, I was smiling from ear-to-ear and spitting dirt and crud out of my mouth at the same time. After that, it was time to get the shop vac out once again!

"The power runs were great, although we found a lot of carbon in the right oil screen. We dumped the oil and installed an oil filter to catch any more carbon that might be swimming around, which worked as the screen was clean the next time we checked it."

Deadline Fast Approaching

The Vintage Aircraft crew finished preparing the aircraft for the ferry flight to Stockton and the time to move the plane was on the horizon. Ramey was working with the local FAA Flight Standards District Office (FSDO) to obtain a letter of authorization, known as an LOA, to fly the Harpoon by himself. For aircraft over 12,500 pounds gross weight

The radar operator's station has been returned to its original condition, showing the attention to detail in outfitting the inside of the bomber. Many of the mounting brackets were built from factory drawings as originals were unobtainable. The navigator's and radio operator's positions received the same attention to detail down to the fuselage fuel tank under the navigator's table.

(the Harpoon weighs in at 33,000 pounds), the Federal Aviation Regulations (FARs) require a type rating, but there are no schools where a pilot can go get typed in the PV-2.

"There is a regulation in the FARs that allows for an LOA in lieu of a type rating for ferry, maintenance, and flight training for those who can demonstrate collateral experience that would allow for the safe operation of the aircraft," Ramey said. "I have a type rating in a B-25 with limited time in the DC-3, B-17, B-24, and some PV-2D time, but that was more than twenty years ago in my friend Doug Lacy's Harpoon. I think the 3,500 hours in the Twin Beech is what helped the most. After flying the Beech, the Harpoon feels like a heavy, slower-responding version of about the same aircraft.

"My local FSDO tossed my request around for two weeks and then decided that I should talk to Sacramento FSDO as the aircraft was in their district. The Sacramento folks were very nice and were familiar with our shop and work and were very helpful. They issued the LOA and a ferry permit within a few hours." Having cleared the paperwork hurdle, it was time to put BuNo 84062 back into the air.

The runway at the Johnson Ranch ends at a road, and across that road are a hill and a number of houses. This meant that Ramey would have to make a sharp right turn after takeoff, and there were not many options if an engine quit as the bomber clawed for altitude. There is only so much ground checking and engine testing that can be done before a flight, thus engine performance was a concern for everyone. After the carburetor overhauls, the engines ran fine on the ground and were not making metal. The oil analysis looked normal, especially for engines that had been sitting for so long.

"The engines are factory new engines and were installed not long [hours wise] before her last flight to California and have around twenty hours since they were built . . . sixty-five years ago!" Ramey said. "They are Ford-built engines and are twenty-five serial numbers apart. Having said that, there was still a big concern as to whether they were going to hold up after all these years. In the air the engines ran great except for the high oil temps, which was a huge concern. Both temps were too high, but the pressure remained steady and solid. Upon landing we found out that we had packed the coolers with weeds and dirt kicked up by the propellers on the takeoff roll. After cleaning, this issue went away.

"Flying the Harpoon was a dream. When I ran her down the runway at fifty-two inches of power, she felt good, and I believe the Twin Beech experience is a wonderful trainer for the Harpoon. Everything felt right so the only real apprehension was over the engines holding together. They did and the flight was wonderful."

Ramey and crew flew the Harpoon off the Johnson Ranch with six days to spare. It had to be off the property on October 9, and it lifted off on October 3!

Preserving and Outfitting

Once the Harpoon was in Stockton and the major mechanical systems were inspected and overhauled, it was time to get to the cosmetics and the details of the interior of the patrol plane. The interior paint was original, but in good shape. "I have always gravitated towards keeping things original as opposed to full-blown restoration even if it's a bit scrappy," Ramey said. "I prefer faded original paint to shiny new paint any day, but not many share my views. It's only original once . . ."

The most visible external change, and one that the Vintage Aircraft crew wanted to tackle first was the removal of the retardant tank. The tank and its fairings came off easily, but the bomber looked naked. A set of bomb bay doors was acquired and installed. Just that one change took the plane from air tanker to bomber and visually demonstrated that the restoration was underway and making progress.

The interior paint was looking good, so the process of locating and installing all of the original equipment began. For the radio operator's station, all of the original components were found and installed, including the automatic direction finder. This was an SCR-269G, an army radio that was installed in navy Harpoons. The SCR-269 was essentially the same as the navy ARN-7, which became standard equipment that was used well after World War II. The ARN-7 used two antennas, namely a loop antenna or football-shaped antenna mounted on the top of the Harpoon and many other bomber aircraft. The loop was a directional antenna that could be rotated to home in on a signal. The other antenna was a simple wire that was called the sense antenna. The two signals were used to compare and determine the direction to the signal. On the Harpoon, the sense antenna was the straight wire from the forward mast to the aft mast.

The radar operator's position is located on the right side of the fuselage and can be seen when the entry door is open. The main radar was the APS-3 search and targeting radar that was widely used throughout World War II. "It must have been a good set to have had such a long run," Ramey said. "There are a lot of attachments and modifications for the basic set, which I am learning were installed in our late Harpoon." The APS-3 could also be used as an IFF (Identification, Friend or Foe) set, which is an early version of today's transponders that now provide aircraft identity, speed, direction, and altitude. The IFF set would send out an interrogation signal and receive responses from aircraft in its vicinity. Used with the APS-3 radar, the operator could see on his scope if a target was friendly or a foe. "The code for the reply was changed daily, so if you used an old code you were treated as a foe," Ramey said. "Ships, submarines, and of course other aircraft had the IFF gear. The IFF was also quite secret as you didn't want the code of the day falling into enemy hands. The transmitter/receiver had explosives installed to destroy the insides of

The exterior of the Harpoon was painted in the correct shades of blue, the fuselage with flat, and the wings with semi-gloss, per the navy specifications. The last three digits of the bureau number have been painted on the nose, and an operational Martin turret occupies the dorsal position once again. *Roger Cain*

the set during a crash through an impact switch or could be manually set off with a destruct switch. IFF gear is hard to find and we are lucky to have a full set to install in the Harpoon."

One of the late war modifications that Harpoons had was the addition of the APA-16 adapter that allowed more accurate bomb, torpedo, and even rocket release through the radar.

"What is more important to me is for any World War II aircrew to get back inside our Harpoon and be able to sit in their old crew position," Ramey said. "I want them to be able to sit down, and be able to fire up the radar or radios. To hear the dynamotors running and to smell the electronics when they are warm is just as important to me as an accurate paint job. If just one Harpoon vet says, 'It's just like

I remember . . .' then I will be happy beyond belief and all of the effort will be worthwhile ten times over."

In addition to the radio operator's and the radar operator's stations, a navigator's position has been installed and fully outfitted. A Martin top turret has been installed along with an F-56 aerial camera that looks out the lower fuselage to record strike damage. It is very impressive to see many of these systems working, and additional ones will be returned to service as the restoration progresses.

Through the generosity of a corporate donor, paint was donated to the Stockton Field Aviation Museum to put the Harpoon back into its original navy colors. Two weeks before the air races in Reno, that deep rich blue was sprayed onto the Harpoon. The next morning, the paint was still wet—not tacky, still wet. It was discovered that the wrong catalyst had been sent, and the paint would never have dried. So the Vintage Aircraft crew, their teenage kids, and a bunch of friends got out their razor blades and began scraping the wet sea-blue paint from the bomber. No matter how fast they worked, it seemed like a monumental, never-ending task—but they got it done.

New paint and the proper catalyst, as well as cleaning supplies that arrived by overnight courier, and the painting process began anew. After working all night, the bomber looked fantastic when rolled out into the central California sunshine.

"I am so proud of my crew at Vintage Aircraft. They are wonderful, and this is just the latest example of what they can do. I think there isn't anything they can't do once we commit to it," Ramey said. And with that, the Harpoon made its first appearance in authentic, flat, non-specular sea-blue paint at the National Aviation Heritage Invitational at the 2012 National Championship Air Races in Reno, Nevada.

Today there are three airworthy PV-2 Harpoons, several in museums on display, and another two dozen in various states of restoration, preservation, or storage. A gun nose Harpoon in the air is a rare sight indeed, and "062" is one of the most authentic of them all.

Some Assembly Required
B-17E/XC-108 *Desert Rat*

Early in World War II the Allies needed long-range transport, and a number of modified bomber schemes were brought forth. Four B-17s were converted to cargo/troop carriers under the C-108 designation, and B-17E 41-2595 became XC-108A. A large cargo door was installed in the left waist gunner's position, the radio operator and navigator were moved to the flight deck, and the armor plate and turrets were removed from the aircraft. The XC-108A is seen during its first combat assignment in India, where it carried troops and supplies over the Hump into China. *via Mike Kellner*

Owning and operating a B-17 Flying Fortress warbird has typically been the purview of large aviation history organizations like the Commemorative Air Force or the Experimental Aircraft Association, or individuals with very substantial financial backing. So many Flying Fortress enthusiasts dream of owning a B-17, but for the majority, operating an aircraft of this size is out of the realm of possibilities. The American dream of a house, having 2.3 kids, and working a day job have a way of taking priority over the desire to push all four throttle levers forward and feeling a B-17 rumble down the runway.

Not so for Mike Kellner. Good with his hands, Kellner was in the flooring business when his dream became a reality. Then his dream consumed his life—but in a good way. Kellner is the proud owner and chief restorer of a unique Boeing-built B-17E, serial number 41-2595, one of 512 "E" models built in Seattle, Washington. During World War II, this aircraft was known as *Desert Rat*, and also wore the name *Tangerine*, presumably after the song of the same name premiered to wartime audiences in the movie *The Fleet's In* (starring William Holden and Dorothy Lamour). The song became a chart-topping hit.

Boeing, Douglas, and Lockheed's Vega Division built 12,731 Flying Fortresses, and B-17 historian Scott Thompson of Aerovintage. com estimates that fifty-four B-17 airframes survive today, of which ten are operational, twenty-four are on display in museums, and four are being restored to fly once again. Kellner's *Tangerine/Desert Rat* is one of the four that will fly again.

X-C-One-Oh-What, Eh?

B-17E 41-2595 was delivered to the U.S. Army Air Forces in February 1942, to serve with the 97th Bomb Group training bomber crews for war in Europe. One year later, in February 1943, 41-2595 was transferred to the 383rd Bomb Group stationed at Ainsworth Field, Nebraska. On March 23, 1943, the bomber was assigned to Wright Field, Ohio.

At this point in the war, the U.S. Army Air Forces still desperately needed airlift capacity. The Douglas C-54 had not come on line in any substantial numbers and Lockheed's C-69 Constellation was some distance away as well. The Army Air Forces had achieved quite a bit of success in modifying Consolidated B-24 Liberators into long-range passenger, cargo (designated C-87), and fuel (C-109) transports, and a program was developed at Patterson Field, Ohio, to convert two B-17Es and two B-17Fs into C-108 transports. The first XC-108 was converted from B-17E 41-2593, and this aircraft became the personal transport of Gen. Douglas MacArthur, christened *Bataan*. The

Undergoing engine maintenance, the XC-108A's large cargo door is visible in this view. The aircraft returned from India in 1945 and was subsequently sold surplus at Dow Field, Maine. *Peter Bowers*

The XC-108A was purchased after the war by an automobile scrapper who let his kids go at the bomber with axes and saws. The boys could keep whatever money they earned from recycling the metal, but the XC-108A proved too tough. The youth's handiwork can be seen in this view of their attempt to separate the cockpit from the bomb bay section. *Mike Kellner*

YC-108 was an executive transport conversion of Vega-built B-17F 42-6036, and the XC-108B was a fuel tanker modified from Boeing-built B-17F 42-30190.

B-17E 41-2595 became the XC-108A prototype. All of the bomber's armament was removed, and a large, upward-swinging cargo door was installed in the left waist position. With the top turret removed, this gave enough room to move the navigator and radio operator's position to the flight deck area. Without the need for a bombardier, the nose section was converted into a cargo space with seats or the capability of carrying litter patients. Access was gained through a solid, up-swinging nose piece. The bomb bay was sealed and the radio room bulkheads were removed and flooring added.

The XC-108A was assigned to India in March 1944, and it was flown down to South America, then across the Atlantic and Africa to its new base at Chabua, India. After flights hauling troops and cargo into and out of China, the XC-108A returned to the United States in October 1944, for duty at Bangor Field, Maine. The plane served as a transport until it was sold as surplus in early 1946.

The troop-carrying bomber was bought by a gentleman who owned an auto scrapyard and he purchased a number of surplus aircraft and dragged them home. Here he let his kids dismantle them for fun, and whatever money they got for the scrap metal they were allowed to keep. A couple of P-51s, a C-47, an O-47, a B-25, and the XC-108A were all beaten upon by the kids. The aircraft components sat in the yard for years, and when it closed, the plane parts were essentially abandoned in place.

Fast forward to 1985 and Mike Kellner is at a museum auction in Ohio, where he meets Jim Gentry, whose hobby is keeping track of restoration projects and matching people and planes. Kellner told Gentry he was looking for a B-17 and he duly made a note of it. "I had been writing looking for a B-17 since high school. Even in high school I used to scrounge *Air Classics*, where they would have write-ups in the Warbird Report about a derelict at an airport. Of course I didn't know then, but by the time the magazine hit the newsstands someone had already snapped up the featured derelict warbird," said

The nose was removed and lost on the property, overgrown by brush and trees. It took Mike Kellner and his friends a couple of days scouting around the property to locate the navigator/bombardier's compartment. *Mike Kellner*

The vertical stabilizer and rudder were completely overgrown when located.
Mike Kellner

Mike Kellner. "I was chasing them. About two weeks after the auction, Gentry introduced me to Steve Alex. He called and said, 'I know where a B-17 is at.' By then I was, 'Yeah, right. Send me pictures,' and I got pictures."

A deal was quickly made. Steve Alex walked away with $7,250 and Mike Kellner's wallet was empty but his dream had come true. Well, part of it, anyway.

Honey, Look What I Bought!

Kellner, his brother Kenneth, and a number of good friends drove from Illinois to Bangor, Maine, to begin the process of making the dream come true. They arrived at the old car junkyard to find that no one had tended the property in years. There were thousands of trees, thirty- to forty-feet tall and a foot in diameter that had grown up all over the yard. The first order of business was to cut down a bunch of trees to make a road back to where the majority of the B-17 sat. Apparently the junkman's kids had tried to cut the Flying Fortress apart, and whatever they had succeed in removing was strewn to the four corners of the property. When Kellner bought the airplane—some assembly required—it was sold without the nose compartment. No one knew where it was, but it was found behind some trees during a parts-recovery search later on.

Kellner took an old house trailer, removed the top, and added ten feet in length to it. With the trailer in place, Kellner's troops began loading the trailer by hand with B-17 parts of all sizes and descriptions. No forklifts, just muscle and a fulcrum here and there. "There was some ingenuity in getting all of the parts loaded," Kellner said. "The biggest section of fuselage was pretty heavy. We strapped two by twelves to the bottom of it where the tires of the trailer would ride and jacked the nose of it up, backed the trailer into it, and then lowered it down onto the tires. Pulling forward it rolled it right up onto the bed without even scratching it. That worked out pretty well for loading the fuselage.

Hauling the first load home, they had overestimated the weight of the parts on the trailer. Figuring they could have carried much more,

Bringing the bomber home was a learning experience not only for Kellner, but for the toll booth collectors as well. The first load was substantially under weight for what they could haul, so when they loaded the second trailer they overcompensated. That load was overweight and only cleared toll booth lanes by one inch on each side. *Mike Kellner*

when they loaded the trailer the second time it was way overweight. "Back then you could get away with a few things on the highway," Kellner said. "We were probably over width too. A couple of the toll booths were starting to question the load as we squeaked through with only about an inch of clearance on each side." It took four loads to recover the B-17, two that Kellner and friends did and two oversize loads that they hired out.

Once the parts were back in Illinois, the problem was where to store them. For a while there were parts, pieces, and large assemblies stored at five different airports in the area. The monthly storage fees were adding up, to the point where more money was going to rent than to restore the Flying Fortress, so Kellner bought a small farmhouse and erected a pole barn next to it. *Desert Rat/Tangerine* now had a permanent home during its restoration.

Getting Down to Business

"When we got it, the nose was totally severed from the fuselage," Kellner said. "The cockpit was nearly severed and the radio room was

All of the flat surfaces made the trip on one trailer. The aircraft's serial number can still be seen on the vertical tail. *Mike Kellner*

more than halfway cut off the fuselage. The rear section was in four pieces. Today we have the radio room, the cockpit, and most of the hull pretty much done. We're just over halfway riveting the nose, so we're almost done with the forward section. When we got the plane, it was cut right in half near the ball turret. We have that all rebuilt and done. Just this year we added the last two pieces, but they're still in Clecos so it's not all riveted yet. There's all new stringers and new skins fitted. We ended up putting a horizontal stabilizer on it to make fairings for another airplane. We're also working on the dorsal fin. The fuselage is getting really close to being externally done and then it has to be fitted out.

"The wing fittings were torched off, but the wings are in a whole lot better shape than the fuselage. There's ax holes in them and stuff like that, but they're intact. They'll probably just be an inspect and repair as necessary. We have started somewhat on the wings, but so far we've just cleaned them, pulled the fuel tanks, and removed the superchargers. We've also removed one main gear from the wing. Our main task is to strip all of the equipment out so we can start inspecting and repairing the components."

Kellner's wife, Cheryl, is responsible for bucking most of the rivets in the aircraft. Proud of her work, her license plate reads: "RosieB17." "She doesn't have any qualms helping me on it; however, she would like to see it get done faster."

Because so many of the fuselage structural members must be replaced to repair the damage done while the plane was under attack by the junkman's kids, many components have to be remade. "I bought the drawings quite a long time ago when you could still get them," Kellner said. "We have around five thousand drawings on paper. I wanted to put everything on paper and then kind of gave up on that. Now everything is stored digitally or on DVD. I still have the original 35mm microfilm.

"We have a couple of different places that make extrusions for us. Early on, Alcoa sponsored us and they made some extrusions and we paid for them, but we paid minimal money. We paid for the dyes and setup fee, and sometimes they would just run it at whatever the cost of material was. They really have helped out. Usually what we try to do is get enough made where we can sell off enough to break even or get out from under the costs of it. Some stuff I wish we'd have made more of because we thought we'd have a lifetime of it and it's already gone.

"Alcoa also gave us a bunch of sheet metal. That was more or less in trade. We ended up sending them a couple of samples of original skin that still had Alcoa stamped on it. I can't say enough about how much we appreciate our vendors' generosity."

Kellner's shop can also turn out stamped parts. They make the forms and stamp pieces or hand-form them and heat treat them. They have also made rollers for rolling the fuselage formers.

Because this aircraft will be restored into a combat aircraft, turrets, gun mounts, and all of the associated armament pieces need to be collected. Kellner is trying to assemble a ball turret from components and has yet to think about a Sperry upper turret.

"In the last couple of months we found a second name on the bomber's nose. We had been calling it *Desert Rat* because we could see that through the paint. Then we sanded it, and of course it pops out and you can see it's in yellow. When we were reskinning the nose, we started drilling rivets out up at the very front and I noticed little flecks of yellow paint," Kellner said. "We start sanding on it and it's got another name that looks like it was its original name because it was under two layers of paint. It's called *Tangerine*. We did some research, and I actually found four other B-17s named *Tangerine* or *Tangerine 2*.

"Both names were on the right side. The name *Tangerine* is written in an italic font. If you look at a lot of E models, that's the way they did it. They put the name right up front, just behind the nose glass. For example, if you look at photos of the famous B-17E *Chief Seattle*, it had its name written in italics. You look at the earlier ones, especially in the South Pacific, and that's usually all they had was just a name on them. No nose art.

"We had thought that we would call the bomber by the name it wore during World War II. But now we have two names. Hopefully

For a number of years the Flying Fortress was stored at the Galt Airport in McHenry County, Illinois, northeast of Chicago. Eventually Mike Kellner was able to find a small farm in Marengo, Illinois, where he could erect a pole barn to begin the restoration effort. *Mike Kellner*

By fall 2012 the nose section had been mated to the fuselage and was receiving new skins. Compared to the condition when it was found, *Desert Rat/Tangerine* looked almost ready to fly. The project welcomes donations to help speed the restoration process. *Bill Stanczak*

this will add more character to the plane. Maybe people will support the aircraft more if it has a nostalgic name like *Tangerine* rather than *Desert Rat*?"

Kellner's B-17E/XC-108A 41-2595 joins a select group of early Flying Fortresses. Only the B-17D *Swoose* (40-3097), currently under restoration at the National Museum of the U.S. Air Force in Dayton, Ohio, and the B-17E 41-2446 *Swamp Ghost* are earlier aircraft. And only two other B-17Es exist—B-17E 41-9032 *My Gal Sal*, which was recently sold to the National World War II Museum in New Orleans, and the Flying Heritage Collection's former Bolivian meat hauler, B-17E 41-9210, under rebuild in Washington State. Only *Desert Rat/Tangerine* and the Flying Heritage Collection's bomber will fly again.

What does Mike Kellner do in his spare time when he's not restoring the B-17E? Why he's working on building a B-17C project with Bill Stanczak, of course. The two gather parts, and when they make a B-17E part that is interchangeable with the B-17C, they make a spare for that project. They have been storing parts and pieces but are not ready to start bolting things together. How's that for ambition?

"It's a heck of a lot of work," Kellner said. "We've had people come to us for advice before buying a warbird project and I tell them, 'Just be prepared to stick to it. It helps if you have more money. If you're buying a project, buy as complete of a project as you possibly can.' When we got this airplane, everybody thought we were nuts. Now this airplane really is a good project. In the scheme of things, we have a pretty nice airplane." Mike Kellner *is* living his dream.

Part Five

Recovering the
Big Fleets
Squadrons Return

There was a point when large caches of World War II warbirds could be found around the globe. Any country that received aircraft as part of a military aid package from the United States and its allies, or had a substantial air arm of their own, was a candidate location for warbird recovery. There were Hawker Furies in Iraq, Thunderbolts in Peru, Messerschmitts and Heinkels in Spain, Kittyhawks and Corsairs in New Zealand, AT-6s in South Africa, and half a dozen countries with substantial supplies of P-51 Mustangs.

In the United States, the air force's Heritage Program kicked off the hunt for large numbers of warbirds as each base museum sought aircraft for display. Many warbirds were supplied to the museum program by fire bomber operators on a trade basis. A World War II–era B-17 might fetch a flyable, early model C-130 that could be equipped for firefighting and would have, in theory, another twenty-five to thirty years of flying left on the airframe. A number of B-25s now displayed at air force base museums came from the air tanker industry and some from the *Catch-22* movie fleet.

Dozens of B-29s came from the gunnery ranges at China Lake and the Aberdeen Proving Ground. Many of these were combat veterans from World War II and Korea, and these collections yielded three aircraft that flew again, plus one close to flying again. The only flying B-29 today, the Commemorative Air Force's *FiFi*, was once a resident at China Lake, and the B-29 *It's Hawg Wild* was flown from China Lake to the Imperial War Museum in England.

One of the most iconic navy fighters of World War II, the gullwing F4U Corsair, was, at one point, almost extinct. There were

The storage pool at NAS Litchfield Park, Arizona, held hundreds of preserved U.S. Navy Corsairs, seen in the foreground. These stocks provided Corsairs that would later equip the air arms of Argentina, El Salvador, and Honduras. *U.S. Navy*

derelicts sitting at airfields here and there, but the number of fliers was less than five. Known affectionately as the "Bent Wing Bird" or "Hose Nose," it took a TV show to rekindle interest in the navy fighter and a pair of adventurers to recover sixteen from the Honduran air force.

With the fire bomber fleets and most foreign air forces picked clean of World War II–era warbirds, aircraft restorers have to go to greater lengths to find large numbers of aircraft. People have not forgotten the five additional P-38s that went down on the Greenland ice cap in 1942. And in the news recently, there has reportedly been a cache of Spitfires located in Burma (today's Myanmar) by adventurer David Cundall. After more than fifteen years of searching, Cundall reports that he's found six Mk. VIII Spitfires buried in a quarry and another twenty to forty crated Spitfires buried on a military base. Many in the warbird community are, understandably, skeptical.

Nearly seventy years after the end of World War II, it appears that the potential for finding large groups of warbirds lies with countries that have had closed borders that have allowed in very few westerners. However, there was a time when dozens of World War II warbirds sat wingtip to wingtip, ready for recovery.

Rescued from a Desert Boneyard
The B-29s of China Lake

Imagine standing in the high desert of California. The temperature is in the mid-eighties; there's a light breeze blowing from the west and you're standing on a plain where nothing but scrub brush grows. Ideal for a navy gunnery range, but not much else. In front of you sit fifty Boeing B-29s in various states of disrepair. Some look like they need fuel and oil, and the engines will be ready to turn while others have suffered a direct hit and all you see is the nose and tail, the outer wing panels, and a black patch were the fuselage once was.

Now imagine dragging one of these aircraft off the target range, prepping her to fly, then heading east, flying across the United States, then across the north Atlantic to the United Kingdom. It was done with B-29A-45-BN serial number 44-61748, known as *It's Hawg Wild*. After *It's Hawg Wild*, it was done successfully two more times.

In the mid-1950s, a large number of B-29s were flown to the Naval Air Weapons Center at China Lake, California, to serve as targets for new generations of missiles. Although a number received direct hits, there were enough intact aircraft to yield fourteen complete B-29s. It is interesting to note that none of the aircraft in this photo survived intact. *Gerald Liang*

B-29A-60-BN 44-62070 was in good enough condition that it could be made flyable again—with a lot of work. Volunteers from the then-Confederate Air Force spent months repairing the aircraft for a ferry flight from California to the aviation history group's home base, then in Harlingen, Texas. After a multi-year restoration, 44-62070 was christened *FiFi*, after the major sponsor's wife, and returned to the air. *Gerald Liang*

This collection of B-29s came from the target ranges at the Naval Air Weapons Station at China Lake, California. An additional nine B-29s were recovered or assembled from multiple airframes rescued from the Aberdeen Proving Ground, north east of Baltimore, Maryland.

In addition to the three ex-China Lake B-29s that were returned to fly, ten additional aircraft were assembled for museum displays, and the restoration of an eleventh aircraft, B-29-70-BW 44-69972, known as the Snow White and the Seven Dwarfs character *Doc*, is ready to fly . . . it just needs engines.

During World II, the Boeing-designed B-29 Superfortress was built by three companies: Boeing, which built 2,766 at its Renton, Washington, factory (abbreviated BN) and its Wichita, Kansas, plant (BW); 668 by Bell Aircraft in Atlanta, Georgia (BA); and 536 by the Glenn L. Martin Co. in Omaha, Nebraska (MO).

Classified as a heavy bomber during World War II, the B-29 is most famous for its incendiary attacks on Japanese cities, and for ushering humankind into the atomic age when single bombs destroyed the cities of Hiroshima and Nagasaki on August 6 and 9, 1945, respectively. After taking the war to the Japanese home islands,

Now known as the Commemorative Air Force (CAF), the group has toured *FiFi* around the United States for more than thirty years. The aircraft was taken down for a major overhaul from late 2005 to 2010, which should keep the aircraft flying for another thirty years.

the B-29 formed the backbone of the new United States Air Force on September 18, 1947, when America's air arm became a separate service.

The introduction of the mammoth B-36 Peacemaker saw the B-29's classification changed from heavy to medium bomber, and in 1948 many of the air force's B-29s were placed into strategic reserve at Warner-Robbins AFB, Georgia and Davis-Monthan AFB, Arizona. In spite of the drawdown of the number of B-29s in service, they served as the main nuclear-capable bomber through the end of the decade.

When war broke out between the Communist-backed North Koreans and the Democratic government of South Korea on June 25, 1950, B-29 bombing raids decimated nearly all of the strategic targets in the north. The introduction of the Soviet-designed and Chinese-built MiG-15 saw twenty-eight B-29s fall to the new jet fighter's cannon. To defend against the MiG, B-29 tactics were changed from bombing targets during the day to night raids against North Korean supply lines. The last B-29 sortie of the Korean War was flown on July 27, 1953, with the bomber having dropped more than 180,000 tons of bombs.

As more, newer aircraft types came on line, the air force began to phase the B-29 out of service with the Strategic Air Command flying its last B-29 bomber flight on November 4, 1954. With the B-29s coming out of service, the navy obtained a number of aircraft for testing at both Aberdeen Proving Ground in Maryland and at China Lake, California. The exact number of B-29s transferred has, to date, never been determined, but it is known that at least fifty went to China Lake and approximately one dozen to Aberdeen.

At Aberdeen, some of the B-29s were used for survivability testing where fuselage and wing sections were positioned as targets for existing and newer calibers and types of aircraft weapons. Damage assessments and warhead fragmentation patterns were determined to how to shield aircrews and equipment.

Because the ranges at China Lake are so remote, the navy is able to launch live weapons at flying drones and to drop live ordnance on stationary targets. China Lake's B-29 fleet was subject to radar-guided bombs and missiles, which did a number on many of the Superfortresses.

Making 'Em Fly

As the B-29s sat out on the target ranges, word started to spread through the military aviation community that there was a cache of the historic bombers sitting in the high desert.

Air Guard pilot Roger Baker saw the fleet of Superfortresses sitting on the target ranges and was the first to take action. He reported his observations to the Commemorative Air Force (CAF—then known as the Confederate Air Force) leadership. With their goal of having one flyable example of every World War II type, a B-29 was a major type missing from the group's collection and they asked Baker to investigate.

Using its political connections, the CAF was granted permission to enter the facility and remove an aircraft. The aircraft they selected was TB-29A 44-62070, built at Boeing's Renton factory and delivered on July 31, 1945. War in the Pacific ended shortly thereafter and 44-62070 spent time as a crew trainer flying from Smokey Hill, Kansas; Dalhart, Texas; and Grand Island, Nebraska, before being stored at Pyote, Texas, beginning in 1947. In April 1952, the air force began the process of removing the bomber from storage, and by September it was on the line at Smoky Hill once again. The B-29 finished out its air force service as a crew trainer at Randolph AFB, Texas, before being flown to China Lake in March 1956.

Once the CAF got to work, it took volunteers only nine weeks to get the bomber flying. After additional work, pilot Randy Sohn ferried the Superfortress to the group's home base at Harlingen, Texas, to begin the restoration. Restoration took more than three years, and when it was done, the bomber emerged ready for the airshow circuit having been christened *FiFi*, in honor of the aircraft's major financial sponsor Victor Agather's wife.

In 2005, the CAF stood *FiFi* down for an extended overhaul, replacing the engines with more-reliable hybrid Curtiss-Wright R-3350 radial engines, reengineering the exhaust system, replacing the fuel cells, and much more. *FiFi* now flies to airshows throughout the United States to educate generations of Americans about the sacrifices made during World War II and Korea.

The second flier from China Lake was brought out by David Tallichet's Military Aircraft Restoration Corp. in 1974. Tallichet's crew got the bomber flyable and hopped the plane a little less than a hundred air miles from China Lake to Barstow-Daggett Field, where additional restoration and repairs was carried out. The aircraft selected by Tallichet's crew was Boeing-Renton-built B-29A-40 44-61669, which was delivered to the U.S. Army Air Forces on May 5, 1945. The bomber was ferried across the Pacific and assigned to the 20th Air Force, 73rd Bomb Wing, 500th Bomb Group's 833rd Bomb Squadron at Saipan. After several postwar assignments, 44-61669 was transferred to the navy and arrived at China Lake on March 18, 1956. There it sat, as a target, although interestingly it escaped damage during the ensuing twenty-five years.

In August 1981, Tallichet's crew air delivered the bomber to the March Field Museum in Riverside, California, wearing the nose art of the B-29 *Mission Inn*. Riverside is home to the historic Mission Inn, and a B-29 with that name flew from the base in the 1950s.

In June 1999 the whole history of 44-61669 came to light. While serving with the 500th Bomb Group, the bomber flew eleven missions before the war ended and had been named *Flagship 500* and dedicated in honor of the Fourth Marine Division that had participated in the invasions of Kwajalein, Saipan, Tinian, and Iwo Jima. The division

Wearing the British aircraft registration G-BHDK, B-29A-45-BN 44-61748 *It's Hawg Wild* is seen at Keflavik, Iceland, en route to the Imperial War Museum at Duxford, England. This aircraft sat in the boneyard at the Naval Air Weapons Station China Lake, California, for twenty years before it was recovered and ferried to Tucson, Arizona. At Tucson the bomber was prepared for the flight to Duxford. *Henry J. Ramey*

took more than seventeen thousand casualties and was awarded a Navy Unit Commendation and two Presidential Unit Citations for its actions during the invasions.

The third and most ambitious of the China Lake flyouts was B-29A-45-BN 44-61748. Built too late to see combat during World War II, this bomber was very busy in Korea. Flying from Kadena Air Base on the island of Okinawa, Japan, and known as *It's Hawg Wild*, 44-61748 flew 105 missions against the North Koreans. The bomber arrived at China Lake in November 1956 where she sat until the U.S. Navy gifted the bomber to the Imperial War Museum in 1979. The Imperial War Museum sent engineers out to inspect the bomber with the intention of dismantling it and shipping it to the United Kingdom. As it turned out, a company known as Aero Services of Tucson, Arizona, bid $10,000 less to fly the bomber to England than the next lowest bid to dismantle and ship the plane.

Surviving B-29 Superfortresses

Serial No.	Model	Location	Status
42-24791	B-29-50-BW	Questmasters, Maryland	S
42-65281	B-29-25-MO	Travis Air Museum, California	PV
42-93967	B-29A-15-BN	Georgia Veterans Memorial State Park, Cordelle, Georgia	PV
44-27297	B-29-40-MO	National Museum of the U.S. Air Force, Ohio	PV
44-27343	B-29-40-BW	Tinker AFB, Oklahoma City, Oklahoma	PV
44-61535	B-29A-35-BN	Castle Air Museum, California	PV
44-61669	B-29A-40-BN	March Field Museum, California	PV
44-61671	B-29A-40-BN	Whiteman AFB, Missouri	PV
44-61739	B-29A-45-BN	Warner-Robbins AFB, Georgia	S
44-61748	B-29A-45-BN	American Air Museum, Duxford, UK	PV
44-61975	B-29A-55-BN	New England Air Museum, Connecticut	PV
44-62022	B-29A-60-BN	Fred E. Weisbroad Museum, Colorado	PV
44-62070	B-29A-60-BN	Commemorative Air Force, Texas	F
44-62220	B-29A-70-BN	History & Traditions Mus., Lackland, Texas	PV
44-69729	B-29-60-BW	Museum of Flight, Washington	PV
44-69972	B-29-70-BW	U.S. Aviation Museum, Kansas	S
44-69983	B-29-55-BW	National Atomic Museum, New Mexico	PV
44-70016	B-29-75-BW	Pima Air & Space Museum, Arizona	PV
44-70102	B-29-75-BW	China Lake NAS Museum, California	S
44-70113	B-29-80-BW	Dobins AFB, Georgia	PV
44-83905	B-29A-70-BN	Eielson AFB, Alaska	in situ
44-84053	B-29B-55-BA	Museum of Aviation, Georgia	PV
44-84076	B-29B-60-BA	Strategic Air Command Museum, Nebraska	PV
44-86292	B-29-35-MO	Smithsonian Institute-Udvar-Hazy Center, Virginia	PV
44-86408	B-29-55-MO	Hill AFB Museum, Utah	PV
44-87627	B-29-80-BW	8th Air Force Museum, Louisiana	PV
44-87657	B-29A-65-BN	National Museum of the U.S. Air Force, Ohio	PV
44-62139	B-29-70-BW	South Dakota Air & Space Museum	PV
45-21739	B-29-90-BW	Korean War Museum, Seoul	PV
45-21787	B-29-95-BW	Fantasy of Flight, Polk City, Florida	S
various	B-29	Aero Trader, Chino, California	S

Boeing, Renton, Washington=BN;
Boeing, Wichita, Kansas=BW;
Bell Aircraft Atlanta, Georgia=BA;
Glenn L. Martin Co. in Omaha, Nebraska=MO.
PV=Public View; F=Flyable, S=Storage.

Aero Services was owned by Jack Kern, and the company specialized in refurbishing aircraft removed from storage at Davis-Monthan AFB, Arizona. Kern's company had been involved in bringing *FiFi* and *Mission Inn* out of China Lake, thus they had plenty of recent experience recovering B-29s. On November 16, 1979, *It's Hawg Wild* was ferried from China Lake to Tucson where the bomber was prepared for the flight from Tucson to Duxford, England.

Notes	Source
Nose section: *The Big Time Operator*; tail gunner's compartment in private collection in California	China Lake
Miss America '62	China Lake
City of Lansford	Aberdeen PG
Bockscar	inventory
Tinker's Heritage	Aberdeen PG
Razin' Hell	China Lake
Flyable at one time (N3299F); *Flagship 500*	China Lake
The Great Artiste	Aberdeen PG
Nose section only	Aberdeen PG
It's Hawg Wild	China Lake
Jack's Hack	Aberdeen PG
Peachy	China Lake
FiFi (N4249)	China Lake
Joltin' Josie the Pacific Pioneer	Aberdeen PG
T-Square-54	China Lake
Doc restored, awaiting engines	China Lake
Duke of Albuquerque	China Lake
Sentimental Journey	inventory
Here's Hopin	China Lake
Sweet Eloise	Aberdeen PG
Lady of the Lake, submerged, intact	inventory
Big Red	Aberdeen PG
Lucky Lady	inventory
Enola Gay	inventory
Haggerty's Hag	Dugway PG
Bossier City	Aberdeen PG
Command Decision, fuselage only	inventory
Legal Eagle II	China Lake
	China Lake
P2B-1S BuNo 84029 *Fertile Myrtle*	Litchfield Park
Flyable project for sale, two airframes	China Lake

Aircraft Source: China Lake, Aberdeen Proving Grounds, U.S. Air Force Inventory, Litchfield Park = aircraft sold surplus from Litchfield Park in the 1960s.

Note that many of the static display examples are composites of multiple airframes. The airframe used to make up the majority of the display aircraft is the serial number listed.

Crew for the trip was Dewitt "Skip" Cregier, pilot; Don Davis, copilot; Aero Services' Jack Kern, flight engineer, and his wife Millie; Dr. Henry Ramey, navigator and World War II B-29 navigator; Henry Zappia, mechanic, and his wife Joann; Ken Kroeger, observer and photographer; and James Miller, Taigh Ramey, and Karen Summers, observers.

The flight departed Tucson on February 17, 1980, flying direct to

Flint, Michigan, at 10,000 feet. All of the flight legs were made under visual flight rules. From Flint, the B-29 headed east to Loring AFB, Maine. "The U.S. Air Force was very generous to us on the trip," said Taigh Ramey. "At Loring AFB they parked the B-29 in a heated hangar, nose-to-nose with a B-52, which was quite a sight in deed. We were at Loring for a week fixing oil leaks to try and cut down on the oil loss/consumption. Number three engine consumed seventy-five gallons of oil on the trip from Tucson to Flint, Michigan. This consumption limited the range of the B-29 to oil range instead of fuel range, which eliminated the possibility of flying across the Atlantic nonstop."

After five days at Loring chasing oil leaks, the war-surplus bomber headed to Gander, Newfoundland, on February 24. The oil consumption situation eliminated the possibility of flying direct to the UK, thus *It's Hawg Wild* had to hopscotch across the North Atlantic. The next day, February 25, the B-29 departed Gander headed for Greenland at an average altitude of 12,000 feet.

"The Air Force loaned us a Herman Nelson ground heater that was secured in the forward bomb bay and ducted into the ventilation system in the old bomber. This worked beautifully until a spark plug stripped out of a cylinder head and killed the engine," Ramey said. "We froze, literally, after the heater flamed out on the leg from Gander, Newfoundland, to Sondrestrom, Greenland. It was so cold (about 20 degrees Fahrenheit below zero) that the moisture from our breath frosted the inside of the cockpit glass. The same freezing moisture jammed up the air filter for the vacuum instrument system and caused the gyros to tumble. Skip jumped back into the seat and kept the B-29 right side up by flying partial panel and saved us from one of several near-death experiences. Skip went on to shoot an instrument approach into Sondrestrom and did a masterful job, as usual, as there was no real missed approach available for us. You fly up the long fjord and there's a wall at the far end of the runway. I believe that this may have been Skip's first night landing in a B-29, but you couldn't tell by looking as he was an awesome pilot indeed."

From Greenland, the flight climbed to 14,000 feet to avoid icing conditions and landed at Iceland on February 26. After a two-day stay at Iceland, the B-29 flew to RAF Mildenhall, landing on March 1. After off-loading all of the spare equipment and personnel, *It's Hawg Wild* made its final flight to Duxford on March 2.

"My father and I were originally just passengers on the flight with no duties except to be in Jack's way," said Ramey. "I remember Skip

Cregier, the aircraft commander, coming into Jack's office at Aero Services and asked who his navigator was going to be. Jack said, 'Dr. Ramey here was a B-29 Navigator in World War II.' Skip turned to my dad and asked him if he had a sextant, to which he replied, 'Yes, I do.' Skip asked him if he could navigate the B-29 across the pond and he said that he could.

"Jack had been trying to have an inertial navigation system loaned to the project, but it didn't work out. He was also trying to get the Flux Gate Compass system operational and had even borrowed parts from Pima's B-29, but he was having trouble getting it to work. The remote transmitter was the biggest problem, which mounted in the wing. There was a big concern as to how the navigation was going to go as the aircraft would be out of radio range a lot of the time and would have to rely on dead reckoning as pilotage was not that useful over the frozen North Atlantic.

World War II B-29 navigator Dr. Henry J. Ramey Jr. takes a turn at the pilot's controls flying the Superfortress over the northeastern United States. Dr. Ramey navigated *It's Hawg Wild* over the North Atlantic using his World War II–vintage A-10A sextant and astrocompass. *Taigh Ramey*

"My dad was welcomed to the crew, but since he was an unknown he would be put to the test on the first few legs of the trip. My dad used dead reckoning from Tucson to Flint and his positions were verified by Skip and Don with their VOR and DME. They were slightly more confident in his abilities, but the true test still was before them.

"My dad navigated the B-29 across the North Atlantic using his old World War II A-10A sextant and astrocompass. The only modern thing he had was a Hewlett Packard HP-65 programmable computer that he used for the navigation tables and calculations. The Flux Gate Compass system was unreliable and the VORs didn't work at our altitude and distance from the station, so he was able to take sun and moon line fixes with the astrocompass. I had the honor of mounting it in the astrodome and aligning it on the sun and moon. I would give it back to him and he would use the readings to calculate a line of position.

"After we landed at Sondestrom, Greenland, my dad, Skip, and I were the last to get off the B-29, and Skip turned to my father and said, 'You are one hell of a tough old World War II navigator,' and he thanked my dad for getting him there safely. I think that this was one of the best compliments that my father ever received. I could not have

Thousands of people lined the runway at Duxford for the arrival of *It's Hawg Wild,* the only complete B-29 on display in the United Kingdom and Europe. It is fitting to have a Superfortress on display at Duxford as the type was flown by the Royal Air Force Bomber Command as the Washington B.1 from 1950 to 1954. *Gary Verver*

been more proud of my dad. How lucky could I possibly be: My father navigated B-29s out of Saipan in World War II and I got to see him do exactly that in 1980. In my eyes, my dad is the last true B-29 Navigator."

Once at Duxford, *It's Hawg Wild* was displayed outside for the next sixteen years. In 1996, *It's Hawg Wild* underwent a complete restoration, stripping it down to bare metal, corrosion removed and inhibited, and then the bomber was primed, painted, and reassembled. She now sits proudly in the American Air Museum on Duxford Airfield.

One of the last B-29s to come off of the China Lake ranges was recovered in 1998. Built as B-29-70-BW, serial number 44-69972 was delivered to the U.S. Army Air Forces on March 23, 1945, and the bomber flew from Barksdale until November of that year. From there it was sent to storage at Pyote, Texas. In July 1951, the B-29 was removed from storage and sent to Kelly AFB, Texas, for overhaul before joining the 4713th Radar Evaluation Calibration Squadron. The 4713th named its aircraft after the characters in the fairy tale *Snow White and the Seven Dwarfs*, and 44-69972 became *Doc.* After serving in the radar evaluation squadron, *Doc* was modified for target tug duty before returning to storage. On March 14, 1956, the bomber was transferred to China Lake to serve as a target where she sat for more than forty-two years.

Tony Mazzolini formed the United States Aviation Museum in 1987 and traded a B-25J Mitchell bomber (44-29035) in display ready condition as a navy PBJ Mitchell in exchange for the title to B-29 44-69972. Mazzolini's group towed the aircraft from the desert and began restoration work at the Inyokern Airport, adjacent to China Lake. They quickly outgrew the space and the lack of infrastructure necessary to rebuild an aircraft the size of a B-29. About the same time, retirees from Boeing Aircraft in Wichita, Kansas, stepped in with an offer of assistance and the plane was moved 1,500 miles east.

The Boeing retirees restored *Doc* about 80 percent of the way to flight, but then the plant closed down, the B-29 was evicted, and it eventually found a new home at the Kansas Aviation Museum across the field. By 2012, *Doc* was in storage on the airport in Wichita while arrangements for a new home were made and work on many subassemblies continued.

More China Lake Veterans

The U.S. Air Force's Heritage Program enabled base museums to collect historic aircraft aligned with the base's mission; thus Strategic Air Command bases went after bombers, Airlift Command bases transports, and Tactical Air Command bases sought fighter types. In addition to the flying aircraft, the B-29 boneyard at China Lake yielded a number of combat veteran Superfortresses that are now displayed at former bomber bases and other museums around the country.

The Castle Air Museum's B-29A-35-BN 44-61535 flew during Korea with the 19th Bomb Group's 28th Bomb Squadron as *Raz'n*

It's Hawg Wild saw combat in the skies over Korea. The bomber has been painstakingly restored and is now on display at the American Air Museum at Duxford. *Peter Langsdale via Taigh Ramey*

Hell, the name a play on the bomb type RAZON, for Range and AZimuth ONly. The bomber flew from Anderson AFB, Guam, and later with the 307th Bomb Wing from Kadena Air Base, Okinawa, Japan, making more than fifty strikes at targets in North Korea. This aircraft was built up from three China Lake B-29s—44-61535, B-29-75-BW 44-70064, and B-29-50-BA 44-84084.

Miss America '62 flew with the 6th Bombardment Group, 24th Bomb Squadron from Tinian Island during the summer of 1945. During the war she accounted for more than forty missions over Japan and her gunners were credited with downing two enemy fighters. Delivered as B-29-25-MO 42-65281, this plane also flew with the 373rd Weather Reconnaissance Squadron during the Korean War. The bomber was recovered and restored by volunteers from the Jimmy Doolittle Air & Space Museum at Travis AFB, in Northern California.

Now at the Museum of Flight at Seattle, Washington's Boeing Field, B-29-60-BW 44-69729 flew thirty-seven combat missions over Japan during World War II with the 498th Bomb Group's 875th Bomb Squadron. Volunteers at the museum have restored the Superfortress to nearly flyable condition, and it currently awaits the construction of an indoor display space.

Although it has been picked over by a number of museums, the nose section of B-29-50-BW 42-24791 was recovered from Mobile Smelters in Mojave during one of the China Lake range cleanups in the early 1980s. The tail gunner's compartment of this B-29 was also rescued at the same time. Serial number 42-24791 was christened *The Big Time Operator* and flew from North Field, Tinian Island with the 20th Air Force's 313th Bomb Wing, 9th Bomb Group making forty-six missions over Japan. This nose section is now under restoration with Questmasters in Maryland.

The target ranges at China Lake consumed a number of historic, combat veteran aircraft, but they also provided a supply of combat veterans for generations to see and touch.

Ben Nattrass's Worldwide Aircraft Recovery Ltd. reduces Kermit Weeks's B-29 *Fertile Myrtle* to components prior to moving the bomber across country. The nose section was moved to Weeks's Florida museum while the remainder of the bomber was sent to storage in the California desert. This aircraft was used by the U.S. Navy and the National Advisory Committee for Aeronautics, or NACA, as the mothership for a number of high-speed test flights in the 1950s. *Fertile Myrtle* is most famous for launching Scott Crossfield in the D-558-2, in which he was the first to fly Mach 2 (1,290 mph/2,076 km/h).

Corsairs Recovered
from Honduras

In the years following World War II, the governments of many Latin American nations were in turmoil. The United States sought to maintain a balance of power and to counter Communist attempts at influence within the region. The United States offered large amounts of surplus military hardware for sale at bargain basement prices under the Military Aid Program.

The Fuerza Aérea Hondureña (FAH—Honduran Air Force) acquired five Bell P-63E Kingcobras, three Lockheed P-38L Lightnings, and one P-38M night fighter from surplus U.S. stocks between October 1948 and September 1949. The aircraft were:

    P-63E FAH400, ex-USAAF 43-11727
    P-63E FAH401, ex-USAAF 43-11728
    P-63E FAH402, ex-USAAF 43-11729
    P-63E FAH403, ex-USAAF 43-11730
    P-63E FAH404, ex-USAAF 43-11731
    P-38M FAH503, ex-USAAF 44-53097
    P-38L FAH 504, ex-USAAF 44-26961
    P-38L FAH 505, ex-USAAF 44-53232
    P-38L FAH506, ex USAAF 44-53095

Operationally, these aircraft are complex to operate, powered by 12-cylinder, water-cooled Allison V-1710 engines. For the next decade, the FAH operated the P-38s and P-63s, and in 1956, when the United States offered air-cooled, radial engine Corsairs to its neighbors south of the border, they quickly acquired ten. The FAH Corsairs were a mix of F4U-5s, -5N night fighters, and -5NL winterized night fighters. As the Corsairs were coming on line, the Allison-powered fighters soldiered on, slowly being cannibalized to keep others of their type in the air.

In 1958, warbird collector and dealer Bob Bean began talks with the FAH to acquire its remaining Allison-powered fighters. Bean proposed swapping ten F4U-4 Corsairs for the FAH's four flyable P-38s, two flyable P-63s, and two wrecked P-63s. He was successful in negotiating with the FAH and the exchange was made.

To maintain the balance of power, the United States also sold Corsairs to El Salvador in June 1957. The Fuerza Aerea Salvadoreña

Vought F4U-4 BuNo 97288 served with the Fuerza Aérea Hondureña (FAH) as FAH 612 from 1960 until it was returned to the United States in 1979. Ed Real is seen at the controls of FAH 612 during its recovery flight from Honduras to Texas. *Vought Aircraft*

(FAS) acquired twenty Goodyear FG-1Ds at a cost of $8,700 each from surplus stocks at the navy's storage depot at Litchfield Park, Arizona. The U.S. government required that five of the twenty aircraft be grounded to provide spares for the fifteen fliers, which would also maintain a balance of air power between Honduras and El Salvador. As soon as the aircraft reached El Salvador, all twenty were maintained in flyable condition and the FAS immediately turned around and asked to buy five more FG-1Ds for use as spares ships. A little more than two years later, in October 1959, the spares aircraft arrived, although they were F4U-4s, not FG-1Ds. Thus the engine, accessory, and oil systems were not completely interchangeable, rendering the planes essentially useless for firewall forward spares.

Corsair versus Corsair in the 100-Hour War

Border tensions between El Salvador and Honduras came to a boiling point in 1969. Honduras has five times the land mass as neighboring El Salvador, and during the 1950s and 1960s tens of thousands of El Salvadorans had illegally migrated across the border. In 1962,

Jim Nettle's Hollywood Wings purchased eight of the nine flyable Corsairs from the Honduran Air Force in 1979. The aircraft had very little time on the airframes, ranging from 1,200 to 2,000 hours, with only one, FAH 614, having 2,649 hours. In addition to the flyable aircraft, a number of "kits" were compiled from the spare subassemblies and parts inventory acquired in the deal. Here one of the Corsairs is inspected before the flight back to the United States. *Vought Aircraft*

Honduras enacted land reform laws that gave the government the power to seize land held by El Salvadorian immigrants and redistribute that land to native-born Hondurans. Salvadorians who returned to their home country were often beaten and abused, igniting anti-Honduran sentiments.

Anti–El Salvador sentiment was running high in Honduras, and the two countries were matched in the 1969 qualifying rounds for the 1970 World Cup soccer tournament. To add fire to the flames, Radio Honduras had been broadcasting anti–El Salvador propaganda during the lead up to the soccer match.

The first game was played on June 8, 1969, in the capital city of Tegucigalpa, and the home team won the match 1-0. The second match was held June 15, 1969, and saw the Honduran team travel to San Salvador. This time the home team won 3-0. Tremendous violence broke out between the fans, adding to the already high tensions.

The series was even, 1-1, and the deciding game in the best two-out-of-three match was held in neutral Mexico City, Mexico. Here the El Salvadoran team won 3-2 in overtime, and tensions between the two nations escalated. On June 26, Honduras and El Salvador broke diplomatic relations.

The "100 Hour" or "Soccer War" began on July 10 when twelve thousand El Salvadoran army troops crossed the border into Honduras. The ground troops were followed by an attack of FAS aircraft against the FAH base at Tocontin, outside of Tegucigalpa. The FAS had a number of North American P-51D Mustangs, Goodyear FG-1D Corsairs, Douglas C-47s, as well as a solitary Douglas A-26B Invader in its air arm. The FAS Corsairs were flying primarily in the ground-attack role. Laden with bombs, they were escorted to their Honduran targets by P-51Ds.

The FG-1Ds of FAS would do battle with the F4U-4s and -5s of the FAH. On July 17, FAH Capt. Fernando Soto was on a ground-attack mission when one of his two wingmen was jumped by a pair of FAS Mustangs. Soto, in FAH-609, an F4U-5N, quickly downed FAS Capt. Humberto Varela flying a Cavalier-converted P-51D Mustang (reported to be 44-73458).

Later in the day, Soto and his wingman were en route to attack San Miguel, El Salvador, when they spotted a pair of FAS FG-1Ds. The Goodyear Corsairs would do battle with the later Vought-built Corsairs in the skies over Latin America. Soto dropped his bombs and began to climb for an altitude advantage over the FG-1Ds. Diving on the FG-1Ds, Soto quickly flamed one (FAS-204, BuNo 67082, Captain Cezena) but overshot the second. Soto's wingman had been bounced by an additional pair of FAS bandits and was unable to cover his attack. After maneuvering behind the second FG-1D, Soto was able to hit the aircraft's port wing, exploding the Corsair (FAS-203, BuNo 67071, Captain Cortez). For the day, Soto had destroyed two FG-1Ds and a P-51D. Although a number of aircraft had been lost on the ground, Soto's three kills on July 17 were the only air-to-air victories during the border conflict.

On July 18, Honduras and El Salvador accepted the Organization of American States' peace plan. Although the peace plan had been accepted, both sides sporadically attacked each other with Honduran forces drawing the last blood on July 27 when they made a number of attacks across the border. El Salvador began to withdraw its troops from Honduras on July 29, thus ending the last aerial battles of the former World War II fighter types.

The FAS flew its last Corsair in the summer of 1971. The FAS subsequently donated FG-1D FAS217 (BuNo 92460) to the Sikorsky

F4U-4 BuNo 96995 flew with the Hondurans as FAH 614. J. K. "Buck" Ridley acquired the Corsair shortly after it was returned to the United States and even put the fighter around the pylons at the National Championship Air Races in Reno, Nevada. The aircraft is now part of the Red Bull air force. *Vought Aircraft*

Memorial Airport, Connecticut, where it serves as a memorial to those who built and flew the Corsair. At least three other FAS Corsairs have been returned to the United States and are now being restored to flying condition.

The FAH retired their Corsairs in favor of the Korean War–vintage North American F-86 Sabre jet, buying six former Venezuelan K models in 1970. The Corsairs were parked in the weeds at Tegucigalpa, awaiting an uncertain future.

Bringing Back the Honduran Corsair Squadron

Jim Nettle was co-owner and mechanic on a DC-4 hauling freight in Honduras. Nettle's partner, Andres Paz Leiva, a Honduran national, had some excellent connections in the military and the two mentioned that they would like to purchase the Corsairs when the government no longer needed them. A few years passed and Nettle sold his interest in the DC-4. While wondering what to do next, the Corsairs were offered to Nettle and his partner by parties within the FAH. Nettle quickly formed Hollywood Wings as the company under which all of the Corsair business would be transacted. The deal would take two years from the day it began until the day they had disposed of the last of the Corsair parts.

The Hondurans had nine flyable Corsairs of different models. Hollywood Wings was able to purchase eight of the aircraft along with five to six container loads of parts—each container was 40-feet long—which would later yield a treasure trove of Corsair parts. The Corsairs all had low airframe times, ranging between 1,200 and 2,000 hours, except for FAH614 (F4U-4 96995), which had 2,649.55 hours.

The ninth Corsair, FAH609, was Captain Soto's aircraft in which he downed the three Salvadoran aircraft during the 1969 border war. It was retained by the Hondurans and currently sits in outside storage awaiting a suitable display space.

Nettle hired and contracted the pilots who would ferry the Corsairs back to the United States. Six of the eight aircraft were flown as an "unarmed squadron of obsolete military fighter aircraft" from Tegucigalpa, Honduras, to Houston, Texas, via Guatemala City, Guatemala; Veracruz, Mexico; and Brownsville, Texas; with final delivery to customers at Houston. The fighters were thoroughly

Howard Pardue, left, and Robert L. Ferguson helped finance the recovery of more than a dozen Corsairs from Honduras by Jim Nettle and Hollywood Wings. Pardue and Ferguson are perched atop BuNo 97288 shortly after the fighters arrived in the United States. *Vought Aircraft*

The attention to detail given to today's restorations is evident in the gunbay of former Fuerza Aérea Salvadorena Goodyear FG-1D FAS-208 (U.S. Navy BuNo 92489). This Corsair was recovered from El Salvador by Frank Arrufat in 1973. John Lane's Airpower Unlimited finished the restoration, and the ex–U.S. Navy fighter is seen at the National Aviation Heritage Invitational competition in Reno, Nevada, in 2010.

checked out on the ground and flight-tested while in Tegucigalpa. Nettle performed most of the maintenance checks himself.

The Corsairs had only VHF radios, no navigational aids, and one-third had no compasses. This did not present a problem as Nettle was to lead the flight of six F4Us in a Cessna 340 from which he could navigate and conduct all radio transmissions for the flight. He had prearranged the overflight permissions and fuel stops with the various governments en route. Pilots for the flight included Ed Real; Lou Remshner; Harold "Bubba" Beale; Mike Penketh; Bob Forbes; and Orrin Carr.

Mike Penketh flew FAH615, BuNo. 97280, in the six-ship formation from Tegucigalpa. At the time, Penketh was a PBY fire bomber pilot and had been a U.S. Marine Corps captain flying Douglas A-4 Skyhawks with the famous VMF-214 Blacksheep squadron. Flying the Corsairs from Honduras to the United States was not only a fitting aside to his aviation career, but the fulfill-ment of a dream for Penketh because his father had served in VMF-214 during Korea when the squadron flew F4U-4 Corsairs.

The crew flew commercial from Los Angeles to New Orleans, then boarded a Sasha Airlines— the national airline of Honduras—flight to Tegucigalpa. Once in Honduras, the pilots shared a single Corsair manual and each made a couple of test hops before all of the aircraft were declared fit to make the journey back to the United States. They looked pretty shabby, but they flew quite well.

Penketh said of the Corsair journey north to the United States, "The flight back was uneventful, except I made an unscheduled landing due to a fuel leak. Three of the guys went on, while two other Corsairs landed with me. We caught up with the others in Brownsville after dark."

After clearing customs in Brownsville, Texas, the six aircraft arrived in Houston on December 19, 1979, where Hollywood Wings turned the Corsairs over to their new owners. Howard Pardue, of Breckenridge, Texas, and his partner Bob Ferguson, of Wellesley, Massachusetts, took delivery of FAH601 (F4U-5NL 124560), FAH604 (F4U-5N 122179), FAH605 (F4U-5 122184), FAH606 (F4U-5N 124486), FAH612 (F4U-4 97288), and FAH615 (F4U-4 97280).

Ferguson retained FAH601 and Pardue kept FAH605, selling the balance of the aircraft to recoup their investment. Ferguson sold his aircraft by 1983 and replaced it with a North American P-51D Mustang, while Pardue kept his until 1987.

Five of the pilots went back to their full-time flying jobs while Ed Real returned to retrieve the last F4U-4, FAH614, BuNo. 96995. Real flew this aircraft back unescorted.

Real was then sent back to Tegucigalpa one more time to retrieve the aircraft Hollywood Wings had decided was special—F4U-5NL, FAH600, BuNo. 124724—and he flew it back to the States unescorted. This plane was the last -5NL built; many claim it is the last true Corsair built, as the AU-1 was primarily a ground attack aircraft and the F4U-7 did not see service with the U.S. Navy or Marines.

While flying from Tegucigalpa, Real was to land in Belize for fuel. As he set up for his landing, the spring-loaded tail wheel dropped, but the main gear failed to extend. He attempted to shake the gear out of the wheel wells with high-G maneuvers, but was unsuccessful, so he decided to belly land FAH600. After dropping the external fuel tanks and stopping the engine, Real dead-sticked the Corsair in and slid to a safe landing. The F4U-4NL slid on the propeller and drop tank hard points, limiting the damage to these items and the inboard flaps. The necessary parts to repair the Corsair were sent from Long Beach, and it was quickly on its way back to the United States.

Hollywood Wings held onto 124724 until it sold the winterized night fighter to Ralph Parker of Wichita Falls, Texas. Parker sold the aircraft in 1986 to the well-known French aeronautical collection Amicale Jean-Baptiste Salis, headed by Jean Baptiste, who then registered the aircraft F-AZEG. The last F4U-5NL is maintained

Honduran Corsairs

FAH serial	U.S. Navy BuNo	Model
FAH-600	124724	F4U-5
FAH-601	124560	F4U-5NL
FAH-602	124447	F4U-5NL
FAH-603	123168	F4U-5N
FAH-604	122179	F4U-5N
FAH-605	122184	F4U-5N
FAH-606	124486	F4U-5N
FAH-607	124692	F4U-5NL
FAH-608	124493	F4U-5
FAH-609	124715	F4U-5
FAH-610	97388	F4U-4
FAH-611	97382	F4U-4
FAH-612	97288	F4U-4
FAH-613	97143	F4U-4
FAH-614	96995	F4U-4
FAH-615	97280	F4U-4
FAH-616	97320	F4U-4
FAH-617	97059	F4U-4
FAH-618	96885	F4U-4

John O'Connor of Downers Grove, Illinois, brings a former El Salvadorean Air Force Corsair in to land at the Thunder Over Michigan Air Show. This Corsair was restored with the early FG-1D three-piece canopy. O'Connor's Corsair was honored with the Grand Champion: World War II award at EAA AirVenture 2010. *Roger Cain*

in flyable condition and is flown regularly from its base at La Ferte-Alais, France.

After disposing of the flyable aircraft, Nettle began to open the containers of parts shipped up from Honduras to Long Beach, California. From the treasure chest of parts, Nettle was able to piece together three complete aircraft, which Hollywood Wings sold as "kits." These kits included FAH602, an F4U-5NL BuNo. 124447 that was rebuilt, registered N100CV, and passed through a couple of owners before ending up on display at the U.S. Marine Corps Command Museum at El Toro, California. The second kit was FAH606, an F4U-5 BuNo. 124486 that was rebuilt by Phil Dear of Jackson, Mississippi, and was registered N49068. The last kit, FAH610, is an F4U-4, BuNo. 97388, that was last reported with Gerald Beck at Wahpeton, North Dakota.

Hollywood Wings donated a number of parts to restorations being undertaken by the National Air and Space Museum and LTV Aerospace. It then sold off the balance of the parts to other F4U owners and went out of the Corsair parts business.

Jim Nettle's chance opportunity of being in the right place at the right time saved eighteen hidden warbirds from an uncertain fate.

Latin American Mustangs Fuel the Warbird Movement

For more than twenty years after the end of World War II, P-51 Mustangs were being used to equip the air forces of ten Latin and South American countries. A couple examples of the P-51A and -51C model went south of the border in the early days, but it was the P-51D and K model and the later Cavalier P-51 conversions that were most numerous. These later models would feed a hungry warbird market in the 1970s and 1980s. New old stock parts that were recovered from these countries are still making their way into civilian hands and have been used in numerous rebuilds.

Mustangs went to Latin and South American through post-war civilian military surplus acquisitions, various U.S. military aid programs, surplus sales by the Swedish Air Force, and the Trans-Florida Aviation/Cavalier Aircraft Corp. refurbishment program. Some were delivered through clandestine means.

The first to receive P-51s was the Fuerza Aérea Dominicana (Dominican Air Force), which began acquiring surplus Mustangs from the American civil aircraft market. Two Allison-equipped Mustangs (P-51 41-37426 and P-51A 43-6007), two P-51Cs, and a pair

Hand-tinted image of the Fuerza Aérea Guatemalteca (Guatemalan Air Force) aerobatic team formation takeoff in the mid-1950s. Note the Douglas B-18 Bolo and the engineless C-47 in the upper right corner of the photo. Aircraft supplied to foreign nations by the U.S. government under various military equipment programs became a big source for the warbird movement. *FAG via Gabriel Contreras/Gaëtan Marie*

of P-51Ds were acquired in the summer and fall of 1948. Four years later, in 1952 and 1953, the Dominicans acquired forty-three P-51D-20s from the Royal Swedish Air Force. Two additional Mustangs were bought bringing the Dominican Air Force's total to fifty-one.

At the other end of Hispaniola, the Corps d'Aviation d'Haiti (Haitian Air Corps) were in the market for Mustangs at the same time as their neighbors, the Dominicans. Perpetually short on cash, the Haitians sought aid from the United States, and although originally turned down in their quest to equalize the balance of air power on the island, they eventually settled for four P-51Ds, which were delivered in May and July 1951. In October 1973, the Haitians sold their Mustangs to help finance the purchase of ten armed T-28E Fennecs. Their neighbors to the east, the Dominicans, acquired the Haitian P-51s and either used them as a source of spares or traded them in to the Cavalier Corp. for services on their existing fleet, which, in 1966, quietly began to go through overhaul at Cavalier.

Mustang Supplier: Trans-Florida Aviation/Cavalier Aircraft Corp

From the end of the 1950s to the 1970s, Trans-Florida Aviation, which was renamed Cavalier Aircraft Corp. in 1967, had its hand in refurbishing and remanufacturing many of the Mustangs operated in Latin and South America.

The company was founded by David B. Lindsay Jr., who had served in the U.S. Army during World War II as an artillery officer in the Pacific. After the war, Lindsay received his bachelor's degree from

FAG 315, believed to be P-51D-25-NA 44-73902, is seen as the maintenance crew swaps out its Rolls-Royce Merlin engine. This aircraft was recovered with other FAG Mustangs in the early 1970s by Don Hull, and is now in storage with Connie Edwards in Big Spring, Texas. *FAG via Gabriel Contreras/Gaëtan Marie*

Purdue University in Indiana, and completed his military service in 1950. The Lindsay family had been in the newspaper business for the two generations prior to David Jr. joining the profession in Indiana and South Carolina. Lindsay Sr. founded the Sarasota (Florida) *Herald* in 1925 and in 1938 acquired the Sarasota *Tribune*. Both papers were merged to form the Sarasota *Herald-Tribune*.

Lindsay Jr. rose to become the paper's publisher in 1955, when his father retired due to a smoking-related illness. With this turn of events, Lindsay Jr. stopped taking cigarette advertising, at the time a very costly decision financially. He also championed what today are environmental causes. Under Lindsay Jr's leadership, the *Herald-Tribune* became the region's largest employer and was sold to the *New York Times* in 1982.

Shortly after assuming the reins at the *Herald-Tribune* in 1955, Lindsay began pursuing his passion for aviation. He used a Cessna 310 for business, but envisioned something faster that could fly up and over weather systems, rather than flying the time consuming path around them. In the days before the Lear Jet, Lindsay realized the P-51 Mustang was the perfect vehicle for the pilot/executive—it could cruise around 325 mph at 10,000 feet and fly above most weather systems in the region.

In 1956, Lindsay started Trans-Florida Aviation at the Sarasota-Bradenton Airport with the intent of selling executive conversions of the P-51 Mustang. At this time, Mustangs were plentiful as surplus U.S. Air National Guard stocks were being sold off and parts were readily available. He started with eight former Royal Canadian Air Force P-51Ds, completely stripped them down removing all military equipment, and added soundproofing, a rear seat, and new, lightweight radios and avionics. Modified V-1650-7 Merlin engines were installed. The airframe and wings were cleaned up aerodynamically, removing any unnecessary antennas, deleting the gun ports in the wing leading edges, and cleaning up the areas formerly used for ordnance hardpoints. The gun bays were turned into baggage compartments while fuel tanks were installed in the ammunition bays.

All eight of the initial aircraft were quickly sold to civilian buyers. From lessons learned with the first aircraft, Trans-Florida Aviation then offered five Cavalier Mustang models, each designated by the aircraft's range: the Cavalier 750 (750-mile range using 184 gallons of internal fuel), Cavalier 1200 (184 gallons plus a 48-gallon tank in each ammunition bay), Cavalier 1500 (184 gallons plus two 63-gallon ammunition bay tanks), Cavalier 2000 (184 gallons plus two 92-gallon wing tip tanks), and Cavalier 2500 (184 gallons plus two 92-gallon wing tip tanks, plus two additional 60-gallon cells added to the tip tanks for a total of 488 gallons). Tall, P-51H-style vertical fin caps were fitted giving the aircraft increased lateral stability and also making the Cavalier conversion stand out among other Mustangs on the ramp.

David Lindsay stands in front of the newly constructed Trans-Florida Aviation building at the Sarasota-Bradenton Airport in 1960. Lindsay had started the Mustang conversion company in 1956, changed its name to Cavalier Aircraft Corp. in 1967, and by 1971 when the company was sold, had supplied reconditioned Mustangs to Bolivia, Guatemala, El Salvador, and Nicaragua. *Ed Lindsay*

By the mid-1960s, Cavalier's Mustang conversion facility had attracted the attention of the U.S. military as well as a number of Latin and South American air forces. Cavalier had the equipment and expertise to overhaul P-51s and supply what were essentially newly manufactured, zero-time aircraft.

Mustangs South of the Border

The U.S. government had planned to provide Republic P-47s to all Latin and South American countries because the Thunderbolt's R-2800 engine was less complex than the Mustang's water-cooled Rolls-Royce V-1650 engine. Uruguay's air force, the Cuerpo Aérea, later Fuerza Aérea Uruguaya (FAU), turned down the American-offered Thunderbolts shortly after the end of World War II, and instead paid for twenty-five Mustangs, which began arriving in November 1950.

The United States' use of the P-51 in the Korean War consumed a fair amount of its spare parts inventory and the war delayed delivery of available parts from U.S. Air Force stocks to Uruguay. The

Bolivian Air Force 519 was a Cavalier conversion that was serial number 67-22579. This aircraft was acquired by Arny Carnegie in 1977 and registered C-CXRG. After passing through a number of owners, the Mustang was acquired by John Bagley of Rexburg, Idaho. *Martin Kyburz Collection*

lack of spare parts, coupled with the complexity of the engine and cooling system, saw the FAU's serviceability rate decline sharply, and by the mid-1950s, less than half of the Mustangs were flyable. The Uruguayans began acquiring Lockheed T-33s and F-80Cs in 1956, which spelled the end of the P-51 Mustang in FAU service. In 1960, the remaining six flyable FAU Mustangs and the complete spares inventory were sold to the Bolivian Air Force.

Bolivia

The Fuerza Aérea Boliviana (Bolivian Air Force) acquired its first Mustangs on the surplus market in July 1954, having bought two P-51Ds and one TF-51D. One of the Ds crashed on the delivery flight and a replacement aircraft was purchased at the end of the year. When the Uruguayans sold off their aircraft, their flying Mustangs and spares inventory went to Bolivia in spring 1960.

In 1967, the Bolivians, fighting rebels led by Che Guevara, received twelve Mustangs under the U.S. project designation "Peace Condor." In all, Bolivia would operate a twenty-five-aircraft strong fleet of P-51Ds and dual control TF-51Ds. In 1977 and 1978, Bolivia traded its Mustangs to Canadair for T-33s.

Costa Rica and Nicaragua

In 1955, Costa Rica was under attack from its Nicaraguan neighbors. Appealing to the United States for assistance, four ex–Texas Air National Guard Mustangs were flown to Costa Rica to bolster its nearly nonexistent air force. Through attrition, 50 percent of its Mustangs were lost in service, with another going down on its delivery flight north from Costa Rica to a new owner in the United States. The last aircraft, 44-74978, was sold to buyers in the United States and was registered N6169U, subsequently N74978. This aircraft was destroyed in a hangar fire in July 1988 at the Shafter Airport in California's Central Valley.

Neighboring Nicaragua's air arm, the Fuerza Aérea de la Guardia Nacional de Nicaragua, operated forty Mustangs between 1955 and the fall of 1963. The service's first twenty-six Mustangs were purchased from the Royal Swedish Air Force and arrived in January 1955. At least ten Mustangs were lost in Nicaraguan service.

Wilson "Connie" Edwards surveys P-51D-20-NA 44-63663, the former Fuerza Aérea Guatemalteca FAG-354. At one time, Edwards owned fifteen P-51s, almost all of which were recovered from Latin and South America. *Martin Kyburz Collection*

Cuba

A trio of Mustangs were flown from south Florida to the Cuban Rebel Air Force in November and December 1958. The P-51s were all D models (44-73978, 44-74505, and 45-11700), of which 44-73978 is today displayed at the Museum de la Revolucionaia in Havana.

Guatemala

The Fuerza Aérea Guatemalteca (Guatemalan Air Force) received its first Mustangs in the summer of 1954. Buying aircraft piecemeal, the service acquired fourteen ex-Royal Canadian Air Force Mustangs in 1957, and in the early 1960s acquired a number of Mustangs from aircraft brokers. Through the years, the Guatemalan Air Force operated a total force of thirty P-51D/TF-51Ds.

Bringing Back the Latin and South American Mustangs

The first of the big Mustang purchases came in the summer of 1963, when fifteen flyable and six partial Guatamalan aircraft were sold to the Maco Sales Financial Corp. of Palos Park, Illinois.

Texans Don Hull and Wilson "Connie" Edwards acquired six of the remaining Guatemalan Air Force flyable P-51Ds and the air arm's spare parts inventory in the summer of 1972. Guatemala had converted to the Cessna A-37 light attack aircraft. The pair acquired six flyable aircraft (P-51Ds 44-63663, 44-72902, 44-72907, 44-74391, 44-74452, and TF-51D 44-84660), which returned to the United States beginning in August 1972.

The ten remaining Guatemalan Air Force Mustangs came north in October 1974. These planes were bought by Jack Flaherty and the majority were Cavalier conversions. The Bolivian Mustangs were bought by Canadians Arny Carnegie and Hector MacGregor in the summer of 1977. This batch of aircraft included three Cavalier P-51D conversions, two other P-51Ds, and a TF-51D.

Brian O'Farrell brought the last big haul of Mustangs from Latin and South America in May 1984. Nine aircraft and tons of spare parts were containerized and sent to O'Farrell's storage facility in Florida. O'Farrell acquired 44-63701, 44-72051, 44-72086, 44-72202,

David Lindsay instructs Salvadoran ground crews in the boresighting of the Mustang's .50-cal. machine guns on the Sarasota-Bradenton Airport in 1968. Lindsay was an artillery officer in the Pacific Theater during World War II, and was able to put his army gunnery training and Spanish language skills to good use. *Ed Lindsay*

44-72339, 44-72364, 44-72438, and 44-74469. The only P-51 left in the Dominican Republic was 44-72123, most recently known as FAD1914. This aircraft served with the U.S. Army Air Forces' 55th Fighter Group and was known as *The Millie G.* This combat veteran Mustang was flown by Capt. Ed Giller of the 343rd Fighter Squadron and passed to the Royal Swedish Air Force in August 1947, and then to the Dominican Air Force in October 1952.

Today, more than fifty Mustangs owe their survival to their service in Latin and South America.

Epilogue
They're Still Out There . . .

Imagine driving down the street and seeing a P-51 fuselage go by in the back of a truck. The truck has the name of a scrapper on the side of it, and that can't be a good thing. You motion to the driver to pull over, and he does. Next thing you're in the back of the truck inspecting the fuselage of one of two XP-51Gs built. The "G" was the lightweight version of the P-51D Mustang. That's what happened to Mustang enthusiast Brian Cooke and a friend. Things like that don't happen every day, but they do happen.

A deal was made with the truck driver and the XP-51G was saved. A few months later, Cooke needed money for this Shelby Cobra Mustang and he sold the project to John Morgan, who has shepherded the project ever since and has built a website devoted to the project (www.xp51G.com). Morgan found the original cockpit panels and has amassed an impressive collection of Mustang parts for the project. He's now looking for a partner to finance the remainder of the restoration process so that this airplane, the fastest of all North American Aviation-built Mustangs (498mph), will fly once again.

More than sixty years after the end of World War II, four 4-engine navy patrol bombers came on the market. These planes were saved from the scrap heap because they were employed as fire bombers by Hawkins and Powers Aviation of Greybull, Wyoming, until 2003. Known as Consolidated PB4Y-2 Privateers, they are the single tail big brother of the B-24 Liberator. During the war, the navy needed an aircraft that could be packed with radar and electronic countermeasures equipment and sent on long-range patrols against the Japanese. To build this airplane they removed the B-24's characteristic twin tails and replaced them with a tall, single tail; added power gun turrets in all positions (nose, two top turrets, two waist turrets, and a tail turret); and fitted Pratt & Whitney R-1830-94 engines without the B-24's high altitude turbochargers. Once these aircraft were sold surplus, the fire bomber operators converted the engines to R-2600 powerplants as flown on the B-25 Mitchell bomber. In addition to the four fire bombers, the Lone Star Flight Museum is restoring a PB4Y-2 that will be fitted with all of its gun turrets. Hopefully the four ex–fire bombers will be returned to military configuration and flown on the airshow circuit.

The Southern Museum of Flight in Birmingham, Alabama, is home to the Lake Murray B-25. The nose section of this bomber

There are hundreds, maybe even thousands, of World War II aircraft wrecks waiting to be located around the globe. Unfortunately, the chances of finding an aircraft wreck as intact as this crashed Corsair are very slim. Most nearly intact aircraft wrecks will be found under water or ice, in the jungle, or in the frozen north, and the degree of completeness depends upon the plane's angle of impact when it crashed. *Vought Aircraft*

is on display in the museum. The plane is B-25C 41-12634 that was on a skip-bombing mission over Lake Murray, South Carolina, on April 4, 1943. After dropping its bombs, the aircraft's left engine lost power and the crew successfully ditched.

Working with a U.S. Navy sonar team, Dr. Bob Seigler was able to pinpoint the bomber's exact location in 150 feet of water. After working with South Carolina Electric and Gas, who owned the lake, the bomber was recovered in September 2005. Following years of conservation work, it was recently put on display for all to see.

One of the more controversial aircraft recoveries was Lex Crawley's recovery of a Brewster F3A Corsair, BuNo 04634. The controversy stems not from Crawley's recovery, but from the heavy-handed response of the Naval Historical Center. Crawley found an aircraft that had lain abandoned in a North Carolina swamp for nearly fifty years before he recovered it. While seeking title to the aircraft, the navy sued Crawley for the aircraft and for "damages" for

The sole surviving Brewster-built Corsair, F3A-1 BuNo 04634 was recovered from a North Carolina swamp, where it crashed in December 1944. One of only 735 Corsairs built by Brewster, this aircraft is now undergoing restoration at Ezell Aviation in Breckenridge, Texas.

the restoration work he had carried out. It took Congressman Walter Jones of North Carolina to add wording to the Defense Authorization Act for 2005 (HR-4200, October 28, 2004) to deed the aircraft to Crawley as a gift from the United States to end the lawsuits. In 2011, Crawley sold the rare bent-wing fighter to warbird collector Jim Slattery, who now has the aircraft under restoration with Ezell Aviation in Breckenridge, Texas.

Another warbird recovered from a former battlefield is Messerschmitt Bf-109-E1, later upgraded to an E7, Werke no. 3523. This aircraft was constructed by Arado GmbH at Warnemünde, Germany, in 1939, and flew in both the Battle of France and the Battle of Britain. The fighter was transferred to the Eastern Front and was being flown by Lt. Wulf-Dietrich Widowitz on April 4, 1942, when the thirty-six-victory ace was shot down by a Soviet pilot flying a lend-lease Hurricane. Widowitz put the Messerschmitt down on a frozen lake where it eventually fell through the ice.

Jim Pearce of Warbird Finders in the United Kingdom recovered this prized Messerschmitt in August 2003, and it has now been acquired by the Freidkin Family Warbirds Collection. It can be seen on display at The Air Museum/Planes of Fame in Chino, California.

From 2007 to 2012, more than a dozen high-profile World War II warbirds were recovered, and are now under restoration or awaiting a decision on their fate. Other World War II crash sites are being discovered on a nearly weekly basis, some found by searchers, some through development, and others by chance.

From the aircraft recovered by chance category comes a Vought F4U Corsair that was discovered off the coast of the island of Sicily in 2007. It was snagged in a fisherman's net and brought into the harbor at Sigonella. Here, sailors cut the wings off the plane and it was sent stateside for further investigation into its history.

Then, beginning in 2009, a spate of recoveries from Lake Michigan were undertaken to round out the aircraft collections of a number of museums. On April 24, 2009, A&T Recovery brought up a Douglas SBD Dauntless for the National Museum of World War II in New Orleans, Louisiana. The museum has a restored SBD on loan. In November of that year, Enterprise Rent-a-Car sponsored the recovery of a Grumman F6F-3 Hellcat; A&T Recovery brought up Lt. Walter Elcock's mount from 250 feet below the surface of Lake Michigan. Enterprise Rent-a-Car was founded by Jack Taylor, who flew Hellcats aboard the USS *Enterprise* (CV-6) and USS *Essex* (CV-9). The following year, A&T Recovery brought up Curtiss SB2C-4 Helldiver BuNo 19866 that was ditched into Lower Otay Reservoir outside of San Diego, California, in June 1945. The plane was discovered by fishermen cruising the surface using a fish scanner. The Helldiver has been trucked back to the National Museum of Naval Aviation for restoration.

In November 2010, A&T Recovery was back on Lake Michigan raising an F4U-1. This recovery was sponsored by warbird collector and veteran Chuck Greenhill. This early model Corsair went into the lake when Ens. Carl H. Johnson tried to trap aboard USS *Wolverine*, but ended up in the water instead. The plane was pulled from 240 feet of water, and it, too, was trucked to the National Museum of Naval Aviation in Pensacola, Florida, for restoration.

One month prior, in October 2010, a Bell P-39 that was recovered from Mart-Yavr lake in Russia above the Arctic Circle was delivered to the Ira G. Roos/Niagara Aerospace Museum in Niagara Falls, New York. The museum is housed in the same building where Bell built the P-39 Airacobra during World War II.

Messerschmitt Bf-109-E1, later upgraded to an E7, Werke no. 3523, was recovered from a lake in the former Soviet Union. The Eastern Front saw extensive combat between the Soviet Air Force and the Luftwaffe. In addition to a large amount of downed Luftwaffe aircraft, the United States and Great Britain sent vast quantities of lend-lease aircraft to the Soviet Union. In recent years, a number of Allied and Axis aircraft have been located, recovered, and are now under restoration. Bf-109-E7, Werke no. 3523, is owned by the Freidkin family and is slated to begin restoration in 2013.

The P-39 was lend-leased to the Soviets and was lost when the engine failed. Lieutenant Ivan Ivanovich Baranovsky wasn't wearing his shoulder harness and perished in the wheels-up landing he made on the frozen lake. The museum plans to display the aircraft in a wheels-up, frozen lake diorama.

One of the most intriguing finds in recent memory was the March 30, 2012, discovery of an intact Curtiss P-40 Kittyhawk, RAF serial number ET574 (ex-USAAF 41-35928), flown by Flight Sgt. Dennis Copping of 260 Squadron. Flight Sergeant Copping was reported missing on June 28, 1942, while ferrying the Curtiss fighter to a repair depot in Egypt. Jakub Perka, a Polish oil company surveyor, located the fighter in the Saharan Desert nearly two hundred miles from the closest town. From evidence at the crash site, it appears that Flight Sergeant Copping made a shelter using his parachute and tried to get the radio working. Copping eventually walked away from the aircraft, but his remains have yet to be discovered. The P-40 was slated to be displayed at the RAF Museum, Hendon, England; however, there have been reports that it will be displayed at the Al-Alamein Museum in Egypt.

In the summer months of 2012, there were a number of interesting warbird recoveries in Europe, including major components of a Heinkel He-219 night fighter found in the sea off the Jutland

Peninsula of Denmark. Substantial pieces of wreckage, including propellers, were brought to the surface and recovered. This was followed by the recovery of a nearly intact Heinkel He-115 floatplane. The He-115 was found on its back in sixty feet of water. After recovery it was disassembled into six sections and immersed in fresh water to stabilize the components before restoration begins. This process will take three to four years.

In June 2012, substantial wreckage from a Junkers Ju-87 Stuka was recovered approximately six miles from the German island of Rügen in the Baltic Sea. The engine was brought up from sixty feet below the surface and the fuselage soon followed. That same month, an Ilyushin Il-2 Sturmovik was recovered from a lake in northern Russia. This ground attack aircraft was forced down on Krivoye Lake on November 23, 1945. Both the pilot and gunner survived. The plane sank through the ice the following spring. The Il-2 has been moved to a restoration facility in the town of Novosibirsk, Siberia.

Each year the National Aviation Heritage Invitational sponsors a competition for the most authentically restored aircraft. The event is held in conjunction with the National Championship Air Races at Reno, Nevada, every September. The winner of the Neil A. Armstrong Aviation Heritage Trophy for 2012 was Duncan Cameron of Lebanon, Tennessee, for his and Tom Westfall's restoration of a 1944 Consolidated Vultee/Stinson OY-1 (U.S. Navy version of the L-5, Bureau No. 02747).

This OY-1 was delivered to the U.S. Marine Corps and saw combat as an artillery spotter in the skies over Iwo Jima in 1945. While flying with Marine Observation Squadron 5 (VMO-5), the plane suffered battle damage, which was discovered during the restoration and shown on the exterior of the aircraft. This airplane was brought back to the United States after the war and was transferred to the Civil Air Patrol, and it was eventually sold to a civilian owner. Mark Holmquist was looking for a wedding gift for his friend Duncan Cameron, and

Although it doesn't look like much right now, this is the fuselage and engine mount of the fastest of the P-51 Mustangs, the XP-51G. After the war it was used as a cockpit procedures trainer and when that career was over, the plane was spotted on its way to a metal recycler. John Morgan acquired the hulk and has been diligently collecting parts for the plane's eventual reassembly and restoration. *A. Kevin Grantham*

Historic aircraft are still out there, like Duncan Cameron's 1944 Stinson OY-1 that saw combat over Iwo Jima. When the aircraft was restored, areas of battle damage were repaired just as they were during the war, with silver fabric over the holes. This aircraft was found in a barn and its restoration was completed in 2012. The plane won the Neil A. Armstrong Aviation Heritage Invitational Trophy during competition held in conjunction with the National Championship Air Races at Reno, Nevada, in September 2012. Posing with the trophy and the OY-1 are (left to right): Mark Holmquist (who found the aircraft in a barn in Marietta, Ga.), former Southwest Airlines CEO Herb Kelleher, Amy Cameron, Duncan Cameron, Duncan Cameron III, and restorer Tom Westphal. *Jim Dunn*

found what he thought was an old, dilapidated L-5 in a barn near Marietta, Georgia. After Cameron married his bride Amy, he set about researching the history of this OY-1 and learned it had flown with VMO-5. Upon pulling the squadron records, he found the name of the pilot who flew this aircraft over Iwo Jima, and to everyone's surprise learned that Merton Hansen was still alive and well.

Cameron's OY-1 demonstrates that hidden warbirds are still out there. The only question is what will be found next?

Bibliography and Suggested Reading

Books

Alexander, Sigmund Col. *B-47 Aircraft Losses*. Spiral bound and available direct from the author (12110 Los Cerdos St., San Antonio, TX 78233-5953); Newspaper clippings, reports, and photos of all B-47 losses. http://www.b-47.com/SAC%20Accidents.htm

Andrade, John M. *U.S. Military Aircraft Designations and Serials Since 1909*. Hinckley, Leic, England. Midland Counties Publications, 1979.

Bailey, Dan E. *World War II Wrecks of the Truk Lagoon*. Redding, California. North Valley Diver Publications. 2000.

_____. *WWII Wrecks of the Kwajalein and Truk Lagoons*. Redding, California. North Valley Diver Publications. 1989.

_____. *World War II Wrecks of Palau*. Redding, California. North Valley Diver Publications. 1991.

Brandt, Trey. *Faded Contrails: Last Flights Over Arizona*. Phoenix, Arizona. Acacia Publishers, 2003.

Cass, William F. *The Last Flight of Liberator 41-1133: The Lives, Times, Training and the Loss of the Bomber Crew Which Crashed on Trail Peak at Philmont Scout Ranch*. West Chester, Pennsylvania. The Winds Aloft Press. 1996.

Childers, Thomas. *Wings of Morning: The Story of the Last American Bomber Shot Down over Germany in World War II*. Reading, Massachussetts. Addison-Wesley Publishing Co. 1995.

Cole, Ben. *Four Down on Old Peachtree Road*. Suwanee, Georgia. Crosswind Publications, Ltd. 2007.

Coggin, Paul. *P-51 Mustang Restored: The Restoration of the Lil' Margaret. An F-6D Photo Reconnaissance Version of the P-51*. Osceola, Wisconsin. Motorbooks International. 1995.

Cupido, Joe. *Chino: Warbird Treasures Past and Present*. Riverside, California. Fox-2 Productions. 2000.

Darby, Charles. *Pacific Aircraft Wrecks . . . And Where to Find Them*. Melbourne, Australia. Kookaburra Technical Publications Party Ltd. 1979.

Doylerush, Edward. *Rocks in the Clouds: High-Ground Aircraft Crashes of South Wales*. Hersham, Surrey, England. Midland Publishing/Ian Allan Publishing Ltd. 2008.

Francillon, René J. *Japanese Aircraft of the Pacific War*. Annapolis, Maryland. Naval Institute Press. 1990.

Gallagher, James P. *Meatballs and Dead Birds: A Photo Gallery of Destroyed Japanese Aircraft in World War II*. Mechanicsburg, Pennsylvania. 2004.

Grantham, A. Kevin. *P Screamers: The History of the Surviving Lockheed P-38 Lightnings*. Missoula, Montana. Pictorial Histories Publishing Co. Inc. 1994.

Green, Brett. *Götterdämmerung: Luftwaffe Wrecks and Relics*. London. Classic/Ian Allan Publishing. 2006.

Havener, J. K. *The Martin B-26 Marauder*. Blue Ridge Summit, Pennsylvania. Tab Books. 1988.

Hayes, David. *The Lost Squadron: A Fleet of Warplanes Locked in Ice for 50 Years . . . Can They be Freed to Fly Again?* New York. Hyperion. 1994.

Hoffman, Carl. *Hunting Warbirds: The Obsessive Quest for the Lost Aircraft of World War II*. New York. Ballantine Books. 2001.

Imparato, Edward T. *Into Darkness: A Pilot's Journey Through Headhunter Territory.* Charlottesville, Virginia. Howell Press, Inc. 1995.

Job, Macarthur. *Air Disaster.* Weston Creek, Australia. Aerospace Publications Pty. Ltd. 1994. Volumes One through Four (published in 1995, 1996, 1999, and 2001, respectively).

Kearns, David A. *Where Hell Freezes Over: A Story of Amazing Bravery and Survival.* New York. Thomas Dunne Books (St. Martin's Press). 2005.

McClendon, Dennis E. *The Lady Be Good: Mystery Bomber of World War II.* Fallbrook, California. Aero Publishers. 1962.

McLachlan, Ian. *Final Flights, Dramatic Wartime Incidents Revealed by Aviation Archaeology.* London. Haynes Publishing. 1995.

Macha, Gary Patric, and Don Jordan. *Aircraft Wrecks in the Mountains and Deserts of California* (1909-2002, Third Edition). Lake Forest, California. InfoNet Publishing. 2002.

Mann, Robert A. *Aircraft Record Cards of the United States Air Force (How to Read the Codes).* Jefferson, North Carolina. McFarland & Co. Publishers. 2008.

Martinez, Mario. *Lady's Men: The Story of World War II's Mystery Bomber and Her Crew.* Annapolis, Maryland. Naval Institute Press. 1995.

Merlin, Peter W., and Tony Moore. *X-Plane Crashes: Exploring Experimental, Rocket Plane, and Spycraft Incidents, Accidents, and Crash Sites.* North Branch, Minnesota. Specialty Press, 2008.

Mikesh, Robert C. *Broken Wings of the Samurai: The Destruction of the Japanese Airforce.* Annapolis, Maryland. Naval Institute Press. 1993.

Mireles, Anthony J. *Fatal Army Air Forces Aviation Accidents in the United States, 1941–1945* (three volumes). Jefferson, North Carolina. McFarland & Co. Publishers, 2006.

Morrison, Lee. B. *Out of the Wilderness: Restoring a Relic.* North Canton, Ohio. Military Aviation Preservation Society. 1995.

Page, Gordon. *Warbird Recovery: The Hunt for a Rare WWII Plane in Siberia, Russia.* New York. iUniverse. 2005.

Panas, John Jr. *Aircraft Mishap Photography: Documenting the Evidence.* Ames, Iowa. Iowa State University Press. 1996.

Quinn, Chuck Marrs. *The Aluminum Trail: China, Burma, India, World War II, 1942–1945.* Self-published. 1989.

Ralph, Barry. *The Crash of Little Eva: The Ultimate World War II Survivor Story.* Gretna, Louisiana. Pelican Publishing Co. 2004.

Sheehan, Susan. *A Missing Plane.* New York. G. P. Putnam's Sons. 1986.

Shepherd, W. Richard. "They Returned: The Story of the Million Dollar Valley Marauders and How They Were Returned to the United States for Preservation in Yesterday's Air Force." *Air Classics Quarterly Review.* Spring 1976.

Skaarup, Harold A. *RCAF War Prize Flights, German and Japanese Warbird Survivors.* New York. iUniverse Inc. 2006.

Smith, David J. *High Ground Wrecks and Relics: Aircraft Hulks on the Mountains of the UK and Ireland.* Leicester, England. Midland Publishing Ltd. 1997.

Spieth, Glen E. *The Swamp Ghost: B-17E 41-2446.* Unpublished manuscript. (Speith's father, Harry E. Spieth Jr. was a pilot in the 7th Bomb Group, 22nd Bomb Squadron and flew on the mission to Rabaul.)

Starks, Richard, and Miriam Murcutt. *Lost in Tibet: The Untold Story of Five American Airmen, A Doomed Plane, and the Will to Survive.* Guilford, Connecticut. The Lyons Press. 2004.

Stekel, Peter. *Final Flight: The Mystery of a WWII Plane Crash and the Frozen Airmen in the High Sierra.* Berkeley, California. Wilderness Press. 2010.

Sturkey, Marion. *Mid-Air: Accident Reports and Voice Transcripts from Military and Airline Mid-Air Collisions*. Plum Branch, South Carolina. Heritage Press International. 2008.

Thompson, Scott A. *B-25 Mitchell in Civil Service*. Elk Grove, California. Aero Vintage Books. 1997.

_____. *Final Cut: The Post-War B-17 Flying Fortress and Survivors* (Third Edition). Missoula, Montana. Pictorial Histories Publishing. 2009.

Van Waarde, Jan. *US Military Aircraft Mishaps 1950-2004*. Schipol, The Netherlands. Scramble/Dutch Aviation Society. 2005.

Veronico, Nicholas A., Ed Davies, et. al. *Wreckchasing: A Guide to Finding Aircraft Crash Sites*, Castro Valley, California. Pacific Aero Press. 1992.

Veronico, N., Ed Davies, Donald B. McComb Jr., and Michael B. McComb. *Wreckchasing 2: Commercial Aircraft Crashes and Crash Sites*. Miami, Florida. World Transport Press. 1996.

Veronico, Nicholas A., A. Kevin Grantham, and Scott Thompson. *Military Aircraft Boneyards*. Osceola, Wisconsin. MBI Publishing. 2000.

Ward, Chris and Andreas Wachtel. *Dambuster Crash Sites: 617 Dambuster Squadron Crash Sites in Holland & Germany*. Pen & Sword Books, England. 2007.

Widner, Robert. *Aircraft Accidents in Florida: From Pearl Harbor to Hiroshima*. Lulu.com. 2009.

Wills, Richard K. *Dauntless in Peace and War: A Preliminary Archaeological and Historical Documentation of Douglas SBD-2 BuNo 2106, Midway Madness*. Washington, D.C. Naval Historical Center. 1997.

Internet Resources

Below is a list of useful and interesting websites that directly relate to warbirds, the recovery of aircraft, and wreckchasing/aviation archaeology. Only sites with dedicated Internet addresses have been included.

Aircraft Wrecks and Aviation Archaeology

Aircraft Wrecks in the Mountains and Deserts of the American West
www.aircraftwrecks.com
Explorer G. Pat Macha's site chronicles the hundreds of sites he's documented and showcases a number of aircraft wreck mysteries he's working to solve. He is currently dedicated to locating missing WASP Gertrude Tompkins Silver, and in the process of looking for her he has located more than seventy other aircraft crash sites in the Santa Monica Bay. Macha is also the host of the History Channel's *Broken Wings*.

Arizona Aviation Archaeology
www.aircraftarchaeology.com
Trey Brandt's excellent site on crash sites in Arizona features visits to a number of interesting wreck sites. Brandt is also the author of *Faded Contrails: Last Flights Over Arizona*.

Aviation Archaeological Investigation and Research (AAIR)
www.aviationarchaeology.com
Craig Fuller, a classically trained archaeologist, is the driving force behind Aviation Archaeology Investigation and Research, the best Internet site for ordering army air force, air force, and navy crash reports as well as missing

air crew reports (MACRs). You can visit a number of crash sites virtually here as well.

Aviation Archaeology in Maine
www.mewreckchasers.com
Pete Noddin's Internet site is devoted to U.S. and Canadian aircraft crashes in Maine. Noddin reports that between 1919 and 1989 there were 741 military crashes in the state. His site features many of the crash sites in the state that have been investigated.

The Bent Prop Project
www.bentprop.org
Patrick Scannon, MD, PhD, has been traveling to the Palau Islands to search for downed aircraft and missing airmen from both sides of the conflict. Follow this outstanding work online.

Colorado Aviation Archaeology
www.coloradoaviationarchaeology.org
A subgroup of the Colorado Aviation Historical Society, this group sponsored the formation of the North American Institute of Aviation Archaeology (NAIAA), which is working to start a national organization to govern and develop standards for aviation archaeology.

Fatal Army Air Forces Aviation Accidents in the United States, 1941–1945
www.warbirdcrash.com
Anthony J. Mirales's site supports his comprehensive listing of more than 7,100 stateside accidents during World War II.

Lost Flights
www.lostflights.org
Author and wreckchaser Michael B. McComb's website features many of the aircraft crash sites he's found in the Southwestern United States. McComb is best known for his explorations of crashes in the Grand Canyon area, and one of his galleries is devoted to aircraft accidents in this area.

Oklahoma Wreckchasing
www.okwreckchasing.org
Jeff Wilkinson's Oklahoma Wreckchasing features a great, active message board as well as a virtual tour of many crash sites in Arkansas and Oklahoma.

Pacific Wrecks
www.pacificwrecks.org
Justin Taylan's online database lists aircraft crashes in the battlegrounds of the Pacific. Taylan has also produced a number of DVDs on these crashes, including the *Swamp Ghost* and the B-17 *Black Jack*, as well as his adventures on many of the islands. Also visit Taylan's sister site: www.pacificghosts.com

TIGHAR – The International Group for Historic Aircraft Recovery
www.tighar.org
TIGHAR is searching for a number of high-profile aircraft crashes, including Amelia Earhart, a TBD, and many others.

Wreckchasing

www.wreckchasing.com

This site was one of the first of the subject online in 1995 and features a very
active message board full of tips, research information, and stories from
people interested in the hobby. Many of today's top aviation archaeologists,
wreckchasers, researchers, and websites can trace their enthusiasm for the
hobby to the books *Wreckchasing: A Guide to Finding Aircraft Crash Sites*
and *Wreckchasing 2: Commerical Aircraft Crashes and Crash Sites*.

X-Hunters Aerospace Archeology Team

www.thexhunters.com

Peter W. Merlin and Tony Moore have been exploring the deserts around
Edwards AFB to honor those who perished while expanding the envelope
of flight. Their website covers every type of experimental aircraft, from
Flying Wings to Blackbirds, to all of the downed X-planes. The duo has also
written a book on the subject, *X-Planes Crashes: Exploring Experimental,
Rocket Plane, and Spycraft Incidents, Accidents, and Crash Sites*, which lists
more than five hundred aircraft crash sites in the Mojave Desert area.

Warbird Restoration/Aviation Museums

Aero Trader

www.aerotrader.net

Known for their B-25 restorations, Carl Scholl and Tony Ritzman have done
everything from Mustangs and Corsairs to A-20s, A-26s, and B-26s.

Airpower Unlimited

www.airpowerunlimited.net

John Lane's shop in Jerome, Idaho, has turned out a number of award-winning
restorations, most recently a pair of Corsairs.

Alaska Aviation Heritage Museum

www.alaskaairmuseum.org

Located in Anchorage, the museum displays and preserves aircraft and artifacts
from the region.

American Aero Services

www.americanaeroservices.com

Just rebuilt the Collings Foundation's award-winning North American
A-36A dive bomber, and maintains the foundation's B-17 *Nine-O-Nine*
and B-24J *Witchcraft*.

American Air Museum

www.aam.iwm.uk

More than thirty thousand U.S. airmen gave their lives during World War II and
the UK remembers their sacrifice in hundreds of locations, none better
than the American Air Museum at Duxford. All of the major World War II
aircraft types are on display here.

Cal-Pacific Airmotive

www.calpacificairmotive.com

Art Teeters shop has restored a number of the best Mustangs flying today.

Cal-Pacific Airmotive holds the Limited Type Certificate for the P-51C, -51D, -51K, and provides certified parts to Mustang restorers around the globe.

Canada Aviation and Space Museum
www.aviation.technomuses.ca/
Canada's National Aviation Collection holds a fantastic variety of aircraft, including a number of World War II–era warbirds.

The New Canadian Air & Space Museum
http://casmuseum.org
Located in North York, Ontario, this museum is home to the Avro CF-105 full-scale replica.

Canadian Warplane Heritage
www.warplane.com
Certainly the largest nongovernment group preserving and flying World War II aircraft in Canada. Home to a fantastic museum at the Hamilton International Airport, Ontario, Canada.

Collings Foundation
www.collingsfoundation.org
Home of the Wings of Freedom air tour, featuring a B-17, B-24, B-25, and two-seat P-51C. A Vietnam flight has been established with an A-4, F-4, F-100, and Huey helicopter.

Commemorative Air Force
www.commemorativeairforce.org
One of the oldest, all-volunteer warbird flying organizations in the country, and operators of the B-29 *FiFi* and more than 140 other warbirds of various types and sizes.

Experimental Aircraft Association (EAA)
www.warbirds-eaa.org and www.eaa.org
Home to the EAA Warbirds and the AirVenture fly-in every July in Oshkosh, Wisconsin. They have an outstanding museum on the Oshkosh airport grounds as well.

Evergreen Aviation Museum
www.evergreenmuseum.org
Howard Hughes's HK-1 Spruce Goose greets you as you drive up to the museum, and there's a tremendous collection of warbirds as well. Check out the waterpark with the Boeing 747 slide.

Ezell Aviation
www.ezellaviation.com
Ezell Aviation has restored just about every type of warbird that has ever flown. Follow their restorations on the website.

Fagen Fighters World War II Museum
www.fagenfighterswwiimuseum.org
Home to flyable, award-winning P-38, P-40, two P-51s, and a number of World War II trainers.

Fantasy of Flight
www.fantasyofflight.com
Located approximately twenty miles from Orlando, Florida, this art deco
    attraction features more than forty flyable aircraft from a variety of
    eras. Warbirds include a P-51C, B-26 Marauder, Short Sunderland, and
    many more.

Flying Heritage Collection
www.flyingheritage.com
Warbirds from all participants of World War II painstakingly restored to as close
    to original configuration as possible.

GossHawk Unlimited
www.gosshawkunlimited.com
Dave Goss's GossHawk Unlimited has rebuilt many rare aircraft, most
    notably an Fw-190D, Spitfire Mk IX, Kawanishi N1K2-J George, and
    a Nakajima Ki-43 Oscar. Currently working on an early variant of the
    Douglas A-20 Havoc.

Historic Flight Foundation
www.historicflight.org
This began operations in 2003 as the John T. Sessions Historic Flight Foundation
    and features a number of World War II warbirds.

Imperial War Museum
www.iwm.org.uk
One of the best collections of World War II warbirds.

Lewis Air Legends
www.lewisairlegends.com
More than two dozen aircraft ranging from the P-38F *Glacier Girl* to the P-39
    Brooklyn Bum, a pair of F7F Tigercats, as well as four F8F Bearcats.

Liberty Foundation
www.libertyfoundation.org
Home of the Salute to Veterans B-17 tour with another B-17G under rebuild.

Mid-Atlantic Air Museum P-61
http://www.maam.org
Follow the P-61 Black Widow restoration at the museum's website.

Midwest Aero
www.midwestaero.com
Numerous award-winning Mustang restorations have come from Midwest Aero,
    including *Lil Margaret*, *Happy Jack's Go Buggy*, and *Daddy's Girl*. The shop
    is now working on a Bf-109 restoration.

Military Aviation Museum
www.militaryaviationmuseum.org
Home to one of the largest private collections of warbirds from all sides of the
    war, everything from a Polikarpov I-16 and Hawker Hurricane to a Curtiss
    P-40 and a B-17G Flying Fortress.

Museum of Flight
www.museumofflight.org
The museum acquired the Champlin Collection and based its new Personal
   Courage Wing around its collection of World War I and II aircraft.

National Air & Space Museum
www.airandspace.si.edu
This nation's collection of history-making aircraft with locations in
   downtown Washington, D.C., and the Steven F. Udvar-Hazy Center in
   Chantilly, Virginia.

National Museum of Naval Aviation
www.navalaviationmuseum.org
The U.S. Navy's repository of historic and record-setting aircraft.

National Museum of the U.S. Air Force
www.nationalmuseum.af.mil
U.S. Air Force aircraft from the world wars to supersonic test birds displayed at
   Wright-Patterson Air Force Base, Ohio.

Pacific Aviation Museum
www.pacificaviationmuseum.org
Warbirds from World War II, Korea, and the Vietnam War on display at
   Ford Island, Oahu, Hawaii. World War II warbirds focus in on the
   Pacific Theater.

Pima Air & Space Museum
www.pimaair.org
More than three hundred aircraft on display with plenty of World War II
   warbirds. This is also the place for tours of the U.S. military's boneyard,
   known as AMARG, at Davis-Monthan AFB.

Planes of Fame Air Museum
www.planesoffame.org
The first aviation museum west of the Mississippi River and boasts one of the
   best private collections of Axis aircraft. Annual airshow in May—not to be
   missed.

Sanders Aeronautics
www.sandersaircraft.com
Warbird restorations on everything from Sea Furies, to Corsairs, to an
   Me-262 replica.

San Diego Aerospace Museum
www.sandiegoairandspace.org
Warbirds in the collection include a Spitfire Mk XVI and Grumman
   F6F Hellcat.

Stallion 51
www.stallion51.com
P-51 flight training in dual-control Mustangs.

The Fighter Collection
www.fighter-collection.com
Europe's largest collection of flyable World War II aircraft.

Tillamook
www.tillamookair.com
More than thirty warbirds on display, nearly all flyable, including a P-38, P-51, F4U-7, J2F-6 Duck, Bf-109, AM-1 Mauler, and many more.

Vintage Aircraft
www.twinbeech.com
Restorers of the Twin Beech series and providers of the Aerospace Products spar strap kit. Restorers and operators of an eight-gun nose PV-2D navy patrol bomber.

Vulture's Row Aviation
www.vulturesrowaviation.com
U.S. Navy tailhook-equipped warbirds are their specialty. Currently restoring an SBD and SB2C side-by-side.

Warhawk Air Museum
www.warhawkairmuseum.org
Home to the P-51B *Boise Bee*, P-51D *Hell-er Bust*, and P-40E *Sneak Attack* and P-40N *Parrot Head* among other warbirds.

Westpac Restorations
www.westpacrestorations.com
Currently working on a number of P-38s, P-47s, an F7F, and an F4U. Co-located with the National Museum of World War II Aviation.

Yanks Air Museum
www.yanksair.com
Home to a large collection of World War II warbirds, from the P-51A and C-47 to an F6F-5 and PB4Y-2.

1941 Historical Aircraft Group Museum
www.1941hag.org
The museum is currently restoring a Douglas B-23 and A-20 Havoc.

Warbirds, Air Racing

A&T Recovery
www.atrecovery.com
A&T Recovery specializes in the underwater recovery of historically significant aircraft. See what they've brought up, and learn about what they're going after.

AAFO: All Aviation Flightline Online
www.aafo.com
Air racing, warbirds, airshows, photo galleries, message board, flight simulators, all in one place.

B-17 Flying Fortress and B-25 Mitchell
www.aerovintage.com
Author Scott Thompson's site for news and information on both the B-17
and the B-25. There's some interesting pages on the Tallmantz operation,
B-17s in the movies, aircraft disposed of through the War Assets
Administration, and pages for the restoration of the B-17E *Desert Rat/
Tangerine* (XC-108A).

B-17E *Swamp Ghost*
http://www.theswampghost.com/
http://www.aeroarchaeology.com
Two sites dedicated to the preservation and recovery of the B-17E *Swamp Ghost*.
TheSwampGhost.com is operated by Justin Taylan, who had made dozens
of trips to the bomber and produced a video about its history and crash.
AeroArchaeology.com is Fred Hagen's website detailing his recovery of the
B-17 and other aircraft.

B-17G *Lacy Lady*
www.b17 wings offreedom.org
Art Lacy flew a B-17 home from the scrapyard and put it on display above his
gas station and motel complex in Milwaukie, Oregon. Follow along as the
family works to restore this Flying Fortress.

B-24 *Lady Be Good*
http://www.376hbgva.com/aircraft/ladybegood.html
www.ladybegood.com
Visit the bomb group's site or LadyBeGood.com for author Mario Martinez's site
on the aircraft and the myths surrounding its loss and discovery.

Courtesy Aircraft
www.courtesyaircraft.com
Mark Clark has been in the warbird sales business for more than thirty-five
years and has sold more than 2,500 warbirds, many multiple times.

National Aviation Heritage Invitational
www.heritagetrophy.com
Home website for information and coverage about the Neil A. Armstrong
Aviation Heritage Trophy and its yearly competitions held every
September in conjunction with the National Championship Air Races in
Reno, Nevada.

P-51 Mustangs
www.MustangsMustangs.com
Mustang automobiles or P-51 Mustang airplanes, both are found at this website.
Up-to-the-minute news on P-51 restorations, history, ace interviews, and
much more.

Swiss Mustangs
www.Swiss Mustangs.ch
Martin Kyburz's site started out focusing on the Swiss Air Force use of the P-51
and what happened to the planes when they were phased out of service.
The site has expanded to cover nearly every aspect of the Mustang's service.

Mustang!
http://www.mustang.gaetanmarie.com/
Gaetan Marie's website dedicated to the P-51 with galleries on many unique uses of the P-51.

XP-51G *Margie Hart*
www.xp51g.com
John Morgan's site to follow the restoration of the sole surviving XP-51G.

P-38 *Glacier Girl*
http://p38assn.org/glacier-girl.htm
The P-38 national association's webpage dedicated to *Glacier Girl*.

Platinum Fighter Sales
www.platinumfighters.com
Own a piece of history! Platinum Fighter Sales has handled some of the highest profile warbird transactions in recent history, including P-38F *Glacier Girl*.

National Championship Air Races
www.airrace.org
Information about upcoming races in Reno, Nevada, plus performer profiles, racing statistics, photos, and videos of air racing past and present. Six classes of air racers turn the pylons every September, some going more than 500 mph. Bucket list item if you've never been.

Society of Air Racing Historians
www.airrace.com
Everything you ever wanted to know about the history of air racing. The group holds an annual symposium each year that attracts many pilots and crewmembers.

Society for Aviation History
www.sfahistory.org
Aviation history presented through educational programs and newsletters. Five programs per year, typically presented by those who made aviation history.

Warbird Information Exchange or WIX
http://warbirdinformationexchange.org/phpBB3/index.php
Message board for all things warbirds and includes the Warbird Registry giving the history of most surviving ex-military types.

Warbird Aero Press
www.warbirdaeropress.com
Hosted by Scott Germain, this site covers "the art, action, and adrenaline of Unlimted Air Racing." Stories, interviews, art, and photography of all aspects of the Unlimiteds.

Worldwide Aircraft Recovery, Ltd.
www.worldwideaircraft.com
You name it, they've moved it, from P-51s to the SR-71.

Index